POE AND THE VISUAL ARTS

POE

=== AND THE ===

VISUAL ARTS

Barbara Cantalupo

THE PENNSYLVANIA STATE UNIVERSITY PRESS

UNIVERSITY PARK, PENNSYLVANIA

An earlier version of chapter 4 appeared as "Poe's Visual Tricks,"
Poe Studies / Dark Romanticism 38, nos. 1–2 (2005): 53–63.

An earlier version of chapter 5 appeared as "Poe's Responses to
Nineteenth-Century American Painting," in *Edgar Allan Poe
(1809–2009): Doscientos años después*, ed. Margarida Rigal
Aragón and Beatriz González Moreno (Cuenca: Ediciones de la
Universidad de Castilla–La Mancha, 2010), 111–20.

Library of Congress Cataloging-in-Publication Data

Cantalupo, Barbara, author.
Poe and the visual arts / Barbara Cantalupo.
p.   cm
Summary: "Explores visual allusions in the writings of
Edgar Allan Poe to paintings and sculptures he saw in
Philadelphia and Manhattan. Examines how his writings
relate to the visual culture of his time"—Provided by publisher.
Includes bibliographical references and index.
ISBN 978-0-271-06309-6 (cloth : alk. paper)
1. Poe, Edgar Allan, 1809–1849—Knowledge—Art.
2. Poe, Edgar Allan, 1809–1849—Criticism and interpretation.
3. Poe, Edgar Allan, 1809–1849—Aesthetics.
4. Poe, Edgar Allan, 1809–1849—Technique.
5. Art and literature—United States—History—19th century.
6. Art in literature.
I. Title.

PS2642.A66C36 2014
818'.309—dc23
2013046957

The Pennsylvania State University Press is a member of the
Association of American University Presses.

It is the policy of The Pennsylvania State University Press to
use acid-free paper. Publications on uncoated stock satisfy the
minimum requirements of American National Standard for
Information Sciences—Permanence of Paper for
Printed Library Material, ANSI z39.48–1992.

This book is printed on paper that contains
30% post-consumer waste.

FOR *Burton R. Pollin*

Contents

Illustrations

Acknowledgments

My most heartfelt thanks go to two men: my mentor and esteemed Poe scholar, the late Burton R. Pollin, and my husband, Charles Cantalupo, poet, scholar, and much-admired professor. Each, in his own way, helped make this book better: Burton's extensive knowledge of Poe's work and Charles's expert advice on clear and engaging writing have both been invaluable guides. A year before his death in 2010, Burton mailed me a folder containing his handwritten notes on Poe's references to painters, carefully matched to pages in James Harrison's edition of Poe's work—what an important key! All of Burton's Poe publications are a scholar's treasures. Throughout the time I had the privilege to know him, Burton was always available at the end of a phone line or in response to an email to help guide me in fruitful directions in my research or to fill in the gaps of my knowledge of Poe. He is much missed. Both Burton and Charles not only shared their expertise but also encouraged me to finish this book because, as they each reiterated many times, this topic is an important contribution to Poe studies. Many thanks also go to Richard Kopley for his encouragement, knowledge of Poe scholarship, and access to his incredible Poe collection; he has been a steadfast friend and colleague.

I have loving regard for my children's respect for my intellectual pursuits: Alicia and Alexandra, my youngest daughters, showed understanding and patience when I was away doing research during their growing-up years, and Elizabeth and Christopher, my two oldest, watched me spend years as a single parent getting my Ph.D. while they were just youngsters. Important to my ongoing commitment to research and learning is knowing that my work has been a model to all of my children. It gives me pleasure to see that Liz and Chris are doing their own publishing in languages I don't know—French and Python, respectively—and that my two youngest will someday make their own marks through violin performance.

My thanks go to The Pennsylvania State University and to my campus, Penn State Lehigh Valley, especially Kenneth Thigpen, director of academic affairs, for their ongoing support of this project. I also want to thank Judy Mishriki, Penn State Lehigh Valley's research librarian, for her guidance and help tracking down obscure references. I am very grateful to Loretta Yenser for her copyediting and organizational help with the final draft of the manuscript; her assistance was invaluable.

Thanks also go to Nicole Joniec, Print Department assistant and Digital Collections manager at the Library Company of Philadelphia; Liz Kurtulik of the Permissions Department at Art Resource; Melanie Neil, assistant registrar at the Chrysler Museum of Art; Allison Munsell, digitization specialist at the Albany Institute of Art; Alexandra Lane, rights and reproductions manager at the White House Historical Association; Joan Albert of the Virginia Historical Association; Sandra Stelts, curator of rare books and manuscripts at The Pennsylvania State University Libraries; Jaclyn Penny, rights and reproductions coordinator at the American Antiquarian Society; and Peter Roiest of the Koninklijk Museum in Antwerp, who provided valuable information on Jean-Baptist De Cuyper, as well as Marcos Pujol for his guidance and support during my research trip to Antwerp.

I have much respect for and feel very grateful to Julie Schoelles at The Pennsylvania State University Press for her incredibly attentive copyediting and the care she gave to the manuscript. And, of course, I am grateful to Kendra Boileau, editor-in-chief, and all of the staff at the press, including Robert Turchick, for their excitement about the project and their support throughout this process.

Note on the Text

The majority of quotations from Poe's works are taken from Thomas Ollive Mabbott's two-volume collection *Tales and Sketches* and his edition of *Complete Poems*. Most of Poe's texts were published multiple times and underwent revisions from printing to printing. The versions printed in Mabbott's *Tales and Sketches* are frequently (though not always) drawn from *The Works of the Late Edgar Allan Poe*, edited by Rufus Griswold and published from 1850 to 1856. Preceding each tale or sketch, Mabbott provides a list of its appearances in earlier publications, and he uses footnotes to identify the changes made to each printing. Using these notes, I have occasionally modified the quotations from *Tales and Sketches* so that they directly reflect the earliest printing of the work under discussion. Where this is the case, I have specified the quoted version in the text or endnotes. However, the dates of publication given for Poe's works throughout this book always refer to their first printings.

Although Edgar Allan Poe's name is most often identified with stories of horror and fear, *Poe and the Visual Arts* stakes a claim for the less familiar Poe—the one who often goes unrecognized or forgotten—the Poe whose early love of beauty was a strong and enduring draw, who "from childhood's hour . . . [had] not seen / As others saw—."[1] The evidence in this book demonstrates that Poe's "deep worship of all beauty," expressed in an 1829 letter to John Neal when Poe was just twenty, never entirely faded, despite the demands of his commercial writing and editorial career. In that letter, Poe appealed to Neal "as a man that loves the same beauty which I adore—the beauty of the natural blue sky and the sunshiny earth."[2] *Poe and the Visual Arts* looks at Poe's connection to such visual beauty, his commitment to "graphicality" (a word he coined), and his knowledge of the visual arts, noting what he saw, how he used what he saw, and how he criticized those who would not see.

Poe valued the artist's vision as well as the ability of a writer to create in words what can be seen by "an artistical eye."[3] His regard for the artist's ability to see how various, seemingly arbitrary combinations can create a composition of beauty is clearly articulated in "The Landscape Garden": "No such combinations of scenery exist in Nature as the painter of genius has in his power to produce. No such Paradises are to be found in reality as have glowed upon the canvass of Claude.[4] In the most enchanting of natural landscapes, there will always be found a defect or an excess. . . . [The artist] positively *knows*, that such and such apparently arbitrary arrangements of matter, or form, constitute, and alone constitute, the true Beauty" (*Tales*, 1:707–8). The explicit references to paintings and painters, such as Claude, in many of Poe's stories and sketches enhance thematic concerns or help produce a preconceived effect. In other works, such as "Landor's Cottage" and "A Tale of the Ragged Mountains," Poe obliquely refers to the Hudson River school painters by evoking their paintings in his own descriptive prose rather than directly naming the paintings he has in mind. In this way, the tales signal a turn in Poe's visual aesthetics from the sublime to the beautiful. In addition, Poe's concern with literary process—as evidenced in "The Philosophy of Composition" and "The Poetic Principle," for example, as well as in many of his (often harsh) reviews of poetry and fiction—reflects his astute awareness of the similarity between the writing and painting processes. He was keenly aware of how a painter uses his medium to produce a "startling effect," a concept essential to Poe's storytelling.

This affinity is evidenced in his February 1838 *Southern Literary Messenger* review of Alexander Slidell's *The American in England*. Poe applauds Slidell's book as being wise by virtue of being superficial and justifies this seeming contradiction by arguing that the "depth of an argument is not, necessarily, its wisdom—this depth lying where Truth is sought more often than where she is found." Poe then compares Slidell's literary effort with the painterly process by observing, "The touches of a painting which, to minute inspection, are 'confusion worse confounded' will not fail to start boldly out to the cursory glance of a connoisseur."[5] In noting that the overall effect of a painting (as seen by a "connoisseur") overrides the minute, seemingly "confused" strokes that produce that effect, Poe once again affirms his belief that truth often lies on the surface. He states this quite clearly in his "Letter to B———": "As regards the greater truths, men oftener err by seeking them at the bottom than at the top."[6] In his review of Slidell's work, Poe also foregrounds his understanding of how a painter creates illusion and how that process applies to literary technique. For example, he compares Slidell's literary finesse with painterly technique as follows: "[Mr. Slidell] has felt that the apparent, not the real, is the province of a painter—and that *to give* (speaking technically) *the idea of any desired object, the toning down, or the utter neglect of certain portions of that object is absolutely necessary to the proper bringing out of other portions—portions by whose sole instrumentality the idea of the object is afforded*."[7]

Three years later, Poe reiterated this understanding in a May 1841 *Graham's Magazine* review of Charles Dickens's *The Old Curiosity Shop, and Other Tales*. Here Poe points out that a painter, rather than attempting to create a direct duplicate of the subject to be depicted, uses his medium to communicate its truth to the viewer through the manipulation of brush stroke, light, composition, line, and shadow—exaggerating elements when necessary and diminishing others to create the desired effect. As he explains, "No critical principle is more firmly based in reason than that a certain amount of exaggeration is essential in the proper depicting of truth itself. We do not paint an object to be true, but to appear true to the beholder. Were we to copy nature with accuracy the object copied would seem unnatural."[8]

In 1845, in Marginalia 243, Poe once again returned to his long-standing idea that the "mere imitation, however accurate, of what *is* in Nature, entitles no man to the sacred name of 'Artist.'" As noted in "The Landscape Garden" and "The Domain of Arnheim," Poe strongly believed that transformation, combination, and composition create beauty beyond what nature can produce, and this belief is evident in the marginalia entry: "We can, at any time, double the true beauty of an actual landscape by half closing our eyes as we look at it. The naked Senses sometimes see too little—but then always they see too much." In this short piece, Poe also provides a definition of "Art": "Were I called upon to define, *very* briefly, the term 'Art,' I should call it 'the reproduction of what the Senses perceive in Nature through the veil of the soul.'"[9]

Often, too, Poe used visual metaphors as high praise. For example, in his September 1839 *Burton's Gentleman's Magazine* review of Friedrich Fouqué's *Undine*, Poe overwhelmingly praises his writing: "'Undine' is a model of models, in regard to the high artistical talent which it evinces. We could write volumes in a detailed commentary upon its various beauties in this respect. Its unity is absolute—its keeping unbroken. Yet every minute point of the picture fills and satisfies the eye" (*Works*, 10:37). Furthermore, in his February 1836 "Autography," Poe applauds John P. Kennedy's handwriting: "This is our *beau ideal* of penmanship. Its prevailing character is *picturesque*. . . . We should suppose Mr. Kennedy to have the eye of a painter, more especially in regard to the picturesque" (*Tales*, 1:273). Poe's praise for the painterly process and for visual art was consistent throughout his literary career.

Chapter 1 of this book, "Poe's Exposure to Art Exhibited in Philadelphia and Manhattan, 1838–1845," suggests that Poe's keen sense of visual aesthetics was nurtured by his exposure to the paintings and sculptures in art venues in Philadelphia and New York, where he lived from 1838 to his death in 1849. The "graphicality" of Poe's own work is enhanced by allusions to painters and paintings, as demonstrated in chapter 2, "Artists and Artwork in Poe's Short Stories and Sketches." This chapter provides a chronological overview of the references to visual artists, paintings, and sculptures in the stories written or revised during Poe's most productive period, from 1838 to 1849. I show how these allusions build on Poe's valuing the artist's vision as well as the ability of the writer to create in words what can be seen by "an artistical eye." The chapter also provides evidence that supports Kent Ljungquist's claim in *The Grand and the Fair: Poe's Landscape Aesthetics and Pictorial Techniques* that "[Poe's] later fiction and criticism mark a general turn away from the sublime." Ljungquist explains, "Beauty becomes Poe's guiding principle, and imagination is the predominant faculty, all other faculties subordinated to it with the sublime added almost as a rather unimportant sub-category."[10]

Chapter 3, "Poe's Homely Interiors," examines the ways Poe's well-known strategy of manipulating the merest detail can reveal undercurrent meanings, thematic resonances, nuanced complications of plot, and/or satirical responses to cultural norms. Specifically, this chapter examines the homely items of interior decoration that function in this way in "The Devil in the Belfry," "William Wilson," "The Philosophy of Furniture," "The Domain of Arnheim," and "Landor's Cottage." Poe also used visual cues in an entirely different way in his tales to confront the propensity to see what is desired and not what is actually there. This phenomenon, studied in chapter 4, "Poe's Visual Tricks," reveals how the act of seeing plays a pivotal role in short stories such as "Ligeia," "The Sphinx," and "The Spectacles." Finally, chapter 5, "Poe's Art Criticism," details the critical responses to visual art that Poe published throughout his career but focuses especially on his responses to the art on display in New York during the time he lived in Manhattan and wrote for the *Columbia Spy* and the *Broadway Journal*.

Poe's attentive response to the visual arts manifests itself in his writing style as well. The "graphicality" of his prose and poetry has influenced visual artists throughout the centuries, including Robert Motherwell, Salvador Dali, Max Ernst, and René Magritte.[11] For example, Kevin Hayes notes that Magritte painted images entitled *The Domain of Arnheim* in 1938, 1949, 1950, and 1962, but "rather than images of Poe's tales, Magritte's works represent images inspired by Poe."[12] Burton Pollin's *Images of Poe's Works: A Comprehensive Descriptive Catalogue of Illustrations* details the remarkable extent of this influence, making it undeniable that Poe's stories and poems are visually provocative. As Pollin notes at the beginning of his introduction, "Edgar Allan Poe has become one of the most widely and most diversely illustrated of authors by virtue of the sketches by Manet, Redon, Doré, Ensor, Gauguin, Beardsley, Whistler, Kubin, and more than seven hundred other artists."[13] In an interview published in the *Edgar Allan Poe Review* in 2001, I asked Dr. Pollin why he believed the residual effect of Poe's work often provokes creative responses from people of all disciplines in the arts—dance, music, and especially the visual arts. He pointedly responded,

> We have to remember, one of Poe's creations . . . : the word was "graphicality"—and Poe coined it. Poe felt that the English language needed to be expanded—and, of course, he felt no hesitation in doing so . . . to express ideas, not necessarily images, but ideas which he felt were needed in the development of talking about the arts, particularly. . . . "Graphicality" is one of the things that Poe aimed at in his tales, at least, and to a certain extent in his poems, it is something an artist can latch onto quite easily—images that are striking and startling, in their nuances and the particular adumbrations that Poe gives to those objects, images, call them what you will, in language, because they convey something to him that he feels has never been done before. That's why the Impressionists were so enormously influenced by Poe, or the Symbolists, people like Redon, for example, or Manet.[14]

Pollin's observation echoes what Washington Irving wrote to Poe in an 1839 letter. After reading "The Fall of the House of Usher," Irving had this to say: "I am much pleased with a tale called 'The House of Usher,' and should think that a collection of tales, equally well written, could not fail of being favorably received. . . . Its graphic effect is powerful."[15] Poe's profound influence on visual artists demonstrates the "graphicality" of his tales.

Poe's keen sense of visual aesthetics was additionally enhanced by exposure to the work of American artists whose paintings appeared as engravings in the magazines and gift books that he reviewed or where his own work was published. For example, Henry Inman's *The Newsboy* appeared in *The Gift Book for 1843* alongside "The Pit and the Pendulum," and William Sidney Mount's *The Trap Sprung* was included in *The Gift Book for 1844* along with "The Purloined Letter." In sketches and short stories such as "The Assignation," "Landor's Cottage," and "The Man of the Crowd," Poe included references to painters and artworks, and many of his tales focus on the art of seeing or the ways visual tricks can be used to dupe, deter, or detract.[16] In addition, Poe's working relationship with Charles Briggs, who wrote most of the reviews of the exhibits at the National Academy of Design and the American Art-Union, brought Poe into close contact with a style of art criticism that went beyond a mere listing of paintings on display—the usual fare found in the daily and weekly newspapers of the time. Poe's own forays into art criticism highlight his visual aesthetics found in sketches and tales such as "The Landscape Garden" and "The Philosophy of Furniture."

The stories, sketches, and art criticism Poe wrote in his later years were enhanced by the art he saw on display in Philadelphia and New York and by his acquaintance with visual artists. In Philadelphia the prominence of the Pennsylvania Academy of the Fine Arts provided a rich resource, as did Poe's friendships with artists Felix O. C. Darley, John Sartain, John Gadsby Chapman, Thomas Sully, and the latter's nephew Robert Sully. Thomas Sully's father, an actor, appeared onstage alongside Poe's mother, and Poe was childhood friends with Robert Sully in Richmond, where the boys attended school together. They renewed their friendship as adults, and "according to tradition, [Robert] Sully entertained Poe and his bride Virginia in 1835."[17] Of special importance is Poe's relationship with Felix O. C. Darley, who signed a contract with Poe and publisher Thomas C. Clarke in 1843 to provide illustrations for Poe's literary journal *Stylus*. Darley also illustrated Poe's short story "The Gold Bug."[18] Writing for the *Home Journal* in 1854, E. Anna Lewis observed that Darley's "pictures not only seem to breathe, they seem to think, which is the highest commendation. They exhibit in the midst of broad humour and satire, a moral pathos which awakens the mind and expands the heart."[19]

Later, when Poe lived in New York, he became acquainted with Hudson River school painter Frederic Church as well as Gabriel Harrison, a painter and daguerreotypist. The latter, "who was also the owner of a tea store on the corner of Broadway and Prince Streets," met Poe when the writer visited his shop. In 1875, Harrison wrote in a reminiscence in the *Brooklyn Daily Eagle*, "From this moment Poe and I became well acquainted with each other, and from 1844 to 1847, whenever he was in the city we frequently met" (*Poe Log*, 472). In the 1850s, Harrison created allegorical daguerreotypes that "found support only in academic, elitist circles."[20] In addition, through his acquaintance with the poet Frances Osgood, Poe would have had conversations about art with her husband, Samuel Stillman Osgood, who also painted a portrait of Poe. Samuel Osgood had two paintings in the 1845 National Academy of Design show—*Girlhood* and *Portrait of a Lady*—that Poe certainly would have seen and discussed with the Osgoods.[21]

Toward the end of Poe's career, his focus on visual aesthetics and the importance of beauty intensified. The two years he spent in New York from 1844 to 1846 were filled with the excitement of a burgeoning arts scene and that of his own newfound fame established by the public's praise for "The Raven," published in January 1845.[22] New York was fast becoming the nation's arts center, and Poe found himself in the midst of this excitement in his varying roles at the *Broadway Journal*. This was a very important time in his career.

Since Poe was drawn to the visual throughout his writing career, this study not only examines his maturing visual appreciation evidenced by his time in Philadelphia and Manhattan but also provides background on his visual allusions, cues, and tricks found in stories, criticism, and sketches written prior to this time. Poe's aesthetic sensibility never faded as he continued to meet the public's desire for "sensational" literature; he never forgot his youthful attachment to beauty. In effect, then, the intent of *Poe and the Visual Arts* is to show how Poe's initial commitment to beauty and his ability to see not "as others saw" affected his work, especially in the last and most productive years of his life.

Setting the Context

Poe spent six years in Philadelphia, from early 1838 to April 1844. He lived in the same "small house" in Philadelphia near Locust Street and North Eighth Street (now Sixteenth Street)[23] for four years after a brief stay at a boarding house at 202 Arch Street in 1839.[24] According to an 1843 map, Poe's North Eighth Street residence was one block west of the Philadelphia Railroad and one block north of the Institution for the Deaf and Dumb (fig. 1). This daunting building, which exists now as Hamilton Hall of the University of the Arts on Broad Street, must have made quite an impression on Poe in all its neoclassical majesty. It brings to mind two lines from Poe's "To Helen," a poem he revised for publication in the February 23, 1843, issue of the *Saturday Museum*, a year before he left Philadelphia for Manhattan: "To the glory that was Greece / And the grandeur that was Rome" (*Poems*, 166). As T. O. Mabbott points out, "[These] two most famous lines, first published in 1843, are among those Poe changed with consummate art" (164).

Within walking distance of Poe's residence lived one of his colleagues: painter, editor, and engraver John Sartain.[25] Sartain's daughter Anne Clarke

Fig. 1 Francis Kearny, *Pennsylvania Institution for the
Deaf and Dumb*, ca. 1826. The Library Company of
Philadelphia, (6)1322.120a.

remembered Poe's visits to her father's home "at Twelfth and Walnut Streets on
[Poe's] way home to Sixteenth Street."[26] Felix O. C. Darley, whose sister married a Sully, was also among Poe's friends in Philadelphia. According to E. Anna
Lewis, "Among the *literati* who took special interest in [Darley] . . . were N. P.
Willis [and] Major Noah," both of whom were friends with Poe.[27] Poe clearly
admired and trusted Darley because Poe asked Darley to be the illustrator for
the *Stylus*, the literary journal Poe tried to establish for so long.

When Poe moved to Philadelphia, the city was still feeling the desperate
effects of the economic panic of 1837, and violence was not unusual. In 1838, riot-
ers destroyed Philadelphia Hall only four days after it was dedicated as an office
space for "free discussion," which included but was not limited to abolitionist

Fig. 2   John Sartain, *Burning of Pennsylvania Hall*, 1838.
The Library Company of Philadelphia, P.2283.2.

speech; it was open "for any purpose not of immoral character."[28] John Sartain
was at the scene of the Philadelphia Hall fire and documented it in an engraving
(fig. 2). As Kathryn Wilson and Jennifer Coval have observed, "Violence in fact
permeated the antebellum city and was often not indiscriminate but highly discriminating, revealing the fears, anxieties, and challenges of an evolving city and
nation. . . . Violence in nineteenth-century Philadelphia had many origins, several of them in the growing pains of a rapidly expanding and industrializing
city. Urbanization fed an increasing influx of 'strangers' into the city from points
abroad as well as the surrounding countryside."[29]

Despite this turmoil, the six years that Poe lived in Philadelphia also saw a
vibrant arts community emerge at the Pennsylvania Academy of the Fine Arts.
Early in the 1830s, the Academy almost closed for financial reasons; however, a
year before the Great Panic of 1837, it had recovered and had enough economic
leeway to buy Benjamin West's *Death on the Pale Horse*. This purchase caused

a lively debate among local artists who felt that not enough of their own work was being shown at the Academy. The Academy listened, and the result was a move toward the exhibition of American art and away from European artists' works. The Academy's website provides the following overview of this period: "While the local artists sought participation in the institution's management and exhibition planning, the affluent gentlemen board members—many descendants of the City's founding elite—were more concerned with the diffusion of cultivated taste to the public. Ultimately both sides gained small victories: the academy focused increasingly on American art and the board remained in the control of laymen city leaders."[30]

After Poe's six-year stay in Philadelphia, he returned to Manhattan with his wife, Virginia, and mother-in-law, Mrs. Clemm, in April 1844. For a short time, Poe had been relatively free of debt because of his successful petition in December 1842 under the 1841 Bankruptcy Act. His bankruptcy petition released him from more than two thousand dollars in financial obligations to numerous people.[31] The New York that Poe found was likewise a much more prosperous place than it had been when he lived there briefly in 1837. By 1844, New York had recovered from the great fire of 1835 and the economic panic of 1837. The city's population had grown by 75 percent; nonetheless, most commerce and residences were still concentrated below Fourteenth Street. What is now Central Park then housed what Eric Homberger describes in *Scenes from the Life of a City* as "squatter encampments."[32] Evidencing Poe's influence in so many disciplines, Homberger enhanced his description of this area of New York with an excerpt from Poe's first installment of "Doings of Gotham," a series of letters he contributed to the Pottsville, Pennsylvania, newspaper *Columbia Spy* right after his move to New York: "I have been roaming far and wide over this island of Mannahatta. Some portions of its interior have a certain air of rocky sterility which may impress some imaginations as simply *dreary*—to me it conveys the sublime. Trees are few; but some of the shrubbery is exceedingly picturesque."[33]

During this stay in New York, Poe saw its first railroad being built; completed in 1846, it extended from City Hall twenty-seven miles to White Plains. By that same year, the first telegraph line connected New York with Philadelphia.[34] These new communication resources indicate a thriving and prosperous city. Wealthy merchants such as Jonathan Sturges and Charles Leupp had both the time and the money to patronize the arts, and they did. Not surprisingly, as a result, a growing number of artists began to settle in New York, and its visual arts scene rapidly expanded. The New-York Gallery of the Fine Arts, the city's first permanent-exhibit art gallery, was founded in 1844, and both the National Academy of Design (dedicated to the display of American artworks) and the American Art-Union (dedicated to the sale of American artists' works) enjoyed marked profits from the substantial increase in attendance at their exhibits during these important years.[35] In fact, more people than ever before were exposed to the arts because the New-York Gallery of the Fine Arts and the American Art-Union provided access to their galleries for little or no charge. The former charged a minimum entrance fee, while the latter was committed to being a "free Picture Gallery, always open and well attended."[36]

This was an exciting time for the arts in New York, and Poe enjoyed a similar excitement in his career. During these two years, he gained great celebrity, became the owner of his own literary magazine, and lived in the most fashionable part of town near Washington Square Park at 85 Amity Street. His time in Manhattan was punctuated by two dramatic literary events: one when he first arrived—the self-proclaimed enthusiastic response to his article "The Balloon Hoax"—and the other early the next year with the publication of "The Raven."

One week after he arrived in New York, Poe's "Balloon Hoax" was issued as a one-page broadside by the *Sun*, followed two days later by publication in Mordecai Noah's *Sunday Times*. "The Balloon-Hoax" created quite a stir, if we can believe Poe's account in his column in the *Columbia Spy* of May 21, 1844: "On the morning (Saturday) of its announcement, the whole square surrounding the 'Sun' building was literally besieged, blocked up—ingress and egress being alike impossible, from a period soon after sunrise until about two o-clock P.M. . . . I never witnessed more intense excitement to get possession of a newspaper."[37] Whether this level of excitement actually occurred could be questioned; nonetheless, Poe unabashedly promoted this "premier" publication in his new hometown of "Mannahatta."

The other pivotal event that pushed Poe into the limelight was the publication of "The Raven." The poem was met with lavish praise, and as a result Poe enjoyed months of celebrity. He was invited to soirees at 116 Waverly Place, the home of poet and socialite Anne Lynch (fig. 3), where he had many opportunities to talk with writers and artists such as Margaret Fuller, Frances Osgood, N. P. Willis, and Horace Greeley. I was struck by the curious Poe-like coincidence that I discovered by coordinating the notes in the *Poe Log* describing both Poe's dramatic reading of "The Raven" at Miss Lynch's home on the evening of

Fig. 3   Savinien Edme
Dubourjal, *Anne Lynch*, ca. 1847.
The Metropolitan Museum of
Art, New York. Bequest of
Vincenzo Botta, 1895, 95.2.3.
Image copyright © The Metro-
politan Museum of Art. Photo:
Art Resource, New York.

July 19, 1845, and the great fire of that year, which broke out on the same day.
The *New-York Mirror*'s description of the night of the fire—"The moon light
falls upon the ruins which are still burning to some extent, and gives a wild and
unnatural aspect to the whole scene"—suggests a particularly eerie setting for
Poe's recitation. While lower Manhattan smoldered and the moon was full, Poe
read "The Raven" to the eager listeners at the Lynch soiree. The setting surely
enhanced his performance, described by Miss Lynch as "electrifying" (*Poe Log*,
553). Not only did this reading increase Poe's popularity and reinforce the reputation he had for his mesmerizing reading style, but the drama that surrounded
the event must have intensified the recitation's lasting effect on its audience.
Before sunrise the next day, the worst fire since the great fire of 1835 had raged
throughout many streets in lower Manhattan.

Although fires had been a constant concern for New Yorkers since the city
was founded, the completion of the Croton Aqueduct in 1842 promised to lessen
the chance that a major fire like the one in 1835 could reoccur. Unfortunately,
this was not the case. Even with the abundant water supply provided by the

aqueduct and the work of a more efficient fire department, the 1845 fire destroyed more than three hundred buildings and killed thirty people. In his diary, George Templeton Strong describes the fire, which began, according to his account of Saturday, July 19, at "half-past three this morning by a couple of explosions in quick succession that shook the house like an earthquake and must have blown me out of bed. . . . The moon was shining full and bright; the dawn just beginning to show itself, and to the southeast there rose into the air a broad column of intense red flame that made the moon look pale."[38]

The weekly edition of the *New-York Mirror* for Saturday, July 26, 1845, began its account of the fire with this claim:

> We are called upon to record a dire calamity, equaled only by that which visited the city in 1835. . . . At about 4 o-clock it communicated to the store of Crocker & Warner, in New Street, in which was stored a huge quantity of salt petre, which blew up with an explosion that shook the city like an earthquake. . . . SATURDAY—MIDNIGHT—The scene at this hour is awfully sublime. The moon light falls upon the ruins which are still burning to some extent, and gives a wild and unnatural aspect to the whole scene. The sentinels perform their duties in silence. They seem to be guarding the remains of some vanquished, sacked and ruined city, and the idea of a place besieged and suffering all the horrors of war is before us.[39]

This description and the picture (fig. 4) that appeared on the first page of the *New-York Mirror* a week after the fire remind the reader of Poe's graphic descriptions of besieged cities and desolate environments. Could Poe have written it himself? Poe worked at the newspaper from October 1844 to February 1845, and either the write-up of the fire was his or the writer who wrote it (possibly N. P. Willis) was influenced by Poe's earlier descriptions of urban disasters. Compare the *Mirror*'s description to this one from Poe's short story "King Pest" (1835): "The paving-stones, loosened from their beds, lay in wild disorder amid the tall, rank grass, which sprang up around the feet and ankles. Fallen houses choked up the streets. The most fetid and poisonous smells everywhere prevailed;—and by the aid of that ghastly light which, even at midnight, never fails to emanate from a vapory and pestilential atmosphere, might be discerned lying in the by-paths and alleys, or rotting in the windowless habitations, the carcass of many a nocturnal plunderer arrested by the hand of the plague"

Fig. 4 "Remains of the Waverley Hotel and Adjacent
Houses on Broadway Two Days After the Fire," *New-
York Mirror: A Reflex of the News, Literature, Arts, and
Elegancies of Our Times,* July 26, 1845.

(*Tales,* 1:243–44). Or compare this similarly bleak description from "Silence: A
Fable" (1838): "And the tall primeval trees rock eternally hither and thither with
a crashing and mighty sound. And from their high summits, one by one, drop
everlasting dews. And at the roots strange poisonous flowers lie writhing in per-
turbed slumber. And overhead, with a rustling and loud noise, the gray clouds
rush westwardly forever, until they roll, a cataract, over the fiery wall of the
horizon" (1:195–96).

While lower Manhattan recovered from the fire's destruction, the New York arts community, on the other hand, was reveling in its newfound prosperity. The visual arts attracted much attention during the two-year period Poe lived in Manhattan. Just after he arrived, the nineteenth annual show at the National Academy of Design opened on April 25, 1844; the number of visitors who saw the show before it closed in July was in the thousands.[40] The 1844 show included about three hundred works of art by American artists, including Frederic Church, Thomas Cole, Thomas Doughty, Asher Durand, Francis Edmonds, Charles Loring Elliott, Henry Peters Gray, and Henry Inman.[41] Since its founding in 1825, the National Academy of Design had gained more and more prominence with each passing year, and by the mid-1840s it was considered "the most influential of all serial exhibitions in this country."[42] In 1841, the Academy moved from its small quarters to "the Society Library building, at the corner of Broadway and Leonard Street. These galleries were larger and more commodious than any yet occupied by the society."[43] Patterned after the Royal Academy in London, the National Academy of Design exhibits were "limited to *contemporary* American art. . . . Exhibitions were planned and executed *by* contemporary artists *for* contemporary artists."[44] Works could only be shown once. The shows attracted viewers who wanted to see the newest work by their favorite artist and those who looked forward to the possibility of discovering a new artist whose work they could follow and support. Unlike the American Academy of Art founded in 1802, which was "primarily concerned with the promotion of civic virtue"[45] and mostly exhibited work by European "masters," the National Academy of Design was established by artists to promote American art and train American artists. By the mid-1840s, New York was considered the center of the arts, primarily because of the quality of the shows at the National Academy of Design.

In addition, in 1844, businessman and art patron Jonathan Sturges organized a group of patrons to establish the New-York Gallery of the Fine Arts, the city's first gallery with a permanent collection. The inaugural exhibit consisted of paintings and drawings from Luman Reed's collection, which included works by prominent contemporary artists such as George Whiting Flagg, Thomas Cole, and William Sidney Mount.[46] Reed began collecting European art in the 1820s but turned to collecting works by American artists in the 1830s. He was one of New York's most generous art patrons, and before his death in 1836 he opened his home at 13 Greenwich Street on a regular basis to those wishing to view his artwork. According to Abigail Gerdts, "Reed's collection remained in his home [after his death] until 1844, when to the alarm of his friends and fellow patrons of the arts, it became known that the family intended to dispose of it."[47] This provided the impetus for the efforts by Sturges and his fellow patrons to establish the New-York Gallery of the Fine Arts and keep Reed's collection intact.

The inaugural exhibit of the New-York Gallery of the Fine Arts was located in rented rooms at the New York Society Library, but soon thereafter, in March 1845, New York City's Common Council voted to allow the gallery to use the Rotunda in the Park "to establish in the city of New-York a permanent gallery of paintings, statuary, and other works of art."[48] It prospered there until 1848, when the city reclaimed the building for another use and the collection was transferred to the New-York Historical Society: "The New-York Gallery of the Fine Arts . . . did propose to the said New-York Historical Society that if the said Society in the construction of their new fire proof Edifice then in progress of erection, would provide a suitable Gallery for the reception, safe keeping, and proper exhibition of the aforesaid collection of art, the said New-York Gallery of the Fine Arts would deposit the same in perpetuity. . . . The New-York Historical Society did cause, at great extra expense, change in the building to provide the Gallery."[49]

An article describing the origin of the New-York Gallery of the Fine Arts, attributed by Burton Pollin to Henry Cood Watson,[50] appears in the September 13, 1845, issue of the *Broadway Journal*. Watson generously commends the individuals who saw in the pending disposal of Reed's collection "a favorable opportunity for founding a Public Gallery": "Too much praise cannot be awarded to these true followers of the beautiful art; while many, and particularly the fashionable many, expend their so-called enthusiasm in wordy expletives and mawkish lamentation upon the fallen state of the Arts in this country, a few gentlemen honorably distinguished as New York merchants, step forward, and give the only substantial proof of their interest in Painters and the Painter's Art."[51] This article is quite unlike the two columns written by Charles Briggs about the founding of the New-York Gallery of the Fine Arts in earlier issues of the *Broadway Journal*. In the March 1, 1845, issue, Briggs chastises the founders of the gallery for showing "bad pictures" (*BJ*, 1:134). He later expressed his disappointment in the founders for hanging copies alongside original works by American artists: "What we had hoped to see, when the New York gallery was first projected, was the foundation of a gallery of American Art; one that we could point to with pride. . . . Our country is so belittled by imitation and copy-ism, that we cannot but think that a collection of Original American works would have a beneficial effect in other departments, and lead to self-dependence in other things of seemingly greater importance than paintings and statues" (1:187). Neither of these sentiments is included in Watson's overview of the founding of the gallery published months later when Briggs was no longer asso-ciated with the *Broadway Journal*.

During this same period, the American Art-Union's lottery shows were thriving. Founded in 1839, the Art-Union was designed to popularize and pro-mote the sale of contemporary American artwork:

> Unlike the AUL [Art Union of London], which was created for both phil-osophical and practical reasons, the AAU [American Art-Union] was founded in 1839 primarily to create a gallery for new art in New York. . . . The AAU borrowed heavily from the AUL's idealized rhetoric about the moral and social benefits of promoting taste among the broader popula-tion and of encouraging artistic production, but openly acknowledged that the form of its particular operations were driven largely by a dual commit-ment to its "Perpetual Free Gallery" (open free to members and at a nomi-nal charge to non-members) and to the purchase of prizes by committee.[52]

By 1845, the gallery had 3,233 members, a significant increase from its original 814 members.[53] In addition to this venue, many artists exhibited their work in "rooms at Broadway."

Poe, like others in artistic circles, would have been caught up in the city's enthusiasm for these new and prospering institutions of art. While working at the *New-York Mirror* and later at the *Broadway Journal*, Poe would have had plenty of opportunities to meet artists and attend art exhibits. He also lived in a neighborhood with painters and other members of the artistic commu-nity; in fact, Asher Durand (91 Amity) and James Hamilton Shegogue (7 Amity), both influential members of the National Academy of Design, were Poe's neighbors when he lived at 85 Amity. Whether Poe came into personal contact with Durand or Shegogue can only be guessed, but since walking to work was a normal means of transportation for those in lower Manhattan, it is highly likely that, as neighbors with similar interests, they came into con-tact with one another.

The underlying contention of this book, then, is that not only did Poe attend art exhibits, write about painting and sculpture, and become acquainted with artists in his neighborhood in both Philadelphia and New York, but his immersion in the visual arts also had a significant impact on his writing, especially immediately following his stay in Manhattan. Poe's exposure to paintings, especially those by the painters of the Hudson River school, similarly influenced his developing visual aesthetics. Of course, as mentioned earlier, Poe had always shown a pointed interest in the visual arts and visual tricks, as his writing prior to 1844 demonstrates; nonetheless, the excitement generated in the arts community at this pivotal time in New York, the nascence of American art criticism, and the impact of Poe's close working relationship with Charles Briggs made this period particularly important and influential, especially as Poe's writing turned from the drama of the sublime to the harmony of the beautiful.

1

POE'S EXPOSURE TO ART EXHIBITED IN
PHILADELPHIA AND MANHATTAN, 1838–1845

This chapter presents a comprehensive listing of the paintings by important American and European artists shown at the Pennsylvania Academy of the Fine Arts while Poe lived in Philadelphia between 1838 and 1844, as well as lists of paintings by significant American artists hung in the 1844 and 1845 annual exhibitions at the National Academy of Design while Poe lived in Manhattan. A number of these paintings are interpreted in relation to Poe's visual aesthetics or his tales—specifically paintings by Nicolas Poussin, Salvator Rosa, Francis Edmonds, William Sidney Mount, Asher Durand, and Thomas Cole. Poe mentioned several of these artists, as well as others, in his work even though he did not specify their particular paintings. Although he saw paintings in homes in Richmond and may have been exposed to paintings in London galleries when he was young, this chapter's discussion of how exposure to art affected his writing and aesthetics begins with his move to Philadelphia in 1838.

Living in Philadelphia for six years (a long time considering Poe's usually unsettled life) afforded Poe the opportunity to see the shows at the Pennsylvania Academy of the Fine Arts and discuss art at "informal social gatherings of artists, actors and writers held at the Falstaff Hotel," where he encountered Thomas Sully, John Sartain, and George R. Bonfield, among others (*Poe Log*, 284). During this time, Poe came to know John Sartain very well, and their friendship lasted from when they met in 1841 until Poe's death in 1849.[1] In fact, just weeks after Poe died, Sartain made a mezzotint portrait of him after Samuel Stillman Osgood's oil painting; this mezzotint was used in Rufus Griswold's *The Works of the Late Edgar Allan Poe*. In the 1840s, Sartain provided engravings for many of the same publications where Poe's work appeared, including *Graham's Magazine*, *Godey's Lady's Book*, and *Burton's Gentleman's Magazine*.[2] In particular, Sartain's engraving after a painting by "Martin," entitled *Landscape with Pan and Syrinx* (1819), became the basis for Poe's plate piece "The Island of the Fay," published in the June 1841 issue of *Graham's Magazine*. F. DeWolfe Miller believes "Martin" to be English artist John Martin, "whom Sartain knew in England before he moved to Philadelphia. In his *Reminiscences*, Sartain notes that he owned several of John Martin's etchings."[3]

While in Philadelphia, Poe also established a friendship with Felix O. C. Darley, often called the father of American illustration. Darley's illustrations accompanied Poe's short story "The Gold Bug" in the June 28, 1843, issue of Philadelphia's *Dollar Newspaper*. Earlier that year, on January 31, 1843, Darley had signed a contract with Poe, agreeing to "furnish original designs, or drawings (on wood or paper as required) of his own composition, in his best manner, and from subjects supplied him by Mess: Clarke and Poe; the said designs to be employed in illustration of the Magazine entitled 'The Stylus'" (*Poe Log*, 396). Poe also renewed his friendship with Thomas Sully's nephew Robert Sully, Poe's childhood friend from Richmond and a painter.[4] In addition, Poe may have become acquainted with Joshua Shaw, who lived in Philadelphia during this time and whose painting Poe praised in a fine arts column in the *Broadway Journal* in 1845. Poe's relationships with artists during his time in Philadelphia clearly afforded him many opportunities to discuss the art he saw on exhibit or in the homes or studios of his artist friends. That Poe mentions Salvator Rosa in his work more than once suggests that the paintings he saw by Rosa and others at the Pennsylvania Academy of the Fine Arts made an impression on him. There Poe also saw paintings by his friend Thomas Sully and by his often-quoted favorite Claude Lorrain.

A year after Poe left Philadelphia, a devastating fire in June 1845 completely destroyed the antique cast collection at the Pennsylvania Academy of the Fine Arts as well as a number of its important European paintings, including some by Rosa. An article in the *New-York Mirror* of June 21, 1845, suggests that the fire was set purposefully:

> The labor of forty years was thus swept away in as many minutes. It seems to have been the work of an incendiary, and what could have induced the fiendish design is most extraordinary. The fire originated among some

lumber in the antique gallery, and no doubt it was placed there intention-
ally, as two persons were seen to leave the building just before the fire
broke out. Many valuable paintings were saved, but the loss is irreparable,
as it includes some of the best paintings in the Union—the works of Salvator Rosa, Rubens, Raphael, Kauffman, Titian, David, many of our best
native artists. . . . Salvator Rosa's landscape, Mercury endeavoring to
deceive Argus, while watching Io is missing.[5]

As a consequence of the Philadelphia fire and because many influential New
York merchants donated significantly to the arts in New York, it fast replaced
Philadelphia as the center of the arts. During Poe's time in Manhattan before
his move to Fordham in 1846, he was a part of this newfound enthusiasm for the
visual arts. Poe had plenty of opportunities to discuss the arts with Charles
Briggs while they were both at the *Broadway Journal*. In addition, Samuel Stillman Osgood attended numerous soirees with Poe, giving the two men opportunities to discuss paintings on display at the various venues on Broadway as well
as Osgood's own paintings. Osgood's 1839 portrait of British poet and feminist
Caroline Sheridan Norton and his portrait of Poe, painted sometime in 1845 or
early 1846, must have been objects of discussion.

Exhibits at the Pennsylvania Academy of the Fine Arts, 1838–1844

The Pennsylvania Academy of the Fine Arts was founded in 1809 by artists
Charles Wilson Peale, Rembrandt Peale, and William Rush as well as by members of the business community. The Academy was established to "provide
America's artists with 'correct and elegant Copies, from the works of the first
Masters' and to 'facilitate' the artists' 'access to such Standards.'" In other
words, "the Academy founders agreed that their primary mission was to bring
classical art education to America, saving artists a difficult and expensive trip to
study in London or on the Continent." However, these idealistic ambitions were
overridden by the desire of wealthy donors to make the Academy "a place for
gentlemen alone to enjoy the connoisseurship of the fine arts."[6] The preservation
of the goals set by the founding charter came into conflict with the practical,
financial realities of the donors' desires. This tension continued until the beginning of the 1840s, when the Academy finally recognized that American artists

needed an academic curriculum and that the Academy could provide that service.

Despite these negotiations, the Academy's exhibits were driven by commercial rather than educational or aesthetic values. It held its first show in 1811, but after 1835 it did not sponsor any group exhibits; instead, the Artists' Fund Society of Philadelphia sponsored group shows at the Academy during this time. Peter Falk's invaluable catalog *The Annual Exhibition Record of the Pennsylvania Academy of the Fine Arts* provides details of these shows during the time Poe lived in Philadelphia. A list of the most important artists on exhibit from 1838 to 1844 from this catalog follows.[7]

John Gadsby Chapman
   1838   *Boy Setting a Snare; Baptism of Col. James Smith, or Ceremony of His Adoption into an Indian Tribe, 1755*
   1840   *View in Virginia; The Partridge Trap*
   1843   Special exhibit: *Vignette—Cottage Scene; Vignette—Blacksmith; Vignette—Milk Maid; Vignette—the Wagoner; Vignette—Mowing; Vignette—Haymakers*
Thomas Cole
   1838   *View on the Catskill*
   1840   *Landscape—Schroon Mountain*
   1842   *The Titan's Goblet*
   1844   Special exhibit: *The Voyage of Life* (series of four paintings)
Asher Brown Durand
   1841   *Landscape*
   1843   *Embarkation of Columbus*
Claude Lorrain (Claude Gellée)
   1844   Special exhibit: *Marine View and Sea Port*
Nicolas Poussin
   1840   *Deluge*
Salvator Rosa
   1843   *Landscape and Figures*
Clarkson Stanfield
   1843   *Caligula's Bridge—Ischia and Procida in the Distance*
Thomas Sully
   1838   *Portrait of a Lady; Portrait of a Lady; Lady Macbeth; The Lost Child*

1840 *Portrait of a Child; The Mantilla; The Country Girl; The Sleeping Girl* (after Reynolds); *Full-Length Portrait of Mrs. Darley and Son; Girl and Bird* (after Reynolds); *The Strawberry Girl* (after Reynolds)

Special exhibit: *Queen Victoria*, St. George's Society (full length, the original from life)

1841 *Portrait of the Late William Kneass; Group of Children; The Farewell* (cabinet picture); *A Group of Children; Portrait of the Hon. Joel R. Poinsett; Portrait of a Lady*

1842 *Portrait of a Lady; Sleeping Infant; Portrait of a Young Lady; Portrait of a Lady; Charity*

1843 *Portrait of a Gentleman; Portrait of a Lady; Equestrian Portrait of Gen. Washington Reviewing His Troops, in the Year 1794, Pending the Whiskey Riots; Portrait of a Lady; Little Nell in the Curiosity Shop* (vide *Master Humphrey's Clock*); *The Sisters; Portrait of a Gentleman; Portrait of a Lady*

Special exhibit: *Whole Length Child and Dog; Great Pitch of the Falls of Niagara, from the American Side; General View of the Falls of Niagara, from the American Side; View of the Falls, from Below, on the Canadian Side, Including Table Rock; Groupe of Children; Child and Dog; Study for a Whole Length, a Lady; Portrait of a Young Lady*

Special exhibit: *Mother and Child, from the Murder of the Innocents; "Isabel"—a Sketch; Full Length Portraits of Mother and Child; Portrait of a Lady; Portrait of a Lady; Portrait of Major Thomas Biddle, 1812*

Special exhibit: *Madonna* (after Battoni)

1844 *Zerlina; The Chip Girl; Portrait of the Rev. T. H. Stockton; Young Harry; Portrait of a Lady; Lady Reading; "Cinderella"; Portrait of a Lady*

Special exhibit: *Portrait of a Lady with a Guitar; Portraits of a Brother and Sister; Whole Length of a Girl and Dog; Portrait of a Lady; Attala* (after Girodet)

Nicolas Poussin (1594–1665)

Poe certainly would have noticed Nicolas Poussin's 1664 painting *The Deluge* (fig. 5) at the 1840 exhibit at the Pennsylvania Academy of the Fine Arts for its powerful depiction of nature and man's vulnerability. During 1840 Poe was writing short pieces of an unfinished novel, *The Journal of Julius Rodman*, which included many framed images of rugged landscapes. Only four years earlier, Poe had reviewed Frances Trollope's *Paris and the Parisians in 1835* in the May 1836 issue of the *Southern Literary Messenger*; in "Letter 5," Trollope deplores the Louvre's "covering up" of Poussin's paintings to give precedence to modern works. She specifically bemoans not seeing *The Deluge*, noting that its "eclipse" was troubling to her and her children. To support her claim that this painting was too important to have been left out of the exhibit, she quotes her brother Henry Milton's response to *The Deluge* in his *Letters on the Fine Arts, Written from Paris, in the Year 1815*: "Colouring was unquestionably Poussin's least excellence; yet in this collection there is one of his pictures—the Deluge—in which the effect produced by the mere colouring is most singular and powerful. The air is burdened and heavy with water; the earth, where it is not as yet overwhelmed seems torn to pieces by its violence: the very light of heaven is absorbed and lost."[8]

In addition to its masterful use of color, this painting, created near the end of Poussin's career, departs dramatically from his usual classical style, according to Richard Verdi. This striking deviation would have been a draw for any art lover but especially for Poe, who was attracted at this time not only to the beautiful but also to the sublime. As Verdi argues, *The Deluge* was "an early masterpiece of the horrific sublime . . . its figures being few and entirely subordinated to an awesome vision of the elemental fury of nature."[9] That "fury of nature" attracts the viewer, and the eye is first drawn to the lightning that breaks through the menacing, dark sky in the middle to left part of the painting. The drama of this white break in the blackened sky leads the eye to the mysterious, cloud-crossed full moon on the far left. The entire upper half of the painting is singularly devoid of man's influence; it is only as the eye moves from the moon downward that a man is seen bathed in light and praying to heaven as his boat sinks into the raging water near a rocky precipice. Because of the way the light hits the waterfall behind the praying man, the eye sweeps upward to the upper-right corner of the painting, again to a scene of harsh, rocky terrain with swaying trees uprooted by the storm, and a barren, dark landscape. Only after that initial sweep does the eye move to the bottom of the painting, where humans are seen struggling, unsuccessfully, against the fury of the floodwaters. Quite to the left of the humans struggling to survive the flood, a huge snake, disproportionately large in comparison to the overall landscape, is seen moving up the rocky cliff.

Fig. 5   Nicolas Poussin, L'hiver (Winter) or Le deluge
(The deluge), 1664. Musée du Louvre, Paris. Photo:
Gianni Dagli Orti / The Art Archive at Art Resource,
New York.

Verdi recounts Horace Walpole's response to *The Deluge* more than twenty years after he saw the painting on exhibit in Luxembourg in 1750 as part of Poussin's four-painting series *The Four Seasons*: "Walpole observed that, of all the works then on view at the Luxembourg, this one was 'worth going to see alone.' 'The three other seasons are good for nothing,' he insisted, 'but the *Deluge* is the first picture in the world of its kind.'" This striking evaluation of *The Deluge* did not lose its merit over time, and certainly Poe recognized the painting's sublime quality when he saw it in 1840. As Verdi suggests, "The *Deluge* has appealed to an unusually diverse and distinguished series of critics and . . . sustained an almost bewildering variety of interpretations. . . . The critical history of this picture can be seen to have paved the way for the modern view of Poussin as an intensely emotional—and even passionate—painter, rather than a learned and philosophical one."[10]

In the same year that Poussin's painting was on exhibit, Poe was publishing chapters from his unfinished novel *The Journal of Julius Rodman* in *Burton's Gentleman's Magazine*. As Burton Pollin so succinctly states in his introduction to his edited edition of *Julius Rodman*, "There is no full study of the truncated novel in the exact context of Poe's life and writings in Philadelphia at the time."[11] One such context would be Poe's exposure to the art on display at the Pennsylvania Academy of the Fine Arts. Even if Poe wrote this serial novel to make money, he nonetheless included passages of landscape description that appear as distinct paintings, suggesting that the landscape paintings he saw were becoming a more important influence on his work than they had been previously. Kent Ljungquist makes note of this textual conceit in his overview of Poe's picturesque aesthetics: "Poe's pictorialism aims . . . to produce the effect of a painting, a piquant combination of details that can be seen as within a frame."[12] Take, for example, the following passage from the third chapter of *Julius Rodman*:

> The banks sloped down very gradually into the water, and were carpeted with a short soft grass of a brilliant green hue, which was visible under the surface of the stream for some distance from the shore; especially on the north side, where the clear creek fell into the river. All round the island, which was probably about twenty acres in extent, was a complete fringe of cotton-wood; the trunks loaded with grape vines in full fruit, and so closely-interlocking with each other, that we could scarcely get a glimpse of the river between the leaves. Within this circle the grass was somewhat

higher, and of a coarser texture, with a pale yellow or white streak down the middle of each blade. . . . Interspersed among it in every direction, were myriads of the most brilliant flowers, in full bloom, and most of them of fine odor—blue, pure white, bright yellow, purple, crimson, gaudy scarlet, and some with streaked leaves like tulips. Little knots of cherry trees and plum bushes grew in various directions about, and there were many narrow winding paths which circled the island, and which had been made by elk or antelopes. Nearly in the centre, was a spring of sweet and clear water, which bubbled up from among a cluster of steep rocks, covered from head to foot with moss and flowering vines. The whole bore a wonderful resemblance to an artificial flower garden, but was infinitely more beautiful.[13]

Similar passages are inserted throughout the six installments of *Julius Rodman*. In the sixth chapter, to cite another instance, Poe describes a "range of high, snow-capped mountains. . . . Two rivers presented the most enchanting appearance as they wound away their long snake-like lengths in the distance, growing thinner and thinner until they looked like faint threads of silver as they vanished in the shadowy mists of the sky."[14] Such passages demonstrate Poe's ability to write with "an artistical eye," a skill that the narrator of "The Landscape Garden" admires in painters. According to this narrator, nature cannot arrange a landscape composition to the best visual advantage: "In the most enchanting of natural landscapes, there will always be found a defect or an excess. . . . The arrangement of the parts will always be susceptible of improvement. In short, no position can be attained, from which an artistical eye, looking steadily, will not find matter of offence, in what is technically termed the *composition* of a natural landscape" (*Tales*, 1:707).

Salvator Rosa (1615–1673)

Salvator Rosa's painting *Landscape with Figures* (fig. 6) was on exhibit at the Pennsylvania Academy of the Fine Arts in 1843. In the painting, the distant light just left of center first attracts the eye, intimating a promised relief to the figures traveling through the rough mountainous terrain. Much in the way that the narrator of "Landor's Cottage" traverses a "precipitous ledge of granite" to find vegetation "less and less lofty and Salvatorish in character" (*Tales*, 2:1331–32), so, too,

Fig. 6   Salvator Rosa, *Landscape with Figures*, ca. 1713.
Uffizi Gallery, Florence. Photo: Finsiel / Alinari / Art
Resource, New York.

do the travelers in Rosa's painting approach treacherous terrain at the beginning
of their trek through the mountains. Although the figures in the foreground
immediately attract the eye, the movement of their party across the river to the
mountain pass is quickly superseded by the grandeur of the mountain peaks and
the brightly lit sky in the distance. As in most of Rosa's paintings, the landscape
dominates; man is diminished.

    Rosa was best known for his rugged, rocky, wild, mountainous landscapes.
Writing in 1846, T. C. Pickering observed that "Salvator Rosa's great excellence
lay in landscape. He delighted in representing scenes of desolation, solitude and
danger, lonely defiles and deep forests, trees scathed by lightning and clouds
lowering with thunder."[15] When Poe was assistant editor at *Burton's Gentleman's
Magazine*, he read (and most likely edited) "A Critical Notice of the Picture
Galleries of the North of Europe" by "A Recent Visitor"; the visitor's review of
the work exhibited in a gallery in Copenhagen's royal palace appears two pages
after an installment of Poe's *Julius Rodman*. The unnamed critic had been

attracted to a very large painting by Rosa entitled *Jonah Preaching to the Ninev-ites*, which notably differs from "the gloomy forests and banditti, or the solitary caverns and rocky passes" that characterize much of Rosa's work.[16]

Sir Joshua Reynolds, in *Lives of the Most Eminent Modern Painters* (1754), admires Rosa's ability to depict "savage and uncultivated nature. . . . What is most to be admired in him, is the perfect correspondence which he observed between the subjects he chose, and his manner of treating them. Everything is of a piece: his Rocks, Trees, Sky, even to his handling, have the same rude and wild character which animated his figures."[17] Years later, an 1801 reprint of William Mason's *Essay on the Different Natural Situations of Gardens* (1774) included another favorable estimation of Rosa: "The author considers Nicolas Poussin and Salvator Rosa the two greatest landscape painters; Salvator for 'terrible and noble natural situations,' with blasted trees and scarce sign of life, and Poussin for views of temples, palaces on hillsides, and rich verdure."[18]

The National Academy of Design's 1844 Exhibit

Although Poe arrived in New York City just before the nineteenth annual show at the National Academy of Design opened on April 25, 1844, he most likely did not attend the opening reception since admission was "on *invitation by the Council* ONLY."[19] Nonetheless, he certainly would have had the opportunity to see the works exhibited that year before the show closed on July 6. The exhibit featured 387 works, including paintings by many well-known artists: Thomas Cole, Thomas Doughty, William Page, and Thomas Sully, each with one painting on exhibit; Peter Frederick Rothermel, with two; Christopher Cranch, Henry Inman, and Joshua Shaw, each with three; Charles Loring Elliott, with four; Jasper Francis Cropsey, Henry Peters Gray, and William Sidney Mount, each with five; George Whiting Flagg, with six; Charles Weir, with seven; and John Gadsby Chapman and Asher Durand, each with nine. James Hamilton Shegogue and Francis Edmonds were on the Committee of Arrangements that year, and as a result they exhibited a large number of their own paintings.

Based on the information in the *National Academy of Design Exhibition Record, 1826–1860*, the following popular artists' paintings were exhibited in the 1844 annual show:

John Gadsby Chapman: *Peasant Girl of Albano*; *Hebrew Women Borrowing the Jewels of the Egyptians*; *Portrait of a Boy in Indian Costume*; *"On the Fence," Town or Country?*; *A Lazy Fisherman*; *The Brush-Wood Gatherer, a Sketch*; *Sketch from Nature*; two portraits

Thomas Cole: *Landscape*

Christopher Cranch: *Landscape*; *The Reapers*; *Landscape*

Jasper Francis Cropsey: *A Shower Coming Up, at Little Falls on the Passaic River*; *View in Orange County, with Greenwood Lake in the Distance*; *Evening, a Composition*; *View of Greenwood Lake*; *Falls of the Greenwood*

Thomas Doughty: *Landscape*; *View from Greenwood Cemetery, Looking over the Bay of New-York*

Asher Brown Durand: *The Solitary Oak*; *Full-Length of a Boy*; *Landscape, Composition*; *Study from Nature*; *Emigrant Family*; *Landscape, Wood Scene*; *Italian Cottage*; two portraits

Francis William Edmonds: *The Beggar's Petition*; *The Image Pedler*; *Sam Weller*; *Vesuvius, from Sorrento*; *Aqueducts on the Campagna of Rome*; *Florence from the Arno*

Charles Loring Elliott: five portraits

George Whiting Flagg: *Half-Length of a Lady*; *Bianca Visconti* (owned by N. P. Willis); *Portrait of J[ames] G. Percival*; *Thomson's Lavinia*; *Girl's Frolic* (owned by N. P. Willis); *The Widow*

Henry Peters Gray: *Portrait of His Wife*; *Magdalen*; *Portrait of a Lady*; *Portrait of Himself*; *Portrait of a Lady*

Henry Inman: *Portrait of the Late Bishop Moore, of Virginia*; *The Ladye with a Mask*; *Landscape*

William Sidney Mount: *Portrait of Rev. S[amuel] Seabury, D.D.*; *Girl Asleep*; *Portrait of Benj[amin] Strong, Esq.*; *Boys Hustling Coppers*; *Farmers Nooning* (engraved by Alfred Jones for the Apollo Association [*sic*] from the original picture by Mount)

Peter Frederick Rothermel: *De Soto Discovering the Mississippi*; *The Novice*

John Sartain: engraving in mezzotint, from an original picture by Thomas Lawrence

Joshua Shaw: *View in Wales, Near Abagavany*; *Scene on the Coast of Cornwall*; *Italian Landscape*

James Hamilton Shegogue: *Senora de Goni*; *The Gift from Brazil*; *Eugene, Alfred, and Marion*; *Fire Island, a Sketch*; two portraits

Thomas Sully: *The Sisters*

Charles Weir: *Compositor Setting Type*; *Boy Feeding Chickens*; *Fish, a Study from Nature*; *Fruit*; three portraits

Francis William Edmonds (1806–1863)

As one of the organizers of the 1844 exhibit, Francis William Edmonds chose six of his own paintings to be hung. Edmonds was by profession a banker, as well as "an artist of considerable talent . . . [and] a man of great personal charm, who played an important part in the cultural life of New York City."[20] His popularity in the arts community is evidenced by his participation in its most important venues. Samuel Morse, the first president of the National Academy of Design, encouraged Edmonds in his artistic pursuits, and his reputation at the Academy grew, as reflected by his quick move through its ranks from student to associate in 1837 and to academician by 1840.[21] Additionally, Edmonds became treasurer of the Apollo Society (later renamed the American Art-Union) in 1839 and was appointed vice president of the New-York Gallery of the Fine Arts when it was founded in 1844. In 1844, as well, Edmonds's painting *The New Scholar* was selected as the engraving to be distributed by the American Art-Union to its members.[22] As Jane Adams explains in her study of nineteenth-century American art unions, "The benefits from purchasing a five-dollar annual subscription were an engraving, a chance in the yearly lottery distribution for a painting or other original art work, free admission to the gallery and a subscription to the *Bulletin*, which was a monthly (published from April to December) compendium of art news, reviews, instruction and engravings."[23] *The New Scholar* also appeared in the National Academy of Design's 1845 annual show.

Edmonds was a member of the Sketch Club, founded in 1829 as a gathering place for painters, patrons, and writers. Its members included Asher Durand, Thomas Cole, Samuel Morse, William Cullen Bryant, John Inman, Jonathan Sturges, and Washington Irving; guests invited to the club included James Fenimore Cooper, James Kirke Paulding, and Ralph Waldo Emerson. Edmonds remained a member of the organization when, in 1844, the Sketch Club became the Artists' Sketch Club, with only painters and sculptors as its members. The first meeting of the new club took place at Edmonds's home at 216 Thompson Street, where he lived from 1844 to 1845. His residence was near the corner of

Thompson and Amity Street and was thus quite close to his good friend Asher Durand, who lived at 91 Amity, two buildings away from Poe's residence at 85 Amity. We have no documentation that Poe ever met Edmonds or Durand in their neighborhood or at a social gathering, but since all three were members of the cultural community, it is probable that they knew each other; if not, they certainly would have known of each other.[24] Since Edmonds was friends with William Page, who, in turn, was friends with Charles Briggs, who published a series of essays by Page in the *Broadway Journal*, Poe might well have made Edmonds's acquaintance through Briggs. However, since Poe did not share Edmonds's aesthetic or political propensities, neither would have desired the other's friendship.

Edmonds often used literary subjects in his art, but his overall concern was to paint homely scenes with an egalitarian bent in the Dutch tradition, such as *The New Scholar*. He was a strong supporter of Andrew Jackson and, later, Martin Van Buren, and his patrons were merchants, bankers, and railroad executives with primarily Democratic sympathies. Politics assumed a prominent role in genre painting during the antebellum decades and is significant to understanding Edmonds's art.[25] Despite the differences between Poe's and Edmonds's political leanings, the cross-references to each other's subject matter suggest that the two men knew of each other's work. This is especially true for Edmonds's painting *Facing the Enemy*, which Poe certainly would have noticed in the National Academy of Design's annual show in 1845 (fig. 7).

Charles Briggs reviewed *Facing the Enemy* in the May 10, 1845, number of the *Broadway Journal* as part of his article on the National Academy of Design exhibit. Briggs praises Edmonds's painting and his storytelling, "which is a point that Mr. Edmonds rarely or never fails in." Briggs describes the "old toper" pictured in *Facing the Enemy* as "one of those hard drinkers with carbuncled noses and crispy hair, who used to be common enough twenty years ago but are now growing very rare." Speaking with all the messianic fervor of a Temperance Movement adherent, Briggs voices his belief that there will come a time in the future when

Fig. 7   Francis William Edmonds, *Facing the Enemy*, 1845. Chrysler Museum of Art, Norfolk, Virginia. Dedicated by the Museum Trustees to William Hennessey in celebration of his tenth anniversary as director, May 2007, 89.92.

"drinking shall have gone entirely out of fashion; the world will scarcely believe that it was indulged in to the excess that books and songs and pictures will tell of" (*BJ*, 1:306). That Poe read Briggs's comments on this painting is unquestionable; that he agreed with Briggs's ardent prediction is highly unlikely.

Poe's "The Black Cat," published in the August 1843 number of the *United States Saturday Post*, can easily be read as a parody of Temperance Movement stories, as T. J. Matheson so convincingly argues. Matheson points to Poe's acquaintance with Timothy Shay Arthur, whom Poe knew in Baltimore in 1833 when both were members of the literary society Seven Stars. Poe was undoubtedly familiar with Arthur's temperance tract *Six Nights with the Washingtonians*, published serially by *Godey's Lady's Book*, since Poe wrote to Joseph Snodgrass in 1841 about Arthur's stories.[26] The unrealistic expectations of the Temperance Movement—the disappearance of all drinking, as Briggs's review suggests and movement enthusiasts predicted—and the dire stories of drunken debauchery that the movement circulated to scare people away from drinking are subverted in Poe's own story of drunkenness and death.

That Poe knew Edmonds's painting is undeniable. *Facing the Enemy* was not only shown in the 1845 National Academy of Design exhibit but also issued as an engraving by the American Art-Union in 1844. Thus, it would have been widely known. Edmonds's painting of the "old toper" was picked up by publisher John Ridner as a good illustration for a broadside that appealed to temperance groups. Ridner wrote a tract around the theme of Edmonds's painting to use in the broadside:

> To give a better idea of this picture, it may be well to relate the incident which supplied the subject. Some years ago, when the cause of Temperance was first agitated, a certain mechanic who had long been addicted to habits of drunkenness, became a convert to the Temperance reform, conscientiously adhering to his "PLEDGE." While sitting with his wife some time afterwards, she observed that he was unusually pensive and his mind apparently disturbed; suddenly he called out to her to "send for a decanter of Rum!" This—it may well be imagined, at once greatly alarmed her, as she had already felt the happy effects of the change from his former habits, and looked forward with still higher hopes to the brighter prospects which his new course of life had led her to anticipate, it is easy to fancy then, that the quickness of woman's imagination immediately conjured up in her

mind the gloomiest forebodings at such an unlooked for request, but, without daring to expostulate, she purchased the liquor and placed it in his hands, he planted it firmly before him, exclaiming "While it was behind me and out of sight I was always thinking of it and fearing it, but now that it is before me and I can face it, I fear it not and defy it." The point represented by the artist is where "the enemy" has been placed before him and he is complacently facing and reflecting upon it.

It will be remembered that the original is by the Artist who painted the popular picture of "SPARKING," published by the American Art-Union a few years since.

A copy of this print should be in the house of every Temperance man, and, to bring it within the means of all, the price has been reduced to

ONE DOLLAR.

John P. Ridner, 497 Broadway, Art-Union Building, New-York.[27]

Interestingly, in both the painting and the sketch on which it was based (fig. 8), the precariously seated carpenter is situated between two emblems also found in Poe's "The Black Cat": alcohol and an ax. Moreover, in Poe's story, the main character's purported nemesis is the "Fiend Intemperance." In Edmonds's painting and sketch, the old man tilts back in his chair as he looks at the "enemy"— the flask purposefully set on a box on the windowsill. Neither Briggs's interpretation that "the man bends back in his chair as if to get out of harm's way" (BJ, 1:306) nor Ridner's story of his determined rejection makes sense if the "old toper's" countenance and position are considered. The posture of leaning back on two chair legs suggests a nervous or vulnerable person, not someone bent on getting out of harm's way. In addition, the man's brow is furrowed rather than determined. The painting's setting—a place of work threatened by the desire for pleasure that the bottle of alcohol implies—includes a subtext of violence, as indicated by the ax.

Kevin Avery mentions the ax in describing how Edmonds carefully changed the drawing when he made the painting. Avery notes that in moving "from preliminary sketch to finished painting, Edmonds defined the setting and subject in the thorough and thoroughly compelling manner to which his viewers and patrons had become accustomed."[28] In the painting, the ax leans against an upright log surrounded by broken chips (in Avery's terms, a "chopping block"),

Fig. 8   Francis William Edmonds, study for *Facing
the Enemy*, ca. 1845. The Metropolitan Museum of Art,
New York. Gift of James C. McGuire, 1926, 26.216.9.
Image copyright © The Metropolitan Museum of Art.
Photo: Art Resource, New York.

indicating that the ax has been used recently. In the sketch, on the other hand,
the ax rests against a longer log that lies on its side, uncut. It appears that
Edmonds decided that the "history" of the setting in the painting should seem
less relaxed than that depicted in the drawing. He purposefully changed the
more relaxed environment by illustrating the strenuous—if not violent—act of
having lodged an ax into a log numerous times. These conscious decisions made
in the move from sketch to painting, in addition to the man's precarious way of
"facing the enemy," all signal a complex and ironic response to the Temperance

Movement—not the determined, purposeful rejection of alcohol that Ridner wanted to see.

Poe incorporates similarly conflicted images of the alcoholic in "The Black Cat" and "King Pest" (first published in 1835 and republished in the October 18, 1845, issue of the *Broadway Journal*). Each story presents a highly dramatized picture of drunken debauchery and its consequences—one excessively violent, the other humorously bawdy. That Edmonds knew "The Black Cat" as the story of an alcoholic who kills his wife by axing her through the head—ostensibly because the "Fiend Intemperance" drove him to do so—cannot be ascertained definitively. However, since "The Black Cat" was published in the Philadelphia magazine *United States Saturday Post* in August 1843, the same year that Poe won first prize in Philadelphia's *Dollar Newspaper*'s contest for "The Gold Bug," Poe's story must have drawn some attention in the Sketch Club's literary discussions. Surely, these two sensationalist stories would not have been overlooked by a society devoted to discussing contemporary literature and art. That Edmonds included an ax in the foreground of his painting is quite purposeful; its prominence could easily be considered a nod to Poe's alcoholic protagonist in "The Black Cat."

Two of Poe's other stories, "The Sphinx" and "The Cask of Amontillado"—both written in 1845 at 85 Amity Street—could easily be read as gesturing toward Edmonds's *Facing the Enemy*. It would have been difficult to overlook or forget this painting, since it appeared in two arts venues and was posted throughout the city in Ridner's broadside in 1845. As in *Facing the Enemy*, the primary image in "The Sphinx" is a man sitting by a window. It is there that he sees what he mistakenly takes to be a monster or enemy; his deranged response would have led to his mental unraveling, if not for his friend's rational explanation. In "The Cask of Amontillado," the narrator uses the lure of amontillado to lead his enemy Fortunato, a former friend who had insulted him, to an untimely death. Due to his drunken lightheartedness, Fortunato is unable to see the obvious signs that indicate he is "facing the enemy." In both stories, the act of seeing plays a prominent role: in the former, distortion causes trauma; in the latter, the unwillingness to see leads to death. Both stories undercut the message of Ridner's broadside, which urges men to forgo alcohol by simply invoking the will to do so. In neither of Poe's stories do men succeed in "facing the enemy" with mere willfulness: in "The Sphinx," the narrator cannot will away his visual hallucination without the help of his friend's rational explanation, and in "The

Cask of Amontillado," Fortunato cannot see how a trowel could foretell his death. Neither man can simply push himself away from danger; one would have gone mad without his friend's helpful research, and the other dies.

William Sidney Mount (1807–1868)

Poe's regard for William Sidney Mount's work can only be surmised, since Poe does not mention Mount in any of his writings. At first, it might seem that Poe would not have been attracted to realistic images of everyday country life, and many of Mount's paintings depict such country scenes, often with children. This is indeed the case in the painting *The Trap Sprung*, which appeared as an engraving in *The Gift Book for 1844* alongside Poe's "The Purloined Letter." Yet to say that Poe would have considered Mount's work too pedestrian or sentimental might not be as apt as this initial surmise suggests. Although Mount's paintings look like homely renderings of country life, often, if not always, they include underlying, wry social critiques that, like Poe's responses to the zealous advocates of the Temperance Movement, reveal a cynical approach to social change. For example, as Deborah Johnson points out, Mount's 1830 painting *School Boys Quarrelling* "is also a sly commentary on the warring camps of the American art establishment of the 1830s, with the young combatants representing the conservative American Academy of Fine Arts, led by John Trumbull, and the upstart National Academy of Design, presided over by Samuel Morse. As a clue to his underlying subject, Mount placed a grammar book in the lower left corner inscribed with the words 'Ocular Analysis.'"[29] Poe was likewise cynical about social change, as evidenced in a letter he wrote to James Russell Lowell on July 2, 1844: "I have no faith in human perfectibility. I think that human exertion will have no appreciable effect upon humanity" (*Letters*, 2:449). This sentiment is again expressed in Poe's 1846 sketch "The Domain of Arnheim" when the narrator reveals his friend Ellison's perspective on social change: "In the possibility of any improvement, properly so called, being effected by man himself in the general condition of man, [Ellison] had (I am sorry to confess it) little faith" (*Tales*, 2:1271). Mount, too, must have held this belief, since his paintings promoted both Whig and Democratic causes, depending on the expediency of the commission. Expediency rather than ideological belief was the underpinning of his political and social scenarios.

Mount was known for using wordplay in his images. For example, as Johnson observes, in *"Bargaining for a Horse* (1835)," two characters cheerfully—and completely calculatingly—negotiate over a horse. The play in this image is around the word 'horse trading,' a derogatory term that had been adopted by political opponents to describe the corrupt deal-making of Democrats."[30] Wordplay thus gives Mount's paintings what Poe called undercurrents of meaning. *Bird-Egging* (1844), another example, initially seems to be a glancing look at a spring day in the country; three children walk along a sunlit, fence-lined pathway, the oldest holding a bird's nest. The narrative turns on the word "egging," which describes what the girl is doing to her older brother—that is, "egging him on"—as well as the actual act of stealing eggs from a bird's nest. The girl is either pleading with her older brother to allow her to carry the nest of eggs or begging him to give it back to the younger brother, who had "egged" it but lost it to the older, bigger boy. The younger boy hides his face, crying because he lost the nest or perhaps because he is ashamed of his older brother's "egging" and, unlike his sister, isn't swayed by the lure of the treasure. This last interpretation would be ironic, of course, since the younger boy is wearing a large plume in his hat, suggesting that he was not altogether innocent of a similar pillage in the past. In either case, the narrative sequence is hardly sentimental.

The children's disregard for nature's cycle contrasts sharply with their innocent, gentle physiognomies. The resulting tension pushes the painting beyond a simple pastoral scene; it becomes a comment on man's relationship to nature and his apparent obliviousness to the destruction that his whims can cause. The viewer is initially drawn into the scene by its homely and pastoral nature, the quiet lighting, and the mannered depiction of the three children walking beneath the trees; these elements signal a safe, domestic space not far from home. However, within this pleasant, comforting space, the viewer can see a forlorn bird sitting on a dead branch in the otherwise verdant, ancient tree whose trunk fills more than a third of the background.

Mount's *The Trap Sprung* (fig. 9) also pictures children drawn in the same mannered way, but the narrative is hardly one of youthful innocence. Two boys, trudging uphill through a late autumn snowfall, eagerly approach a rabbit trap, anticipating the kill and the reward. Holding a dead rabbit in his hand, one boy, dressed warmly in an overcoat, scarf, cap, thick pants, and boots, encourages the other, dressed in a torn, lightweight jacket, to get the trapped rabbit. With no means of killing it except their bare hands, the boys' smiles indicate the

Fig. 9 William Sidney Mount, *The Trap Sprung*, 1844.
Terra Foundation for American Art, Chicago. Daniel J.
Terra Collection, 1992.52. Photo: Terra Foundation for
American Art, Chicago / Art Resource, New York.

anticipated pleasure of wringing the rabbit's neck. The cloud-filled sky and vast vista of the mountains in the background, along with the snow-covered hillside and the red leaves still lingering on the branches in the foreground, signal both the life that is and the cold death soon to follow.

Mount's paintings were clearly more than depictions of pleasant pastoral life. As Johnson argues, "Mount [often] employed popular puns that themselves sprang from a nervousness in the culture about the discrepancies between what is seen and what is hidden."[31] Other critics discuss the political implications of his farmyard imagery. Differing from the landscape painters of what would become known as the Hudson River school, Mount preferred to paint the "everyday" in all its complex contradictions rather than simply portraying the beauty of nature.

The National Academy of Design's 1845 Exhibit

The twentieth annual show at the National Academy of Design opened on April 17, 1845, featuring 369 works by 145 artists. These included 152 portraits, 30 miniatures, 97 landscapes, 15 history paintings, 12 watercolors, and 2 sculptures.[32] The following works by prominent artists of the time were exhibited in the 1845 show:

Frederick Catherwood: fifteen works, mostly scenes from Mexico and designs for a fountain in Gramercy Park, Gothic buildings, and the pedestal for a statue of Washington in New York City

John Gadsby Chapman: *Portrait of a Boy*; *"Rachel Envied Her Sister"*

Frederic Edwin Church: *Twilight Among the Mountains*; *Hudson Scenery*

Thomas Cole: *Elijah at the Entrance of the Cave*; *The Mill, Sunset*; *View Across Frenchman's Bay, from Mount Desert Island, Maine, After a Squall*; *A View of the Two Lakes and Mountain House, Catskill Mountains, Morning*

Christopher Cranch: *Landscape, Sunset*; *Landscape, Study from Nature*; *View on the Hudson, Near Cold Spring*; *Cloudy Twilight*; *View from the Palisades Opposite Hastings*

Jasper Francis Cropsey: *The Forest on Fire*; *Twilight, View in Sullivan County*; *View on Esopus Creek*; *Landscape, a Study from Nature*

Thomas Doughty: *Land Storm*

Asher Brown Durand: *Landscape, Composition, "An Old Man's Reminiscences";*
 Close of a Sultry Day; Landscape, Composition; The Bride

Francis William Edmonds: *"Facing the Enemy"; The New Scholar; Sparking*
 (engraving by Alfred Jones from a picture by Edmonds)

Charles Loring Elliott: *Portrait of an Artist; Capt. Ericsson; Frederick R. Spencer,*
 N. A.; Study from Life; Portrait of a Gentleman; Portrait of a Lady; Horace
 Kneeland, Sculptor; Portrait of a Child

Henry Peters Gray: *Cupid Begging for His Arrows;* three portraits

Henry Inman: *Rydal Water; Jacob Barker, Esq.*

William Sidney Mount: *Dance of the Haymakers; G[eorge] W[ashington] Strong,*
 Esq.; Bird-Egging; Pencil Sketches of Children

Samuel Stillman Osgood: *Girlhood; Portrait of a Lady*

Peter Frederick Rothermel: *Surrender of Guatemozin*

Joshua Shaw: *Landscape*

James Hamilton Shegogue: *Evening—Landscape Composition; Portrait of a*
 Gentleman; Cabinet Portrait of a Lady; Portrait of a Gentleman; Sadi Edrehi;
 The Country Pedlar; Portrait of a Lady

Charles Weir: *Portrait of a Gentleman; The Young Connoisseur; Blind Old Man*
 Listening to His Nephew Reading; Fruit

Asher Brown Durand (1796–1886)

Unlike William Sidney Mount, Asher Brown Durand was not interested in social critique but was influenced, rather, by Thomas Cole's spiritual landscapes. Durand was a good friend of Cole, who was held in high regard as a landscape painter by the mid-1840s and was considered the leader of the Hudson River school of painting. Unlike Cole, however, Durand had to depend on portraiture to earn his living in Manhattan. Nonetheless, Cole encouraged Durand "to come to live in the country" because Cole believed that Durand's work would benefit. "The desire to produce excellence feeds the flame of our enthusiasm," Cole wrote to Durand, "and I believe the product is worthier than that which is wrought out to the approbation of the many around us. In the country we have necessarily to defer the reward of the approbation of our fellows, and have time to examine critically our own works."[33] However tempting, Cole's letter did not persuade Durand to move from the city, since he believed that proximity to his clients was essential; therefore, he remained in Manhattan. Yet, after a trip abroad in 1840, where he was joined by his friend and fellow artist Francis Edmonds, Durand returned home with a renewed sense of his own abilities and a strong desire to give up portraiture and concentrate on landscape painting. One of Durand's paintings in the 1845 National Academy of Design exhibit, *An Old Man's Reminiscences* (fig. 10), was inspired, according to his son, by "the sentiment of Goldsmith's poetry" and marks the transition from Durand's dependence on portraiture to his embrace of landscape painting.[34]

The painting depicts an old man in the left foreground observing the idyllic country scene before him and, as the title suggests, "reminiscing" about a serene life full of love (represented by the intimate couple under the trees next to the old man), peaceful pastimes (men playing baseball across the stream), fruitful employment (the man guiding his cart overfilled with the harvest of hay), domestic tranquility (the cows grazing in the pasture), and natural beauty (the wispy clouds in the blue sky and the general sweep of the composition toward a distant light). Durand depicts the various stages of the old man's life in a way that suggests it has been full, satisfying, and peaceful. Durand's painting evokes the peaceful domesticity found in "Landor's Cottage," a sketch Poe wrote just before his untimely death. It is as if we are looking at Landor many years after the narrator finds him in his home, which is simply but tastefully decorated and full of repose, two of Poe's most admired aesthetic principles.

The exhibition of *An Old Man's Reminiscences* at the National Academy of Design's annual show was a turning point for Durand's acceptance as a landscape painter, and from then on he depended less and less on portraiture. Upon Thomas Cole's unexpected death in 1848, Durand assumed his role as leader of the Hudson River school of painting.

Thomas Cole (1801–1848)

Sarah Burns argues in *Painting the Dark Side: Art and the Gothic Imagination in Nineteenth-Century America* that Poe's and Cole's work shared a similar concern for politics: "For Cole and Poe alike, the idea of democracy raised specters of disaster and decline."[35] Burns maintains this argument throughout her book, aligning Poe's tales of gothic horror and fear with Cole's paintings: "Cole's scenes of ruined castles and towers find a literary analogue in the tales and poems of Edgar Allan Poe, obsessed like Cole with contempt for and dread of the multitude that the new democratic order had spawned, and bedeviled like Cole by the

Fig. 10   Asher Brown Durand, *An Old Man's Reminiscences*, 1845. Albany Institute of History and Art. Gift of the Albany Gallery of Fine Arts, 1900.5.3.

conflicting demands of art and an increasingly commercial market." However convenient that comparison may be for some of Poe's works, Burns totally ignores Poe's other aesthetic regarding the importance of beauty, which he expressed numerous times throughout his life in essays like "The Philosophy of Composition" and in sketches like "The Domain of Arnheim." Poe's work is not simply about gothic horror and fear. Burns's claim that "Cole's paintings were influenced by the gothic effects of Salvator Rosa . . . whose landscapes were visual textbooks of terror for romantic painters" does seem to connect some of Poe's work to Cole, and Poe does refer to Rosa in "Landor's Cottage."[36] However, Burns ignores how Poe uses Rosa in this sketch.

The scene in question begins with the "Salvatorish" imagery that Burns observes, though she ignores the way that that landscape moves from the sublime toward the beautiful as the narrator approaches Landor's cottage. Poe uses the reference to Rosa to create a contrast between the aesthetic the narrator approaches and the one he leaves behind. He comes down from the ragged peaks to find solace in the landscape surrounding Landor's cottage. The narrator shares the following description in remembering his travels through the mountains to the valley that houses the cottage:

> To the north—on the craggy precipice—a few paces from the verge— upsprang the magnificent trunks of numerous hickories, black walnuts, and chestnuts, interspersed with occasional oak; and the strong lateral branches thrown out by the walnuts especially, spread far over the edge of the cliff. Proceeding southwardly, the explorer saw, at first, the same class of trees, but less and less lofty and Salvatorish in character; then he saw the gentler elm, succeeded by the sassafras and locust—these again by the softer linden, red-bud, catalpa, and maple—these yet again by still more graceful and more modest varieties. (*Tales*, 2:1332)

In this passage, the narrator's vision shifts from the dramatic precipices or "Salvatorish" imagery to a more pastoral, cultivated, and designed landscape that evidences man's influence. This human influence moves the landscape away from the dreadful, sublime terror that Burns associates with both Cole and Poe and toward a beauty resulting from the artistic transformation of landscape gardening and peaceful domesticity. In an effort to link Poe to the "dark side" of American experience, Burns ignores this more domestic aspect of his sensibility—a sensibility also expressed in "The Domain of Arnheim" (a pendant to "Landor's Cottage") and seen in the landscape paintings composed by Asher Durand and Frederic Church during the mid-1840s. This sensibility and its importance to Poe are revealed in a most personal way in his letter to Helen Whitman dated October 18, 1848:

> I suffered my imagination to stray with you, and with the few who love us both, to the banks of some quiet river, in some lovely valley of our land. Here, not *too* far secluded from the world, we exercised a taste controlled by no conventionalities, but the sworn slave of a Natural Art, in the building for ourselves a cottage which no human being could ever pass without an ejaculation of wonder at its strange, weird, and incomprehensible yet most simple beauty. Oh, the sweet and gorgeous, but not often rare flowers in which we half buried it!—the grandeur of the little-distant magnolias and tulip-trees which stood guarding it—the luxurious velvet of its lawn—the lustre of the rivulet that ran by the very door—the tasteful yet quiet comfort of the interior—the music—the books—the unostentatious pictures—and, above all, the love—the *love* that threw an unfading *glory* over the whole! (*Letters*, 2:712)

Such is the sentiment that Poe longed for not only in his life but also in his work. The paintings he saw by Cole, Church, and Durand are portrayals of natural beauty or idealized portraits of human intercourse with nature. The latter description is especially true of Asher Durand's *An Old Man's Reminiscences*. Nothing in the painting is threatening or remiss, bringing to mind Poe's sketch of Ellison's life in "The Domain of Arnheim" and Landor's life in "Landor's Cottage."

Poe's fascination with landscape and landscape gardening is evident in his mature sketch "The Domain of Arnheim," written in 1846. This sketch not only reflects a desire for peace but also articulates Poe's visual aesthetics. Here the narrator asserts that "the art of landscape gardening exhibits those qualities of the poet" that Poe held in high esteem:[37]

> The landscape-garden offered to the proper Muse the most magnificent of opportunities. Here, indeed, was the fairest field for the display of imagination in the endless combining of forms of novel beauty; the elements to

enter into combination being, by a vast superiority, the most glorious which the earth could afford. In the multiform and multicolor of the flower and the trees, [Ellison] recognised the most direct and energetic efforts of Nature at physical loveliness. And in the direction or concentration of this effort—or, more properly, in its adaptation to the eyes which were to behold it on earth—he perceived that he should be employing the best means—laboring to the greatest advantage—in the fulfillment, not only of his own destiny as a poet, but of the august purposes for which the Deity had implanted the poetic sentiment in man. . . . Mr. Ellison did much toward solving what has always seemed to me an enigma:—I mean the fact (which none but the ignorant dispute) that no such combination of scenery exists in nature as the painter of genius may produce. No such Paradises are to be found in reality as have glowed on the canvass of Claude. (*Tales*, 2:1272)

It may seem curious that Poe chose as his example the seventeenth-century French painter Claude Lorrain rather than a contemporary American artist. But, in fact, of the thirty-seven painters Poe mentions in his works, only five are American: Charles Weir, Asher Durand, John Sartain, John Gadsby Chapman, and Thomas Sully. Claude was an important influence on American landscape painters, including Cole and Durand; Cole's paintings, as Burns observes, often embrace the intensity of Rosa's work, but others reflect the peaceful beauty of Claude's. That Poe cites Claude in "The Domain of Arnheim" rather than Cole could have simply resulted from his having read Andrew Jackson Downing's 1841 edition of *A Treatise on the Theory and Practice of Landscape Gardening*; Downing repeatedly praises Claude with such statements as "To the lover of Fine Arts, the name of Claude Lorrain cannot fail to suggest examples of beauty in some of its purest and most simple forms."[38] Or it might have been Poe's way of avoiding any association with the opinions of Charles Briggs, who had harshly criticized Cole's work for being didactic. "We dislike exceedingly Cole's allegorical landscapes," Briggs wrote. "The pictures in themselves are truly beautiful, but the plan of them is against nature. . . . The charm of nature is destroyed. . . . We turn from them in disgust" (*BJ*, 1:103). Poe publicly rejected Briggs's art criticism in "The Literati of New York City," published in the May 1846 issue of *Godey's Lady's Book*: "Among the principal papers contributed by Mr. B. [to the *Broadway Journal*] were those discussing the paintings at the last exhibition of the Academy of Fine Arts in New York. I may be permitted to say that there was scarcely a point in his whole series of criticisms on this subject at which I did not radically disagree with him."[39] However, in a letter to Helen Whitman, Poe revealed that "Landor's Cottage," as a pendant to "The Domain of Arnheim," provides insight into his soul and reveals his love of nature's beauty and the artist's ability to capture that loveliness in a painting. Using Claude rather than Cole, then, allowed Poe to avoid the perception that he was simply deferring to Downing or rebutting Briggs, and yet allowed him to show his long-held love of nature's beauty and domestic repose. The aesthetic precepts outlined in these two sketches could thus be read as a true reflection of Poe's aesthetic principles and beliefs, ones that he had professed to John Neal at the age of twenty and that he kept until his death.

Of course, we do not have any direct quotes to confirm what Poe thought of the paintings by Thomas Cole—or Asher Durand or Frederic Church (specifically the latter's ethereal *Twilight Among the Mountains*, which hung in the National Academy of Design's 1845 show). However, Poe's own landscape writing strongly suggests that he would have been drawn to these works, especially to Cole's romantic imagery, dramatic color, and fine craftsmanship. Like Briggs, Poe would have faulted Cole for the didactic nature of his *Course of Empire* series, but he could not have faulted Cole's overall technique, which produced profound effects. Poe had already shown that he could quite harshly criticize even highly regarded painters such as Henry Inman—one of the founders of the National Academy of Design—for poor technique. However, Poe saw Cole's work a number of times both in Philadelphia and in New York, and he must have viewed it in a positive light since he applauds Cole's predecessor Claude Lorrain.

2

ARTISTS AND ARTWORK IN POE'S
SHORT STORIES AND SKETCHES

This chapter provides a chronological overview of Poe's references to visual artists and paintings in the stories and sketches he wrote or revised while living in
Philadelphia and New York from 1838 until his death in 1849. In some of Poe's
works, references to specific painters enhance thematic concerns or help produce a preconceived effect. In others, such as "Landor's Cottage" and "A Tale of
the Ragged Mountains" (both written later in his career), Poe obliquely admires
the Hudson River school painters by evoking their landscape paintings in
words. This nod to painters such as Thomas Cole and Asher Durand signals a
change in Poe's aesthetics from valuing the power of the sublime to appreciating
the harmony of the beautiful. In addition to the painterly references in his stories and sketches, Poe articulates quite specifically in his criticism his belief in
the affinity between the writing and painting processes. He is keenly aware of
how a painter uses his medium to produce a "startling effect" and how that
method can be replicated in the writing process.

In this overview of Poe's references to visual artists, it will become clear that
Poe prefers referring to European artists as models of great artists. He does
refer to some American painters, but more often he mentions European painters and sculptors such as Henry Fuseli, Claude Lorrain, Nicolas Poussin, Clarkson Stanfield, Antonio Canova, Giovanni Cimabue, Leonardo da Vinci,[1] Peter
Paul Rubens, Michelangelo, Raphael, Moritz Retzsch, and Salvator Rosa.[2] For
example, instead of alluding to American painters Frederic Church or Thomas
Cole in "The Landscape Garden," "The Domain of Arnheim," and "Landor's
Cottage," Poe makes reference to Claude and Rosa. This is particularly ironic

with regard to Cole, since his work was influenced by both Claude and Rosa, as art historian Barbara Gallanti observes: "By drawing on the time-honored art of Claude Lorrain and Salvator Rosa . . . and by applying the aesthetic principles of English landscape to a distinctly American geography, Cole developed—or invented—a uniquely American content."[3] Gallanti is not alone in this assessment; in his late nineteenth-century text *Art in America*, S. G. W. Benjamin wrote, "So far as foreign technical influences can be traced in the compositions of Cole, they are those of Claude and Salvator Rosa. . . . In all of [Cole's] compositions there are evident a rapturous love of nature, and the energy and yearning of a mind seeking to find expression for a vast ideal. Cole was what very few of our artists have been—an idealist."[4] And, more recently, Erica Hirshler has recognized that "it was Cole who . . . employed the idiom of Salvatore [*sic*] Rosa when seeking to portray the elemental forces of nature. But it was also Cole who introduced to the United States Claude Lorrain's concept of landscape: the interaction of nature and human civilization, and the resulting beauty of cultivated nature."[5] Clearly, Poe could have easily chosen Cole over Claude and Rosa, but he preferred to let American painters of the Hudson River school go unnamed, perhaps because they had been so highly praised by American critics—especially by Charles Briggs—or perhaps because they had not developed the cachet that European artists had already established in the United States. Or, quite simply, Poe was picking up on the English literary tradition of admiring Claude and Rosa, as Elizabeth Manwaring so aptly suggests: "Of all landscape painters, Claude and Salvator are named most often. . . . They are presented in contrast, especially after the appearance of Burke's *Essay*, one representing the beautiful and rural, the other the sublime and wild."[6]

"The Fall of the House of Usher" (1839)

In Poe's well-known story "The Fall of the House of Usher," the narrator describes Roderick Usher's dwelling in detail but, curiously, makes no mention of any paintings on the walls, even though Usher is a painter, as was his family, whose "peculiar sensibility of temperament" had "display[ed] itself, through long ages, in many works of exalted art" (*Tales*, 1:398–99). The narrator discusses the exterior and interior architecture and mentions the "phantasmagoric armorial trophies" lining the walls of the entryway (1:400). However, the only paintings that he describes are those still in progress in Usher's studio. In this story of an artist, Poe makes only one reference to a well-known European artist— Henry Fuseli, a Swiss-born British painter. In a cursory reference, the narrator compares what he feels when looking at Usher's paintings with what he had felt upon seeing paintings by Fuseli. He concludes that Fuseli's reveries are "too concrete," unlike the reveries that Usher's canvases evoke. Usher's imagery is ethereal, abstract, and atmospheric—not at all "concrete." The narrator remembers suffering from "an intensity of intolerable awe" upon viewing Usher's paintings (1:405).

When the narrator refers to the style of Fuseli's paintings, he could be alluding to Fuseli's best-known painting *The Nightmare* (ca. 1781; fig. 11), first exhibited at the Royal Academy in London in 1782 and soon thereafter reproduced as an engraving and distributed throughout Europe. According to the English painter B. R. Haydon, "Prints were transmitted very quickly from one country to another and Fuseli's composition became widely available in 1783, as soon as an engraving of it was issued."[7] The conjecture that Poe is referring to Fuseli's *Nightmare* in "The Fall of the House of Usher" is reinforced by a description in "The Black Cat" that comes very close to describing the painting: "I started, hourly, from dreams of unutterable fear, to find the hot breath of *the thing* upon my face, and its vast weight—an incarnate Night-Mare that I had no power to shake off—incumbent eternally upon my *heart*!" (*Tales*, 2:856).[8]

When first exhibited at the Royal Academy in 1782, *The Nightmare* was considered "shocking." Nicolas Powell notes that it "involve[d] [viewers] in the equivocal, lubricious sensations [it] depicted. . . . *The Nightmare* required some mythological or other 'distancing' to render [these sensations] acceptable,"[9] and clearly Fuseli did not choose to include this "distancing" feature. *The Nightmare* pictures a triumphant, muscular, hairy, gnome-like incubus crouching on top of a young, beautiful, sleeping woman whose limp arms and body fall voluptuously over the end of her bed. The self-satisfied posture and gloating visage of the incubus would be enough to suggest a lascivious conquest, but Fuseli did not stop there. From the dark background of the painting, a horse's head appears through the parted curtains. The horse's glaring, vacant stare and its eager, manic expression add to the mix of sexuality and horror that blatantly represents the unsettling nature of dreams out of control. Powell describes the painting in this way: "The composition consists of three main elements, a sleeping girl, an incubus or nightmare squatting on her belly, and the head of a horse

Fig. 11   Henry Fuseli, *The Nightmare*, ca. 1781. Goethe
House and Museum, Frankfurt am Main. Photo: Foto
Marburg / Art Resource, New York.

peering through the curtains with wildly staring eyes. . . . Its explicit meaning is
immediately apparent." However, he then posits his interpretation of a detail
that might go unobserved because of the powerful force of these other three elements: "By including in *The Nightmare* a looking-glass which in fact reflects
nothing, [Fuseli] seems to tell us that the painting faithfully records an image
which would otherwise fade away, and also that the nocturnal visitation

depicted is a mere figment of the imagination."[10] The sexuality that characterizes *The Nightmare* is also evoked in the illustrations that Fuseli did for the popular 1805 Chalmers edition of Shakespeare's plays (see fig. 12). These illustrations drew public praise and contributed immensely to the work's popularity: "The enormous vitality of Fuseli's drawings makes his Shakespeare series exhilarating. . . . He brought Elizabethan passion into book illustration (as he had already into painting), the violence, sexuality, and the darker sides of the human spirit as well as its nobler."[11]

When Poe's narrator in "The Fall of the House of Usher" alludes to the concreteness of Fuseli's paintings, he contrasts them with Usher's "vaguenesses," and in doing so he subtly refers to the atmospheric and ephemeral nature of J. M. W. Turner's paintings. The narrator has difficulty describing Usher's atmospheric paintings with words, despite the vividness with which he sees them in his mind's eye as he tells his story:

> The paintings over which [Usher's] elaborate fancy brooded, and which grew, touch by touch, into vaguenesses at which I shuddered the more thrillingly, because I shuddered knowing not why;—from these paintings (vivid as their images now are before me) I would in vain endeavor to educe more than a small portion which should lie within the compass of merely written words. By the utter simplicity, by the nakedness of his designs, he arrested and overawed attention. . . . There arose out of the pure abstractions which the hypochondriac contrived to thrown upon his canvass, an intensity of intolerable awe, no shadow of which felt I ever yet in the contemplation of the certainly glowing yet too concrete reveries of Fuseli. (*Tales*, 1:405)

The visual "vaguenesses" of Usher's paintings are closely akin to the diaphanous, vague, abstract nature of Turner's paintings. Turner's work, however, was not shown in the United States during Poe's lifetime, and although Poe may have seen Turner's illustrations in *The Rivers of France* (1837), these line drawings have none of the atmospheric "vaguenesses" of Turner's sea paintings. Nonetheless, it is possible that Poe had a childhood memory of Turner's paintings from a visit to a London museum or gallery. And he would have had the opportunity to see Turner's work in his illustrations for Sir Walter Scott's *Poetical Works* (1833).

Fig. 12   Henry Fuseli, illustration for *A Midsummer Night's Dream*, in *A Collection of Prints, from Pictures Painted for the Purpose of Illustrating the Dramatic Works of Shakspeare by Artists of Great-Britain* (London: John and Josiah Boydell, 1803). Reproduced with the permission of Rare Books and Manuscripts, Special Collections Library, Pennsylvania State University Libraries.

Fig. 13   Joseph Mallord William Turner, *Fingal's Cave, Staffa*, in *Poetical Works*, by Walter Scott, vol. 10 (Edinburgh: Robert Cadell, 1833–34). Engraving by Edward Goodall. Tate Gallery, London. Photo: Tate, London / Art Resource, New York.

Curiously, however, when the narrator describes the painting Usher is working on when he arrives, he notes that it differs from the other "vaguenesses" Usher had painted. Although small, this painting depicts an "immensely long and rectangular vault or tunnel" that "lay at an exceeding depth below the surface of the earth. . . . Yet a flood of intense rays rolled throughout, and bathed the whole in a ghastly and inappropriate splendor" (*Tales*, 1:405–6). This could easily be an allusion to Turner's drawing *Fingal's Cave, Staffa* (fig. 13), which appears on the title page of Scott's *Poetical Works*. The drawing resembles the small painting that Usher produces, albeit of a different subject. Turner's depiction of nature—water rushing through a cavernous passageway from a brightly sunlit ocean source—is much like Usher's painting of an "immensely long and rectangular vault or tunnel" lit with a "flood of intense rays." The strong source of light in both pictures is "otherworldly" and empty of human effect. Although

Turner's other illustrations in *Poetical Works* are not the "vaguenesses" that inspire so much awe in Poe's narrator, they do include the atmospheric quality characteristic of Turner's paintings. Moreover, Poe may have found something akin to Turner's atmospheric renderings in the paintings of Clarkson Stanfield, whom Poe admired, as evidenced by his reference to Stanfield in "The Philosophy of Furniture."[12] John Ruskin, a strong and vocal admirer of Turner's work, was particularly attracted to the atmospheric aspect of Stanfield's painting. However, although Stanfield's skies come close to Turner's atmospheric paintings, Stanfield's work always includes concrete images, unlike Turner's seascapes, which are almost completely abstract.

Matthew Brennan and Paul Ramsey both interpret Usher's overall artistic style as important to Poe's tale. Ramsey argues that "the kind of painting Usher does shows us what he is, and what he suffers. . . . As artist, he is exactly like Poe, whose theory of art rejected all claims of conscience and intellect, in favor of a pure aestheticism which was to respond, not to any beauty of the world, but to a beauty beyond the world's reach."[13] Most critics, including H. Wells Phillips, Paul Ramsey, Matthew Brennan, and G. R. Thompson, have interpreted the small painting the narrator describes in detail and link its relevance to understanding the tale's denouement.[14] The narrator, however, says nothing further about this painting after describing it and abruptly turns to consider Usher's "morbid condition of the auditory nerve" (*Tales*, 1:406). It is important to note that the narrator's overall response to Usher's abstract paintings is much more intense than his response to the small painting, even though he is able to describe the latter in detail. The awe inspired by the abstract paintings is more in keeping with his startling vision at the end of the tale, when the "deep and dank tarn . . . closed sullenly and silently over the fragments of the '*House of Usher*'" (1:417).

Although he has no words to describe the abstract paintings themselves, he can describe his reactions to them with vivid language: "I shuddered the more thrillingly, because I shuddered knowing not why. . . . By the utter simplicity, by the nakedness of his designs, he arrested and overawed attention" (*Tales*, 1:405). This "utter simplicity" and thrilling shudder come, again, at the end of the narrator's tale as he stands in the very spot where he had turned to seek relief from "an iciness, a sinking, a sickening of the heart" (1:397) upon first approaching Usher's home. He returns again to the dank tarn, which had been a reflective surface. Having just escaped the utter destruction of Usher's house, the narrator watches as the tarn becomes an endless vortex that swallows all the horror that Usher's life and home had been for the narrator (or that he imagines they would have been).

The image of the house and surrounding landscape that the narrator sees upon his initial arrival is deeply depressing, prompting his unsuccessful attempt to mentally "repaint" the scene. He understands full well a painter's ability to recombine forms to recreate an image: "There *are* combinations of very simple natural objects which have the power of thus affecting us. . . . It was possible, I reflected, that a mere different arrangement of the particulars of the scene, of the details of the picture, would be sufficient to modify, or perhaps to annihilate its capacity for sorrowful impression." Thus the narrator recalls how he positioned himself on the "precipitous brink" of the tarn to try to undo what he had seen there (*Tales*, 1:398). Unfortunately for him, this attempt at re-arranging the forms of the initial picture horrifies rather than relieves him. Only at the end of the tale, when the tarn absorbs the "House of Usher," does the narrator find a way to reconfigure all that he has seen: all disappears "sul-lenly and silently" into the dark water of the dank tarn, leaving only a black blankness in its stead. This finally provides relief for the narrator and a reassur-ance that, in fact, he was able to recombine the forms and transform the con-crete horror into a blank nothingness, thereby erasing the utter depression that had overwhelmed him upon first seeing the "House of Usher." The narra-tor, after all, is a painter, too, as he subtly notes in passing: "We painted and read together" (1:404). Or perhaps, as Richard Wilbur has argued, the narra-tor *is* Roderick Usher: "We must understand *The Fall of the House of Usher* as a dream of the narrator's. . . . Roderick Usher, then, is part of the narrator's self, which the narrator reaches by way of reverie. . . . And as for Usher's paintings, which the narrator describes as 'pure abstraction,' they quite simply are hypnagogic images."[15]

Ultimately, the narrator's tale of a horrific, incestuous murder is told with the vivid and "concrete" sensuality of a Fuseli painting. The reader, in picturing Usher's tortured sensibility, feels perhaps even more strongly the thrilling shud-der that the narrator experiences when looking at the "vaguenesses" of Usher's paintings, despite Wilbur's claim that "the narrator, in reaching that state of mind which he calls Roderick Usher, has very nearly dreamt himself free of his physical body. . . . Roderick Usher has become all soul." Wilbur concludes, "[The tale] is a triumphant report by the narrator that it is possible for the poetic soul to shake off this temporal, rational, physical world and escape, if only for a moment, to a realm of unfettered vision."[16]

"The Man of the Crowd" (1840)

Although Poe's short story "The Man of the Crowd" is frequently interpreted, only one critic, Kevin Hayes, has written about a minor detail related to an artist in the tale—specifically, the German painter and illustrator Moritz Retzsch. However, Hayes used this detail solely to characterize the first-person narrator as a bourgeois, a descriptor that Louis Renza had employed earlier.[17] According to Hayes, in "referring to Retzsch in 'The Man of the Crowd,' the story's narrator reveals his familiarity with contemporary bourgeois culture and thus identifies with his modestly sophisticated, middle-class readers. As he drops Retzsch's name, he performs an analogous act to those who prominently displayed copies of Retzsch in their homes." Hayes also reminds readers that Baudelaire "drew an analogy between Poe's story and the visual arts as he asked his readers: 'Do you remember a picture (it really is a picture!), painted—or rather written—by the most powerful pen of our age, and entitled *The Man of the Crowd*'?"[18]

Poe admired Retzsch for his allusive but simple outline drawings. In a review of Henry Wadsworth Longfellow's *Ballads and Other Poems* in *Graham's Magazine* for April 1842, Poe clearly states his preference for the subtlety of line drawings: "Indeed it is curious to observe how very slight a degree of truth is sufficient to satisfy the mind, which acquiesces in the absence of numerous essentials in the thing depicted. An outline frequently stirs the spirit more pleasantly than the most elaborate picture. We need only refer to the compositions of Flaxman and of Retzsch. Here all details are omitted—nothing can be farther from *truth*. Without even color the most thrilling effects are produced" (*Works*, 11:84). This preference is particularly significant in the context of "The Man of the Crowd," since the narrator directly refers to Retzsch's work at a crucial moment in the telling of his tale.

At what can be considered the turning point of the story, when the narrator sees "the man of the crowd" through a London coffeehouse window, he thinks immediately of Moritz Retzsch: "With my brow to the glass, I was thus occupied in scrutinizing the mob, when suddenly there came into view a countenance (that of a decrepid old man, some sixty-five or seventy years of age,)—

a countenance which at once arrested and absorbed my whole attention. . . . I well remember that *my first thought*, upon beholding it, was that Retzsch, had he viewed it, would have greatly preferred it to his own pictural incarnations of the fiend" (*Tales*, 1:511; emphasis added). Startled by the old man's countenance "on account of the absolute idiosyncrasy of its expression" (1:511), the narrator instantly recalls the illustrator of Goethe's *Faust*, Moritz Retzsch (see fig. 14). This curious detail provides a clue to an undercurrent meaning of the overall story, not just the tale proper that the narrator chooses to tell.

The narrator remarks that he had never before seen an expression "even remotely resembling" what he saw in the old man's countenance. At first, the reference to Retzsch, above all the other choices Poe could have made, seems

Fig. 14   Moritz Retzsch, *The Study, with Faust at His Desk and Mephistopheles as a Dog*, in *Faust*, by Johann Wolfgang von Goethe (London: Thomas Boosey and Sons, 1821). Photo: bpk, Berlin / Art Resource, New York.

puzzling in this context, since Retzsch's renderings do not promote the kind of confusion or obfuscation that the narrator feels and that prompts him to pursue the old man. As William Vaughan explains, "Retzsch was an artist of significance [in the 1830s]; and it would seem that, above all, this significance lay in the clarity and dramatic power of his visualizations. . . . By a skillful use of half-suggested lines, Retzsch was able to . . . avoid the confusion encountered in the works of many other illustrators." In fact, Vaughan continues, "through Retzsch's Faust, Goethe's work itself became better known, the first full translation appearing as a direct result of the success of Retzsch's outlines."[19] So why would Poe allude to Retzsch, whose drawings brought clarity of expression to Goethe's text, when clarity is the exact opposite of what the narrator feels when he sees the countenance of "the man of the crowd"? The narrator makes it clear that his impressions "arose confusedly and paradoxically within my mind" (*Tales*, 1:511), and these confused impressions prompt him to fervently chase after the old man.

The narrator, who is aptly characterized by Louis Renza as "a budding, bourgeois sociologist,"[20] believes that he can easily classify all of the visages passing by as he sits at the window, and this is true until he sees the old man. Yet, when startled by his inscrutable face, rather than relying on the convenient, scientific classification system that he had been employing, he recalls that his first thought was of how Moritz Retzsch would have preferred the old man's visage to that of "his own pictural incarnations of the fiend." For an American author, this mention of Retzsch may, at first, seem to be a recherché reference, akin to one of Poe's allusions. However, the narrator's referring to Retzsch would not have been out of the ordinary for an Englishman in the 1830s. Just as the English version of the prayer book *Hortulus Animae*[21] was well known to those in England in the sixteenth century, so, too, would the English translation of Goethe's *Faust*, illustrated by Retzsch, have been a commonplace in the early nineteenth century.

T. O. Mabbott understands Poe's reference to "Hortulus Animae" in the 1840 version of "The Man of the Crowd" to refer to what Poe added in a footnote in his revised 1845 version, but Mabbott calls it "the *Ortulus anime cum oratiunculis* printed at Strassburg by Johann Reinhard Grüninger" (*Tales*, 1:518n19); the actual title given in the footnote is "the *Hortulus Animae cum Oratiunculis Aliquibus Superadditis*" (*Some Short Orations of the Little Garden of the Soul*) (1:515n). The *Hortulus Animae* (*Little Garden of the Soul*) was a common and very popular prayer book in both its Latin and German forms in the early years of the sixteenth century. Mabbott suggests that Poe took the title *Hortulus Animae* from Israel D'Israeli's essay "Religious *Nouvellettes*" in *Curiosities of Literature*. There D'Israeli describes the prayer book as follows:

> The chief part of these meditations are as puerile as they are superstitious. This we might excuse, because the ignorance and superstition of the times allowed such things; but the *figures* which accompany the work are to be condemned in all ages; one represents Saint Ursula and some of her eleven thousand virgins, with all the licentious inventions of an Aretine. What strikes the ear does not so much irritate the senses, observes the sage Horace, as what is presented in all its nudity to the eye. One of these designs is only ridiculous: David is represented as examining Bathsheba bathing, while Cupid hovering round him throws his dart, and with a malicious smile triumphs in his success: we have had many gross and strange designs like this.[22]

Clearly, according to D'Israeli's interpretation, the *Hortulus Animae* would have been an "unreadable" book for the reader who did not want to be directly embroiled in licentiousness. In truth, however, the common—and popular— prayer book of the sixteenth century and Retzch's image of the fiend are both eminently "readable." In other words, both "permit themselves to be read." The latter portrays the horror emanating from the fiend's countenance, while the former provides the means to resist such horrors.

Poe has the narrator refer to the common prayer book as "unreadable" in both the preface and afterword of the tale proper with purpose. Before beginning his story, the narrator reveals the reason why "the essence of all crime" ostensibly cannot be discovered: the burden of such insight is "so heavy in horror that it can be thrown down only into the grave" (*Tales*, 1:507). In providing this precaution, the narrator tempts the curious reader into thinking that the narrator has found a way to wrench open the cover to reveal the secret of what lies at the heart of all crime, without having been overwhelmed by that insight himself. He also offers the hope that he will reveal this knowledge to the reader. However, at the tale's end, the reader knows no more about the "essence of all crime" than before the story began; the reader only knows that the narrator finally stopped his chase and stood "fully in front of the wanderer, [and] gazed at him steadfastly in the face" long enough to claim that he is "the type and the genius of deep crime."[23] After telling of how his chase ended, the narrator appears to try to pacify the reader's disappointment in not discovering "the type and the genius of deep crime" by providing an answer that he hopes will sate the reader's curiosity. Although the reader remains ignorant of "the essence of all crime," the narrator claims that this ignorance is "one of the great mercies of God" (1:515).

The clear simplicity of Retzsch's drawing is the pivot for this interpretation. Just as Retzsch's drawing of the fiend can be easily read, so too could the *Hortulus Animae*; neither is a text *"er lässt sich nicht lesen"* (*Tales*, 1:506). Acknowledging this contradiction suggests that the reader has been confronted, yet once more, with one of Poe's unreliable narrators—one who, having "gazed at [the man of the crowd] steadfastly in the face," has neither died from seeing "the genius of deep crime" nor told his tale for any purpose other than to appear superior to the reader, who, he so conveniently concludes, remains ignorant through God's grace. The narrator, however, can claim otherwise. He can claim to have read the "unreadable"—just as easily as he classified the rest of the crowd—and lived to tell the tale.

"The Philosophy of Furniture" (1840)

An analysis of "The Philosophy of Furniture" in relation to Poe's aesthetic principles will be presented in a later chapter; the interpretation here will focus on the painters whose works hang in the ideal room described in this sketch, in order to further understand Poe's painterly preferences. "Many paintings relieve the expanse of the [wall]paper," Poe writes. "These are chiefly landscapes of an imaginative cast—such as the fairy grottoes of Stanfield, or the lake of the Dismal Swamp of Chapman. There are, nevertheless, three or four female heads, of an ethereal beauty—portraits in the manner of Sully. The tone of each picture is warm, but dark. There are no 'brilliant effects.' *Repose* speaks in all. Not one is of small size. Diminutive paintings give that *spotty* look to a room, which is the blemish of so many a fine work of Art overtouched" (*Tales*, 1:502). Poe chooses as his ideal paintings "landscapes of an imaginative cast" by artists such as Stanfield and Chapman, as well as portraits of women such as those painted by Thomas Sully. These choices exclude paintings of the Dutch school of realism; Poe disdained these mundane images, as evidenced by his dismissive comment in a March 1842 review in *Graham's Magazine* of Charles James Lever's novel *Charles O'Malley*, edited by Harry Lorrequer: "The holy—the electric spark of genius is the medium of intercourse between the noble and more noble mind. For lesser purposes there are humbler agents. . . . For one Angelo there are five hundred Jan Steens" (*Works*, 11:90). Jan Steen is best known for his genre and still-life paintings. Peter Sutton and Marigene Butler describe his genre scenes as "filled to bursting with drunken louts reeling about rustic inns, singing and brawling, or attempting to lure the tavern mistress into a game of 'slap and tickle.'" However, they note, "Steen's images of licentious havoc are never haphazard jumbles of riotous anecdote; rather, by their very programmatic nature they reflect an ethical point of view. . . . Steen's comic vision of disintegration implies a moral order; the many symbols in his pictures, to say nothing of the actual inscriptions of proverbs . . . encode moral lessons."[24] Such "moral lessons," of course, would be anathema to Poe.

Poe expresses similar disdain with regard to painting and verisimilitude in his review of Henry Wadsworth Longfellow's *Ballads and Other Poems* in the April 1842 issue of *Graham's Magazine*: "That the chief merit of a picture is its *truth*, is an assertion deplorably erroneous. Even in Painting, which is, more essentially than Poetry, a mimetic art, the proposition cannot be sustained. Truth is not even *the aim*" (*Works*, 11:84). This sentiment appears again in Marginalia 243; here Poe dismisses German artist Balthasar Denner for his "accurate" painting style.[25] Clearly, Poe would not have found genre painting or still-life imagery a means of communicating an "electric spark of genius." His contempt for accurate "rendering," combined with his contempt for the whims of fashion and popular taste, would have inclined him to be uninterested in Dutch realism. In Poe's review of *Charles O'Malley*, he deplores deference to popular taste: "We shall not insult our readers by supposing any one of them unaware of the fact, that a book may be even exceedingly *popular* without *any* legitimate literary merit. . . . [Popularity] is evidence of the book's *demerit*, inasmuch as it shows a 'stooping to conquer'—inasmuch as it shows that the author has dealt largely, if not altogether, in matters which are susceptible of appreciation by the mass of mankind—by uneducated thought—by uncultivated taste, by unrefined and unguided passion" (*Works*, 11:86–87). In the same way, as Nicolai Cikovsky observes, "the 'exactness of imitation' of still lifes made them 'intelligible to all,' available, like panoramas, to 'all classes of spectators' because 'no study or cultivated taste' was needed to appreciate them."[26]

Poe preferred, instead, the romantic rendering of portraits by Thomas Sully or the otherworldliness of landscape paintings such as John Gadsby Chapman's *Lake of the Dismal Swamp*. Such mysterious landscapes and romantic portraits invite both inquisitiveness and reverie. For Poe, repose is an essential quality of an artwork displayed in his ideal room. The viewer becomes lost in the mystery of the landscape or the fantasy of the romantic portrait, providing a release from the realities of day-to-day concerns. Poe saw such portraits by Sully in the Pennsylvania Academy of the Fine Arts, in the homes of his wealthy acquaintances, and in artists' studios while he lived in Philadelphia and as a youth in Richmond or England.

Thomas Sully (1783–1872)

Poe's favoring Thomas Sully as a portrait painter over, for example, Asher Durand or Charles Loring Elliott, whose work he also saw, reveals Poe's preference for idealized renderings of beautiful women. Sully is described as "the foremost American exponent of the romanticized, painterly, and fluid style of portraiture. . . . Sully's fame rests mainly on his exaggeratedly elegant and idealized portraits of fashionable society women."[27] A prolific painter, he is known to have painted at least two thousand portraits.[28] His portrait of Mary Anne Heide Norris (1830; fig. 15), for instance, would have met with Poe's approval due to the soft brushstrokes that create a dreamy countenance set against a vague, atmospheric background of dark clouds and an emerging patch of blue sky. When looking at the portrait, the eye is led diagonally across the image; starting at the bottom right, it travels up along Norris's white fur wrap to her face and then continues on to the bit of blue sky in the top-left corner. The dreamy, enticing draw of Norris's dark, intelligent eyes and expressive mouth create that "spark" that Poe admired, especially as her soft visage is contrasted with the sharp detail of her gold brooch, causing the eye to shift back and forth between them.

Fig. 15 Thomas Sully, *Portrait of Mary Anne Heide Norris*, 1830. Philadelphia Museum of Art. Bequest of G. Heide Norris, 1960, 1960–78–2. Photo: Philadelphia Museum of Art / Art Resource, New York.

Originally from England, Thomas Sully's family immigrated to the United States in 1792, when he was still a young child; at the age of twenty-four, he moved to Philadelphia, where he lived most of his adult life and ran a commercial art gallery with James S. Earle, a carver and gilder. Their partnership began in 1819, and the gallery was successful until 1846; Sully showed his own works for sale there, as well as paintings by artists from Philadelphia. He was also associated for many years with the Pennsylvania Academy of the Fine Arts as a member of its Committee of Correspondence, Committee of Instruction, and board of directors.[29] Poe met Sully while attending informal social gatherings of artists and writers in Philadelphia in 1839 (*Poe Log*, 284). In fact, art collector Isaac Winter Heysinger claimed to own a portrait of Poe painted by Sully in 1839 or 1840: "It was the fashion at this time to call Poe the American Byron . . . and Sully posed him, for his own pleasure, in the Byron attitude." Heysinger supports his claims about the sitter's identity by citing John Sartain's description of Poe: "'Poe's face was handsome. . . . Viewed from the front [his forehead] presented a broad and noble expanse, very large at and above the temples. His lips were thin and delicately moulded.' This picture alone shows these features."[30] However, Michael Deas's authoritative study of Poe portraits demonstrates that a scenario in which Sully painted Poe and Heysinger's claims to own the resulting portrait are questionable, at best; both are most likely fictional accounts.[31] Nonetheless, it is clear that Poe knew Sully's work from exhibits at the Pennsylvania Academy of the Fine Arts, where many of his works were shown while Poe lived in Philadelphia.

Poe and Thomas Sully's nephew Robert Sully were childhood friends in Richmond. Robert Sully, like his uncle, became a painter and moved from Richmond to Philadelphia, where he renewed his friendship with Poe (*Poe Log*, xliv). According to Deas, the possibility that Poe sat for Robert Sully is more likely than Heysinger's account of the Poe portrait by Thomas Sully: "Rumors of one or more portraits of Poe by [Robert] Sully . . . have circulated since the late nineteenth century. Although the existence of these portraits has never

Fig. 16   Thomas Sully, *Portrait of Fanny Kemble*, 1834. The White House Historical Association (White House Collection). Gift of the Daniel W. Dietrich Foundation, 965.566.1.

been completely substantiated, it seems likely that Poe did pose for the artist on at least one occasion, in the late 1840s."[32]

In any case, it is clear why Poe chose to cite Thomas Sully rather than any other portrait painter of the time in his "Philosophy of Furniture. " Poe valued Sully's work not only because they were personally acquainted (and because of his friendship with Sully's nephew) but also because Poe preferred the romantic ambience of Sully's portraits over the more "realistic" portrayals by other portrait painters. Poe specifically praised Sully's work in his review of *The Gift for 1836*, printed in the September 1835 issue of the *Southern Literary Messenger*. Sully's portrait of Fanny Kemble (fig. 16), Poe notes, is "one of the finest things in the world. . . . The likeness is admirable—and the attitude exquisite—and the countenance is beaming all over with intelligence."[33]

Clarkson Stanfield (1793–1867)

British painter Clarkson Stanfield was well known for his watercolor paintings of seascapes and for his book illustrations. He worked collaboratively with Charles Dickens to illustrate four of his books: two engravings of Stanfield's paintings appear in *The Chimes* (1844), three in *The Battle of Life* (1846), one in *The Cricket on the Hearth: A Fairy Tale of Home* (1846), and three in *The Haunted Man* (1848). Poe also could have become familiar with Stanfield's images years earlier from a variety of sources, including *Heath's Picturesque Annual* (1832), which contains more than twenty-five engravings after paintings by Stanfield; the background in almost all of these paintings features a romantic rendering of swirled clouds in a blue sky.

Additionally, engravings of nineteen of Stanfield's paintings illustrate *The Naval Annual, or Stories of the Sea* by Captain Frederick Marryat (1836). These include the romantic image *The Cave of Caicos*, which pictures a wounded man in a cave lying in the arms of a woman. Poe may also have become acquainted with Stanfield's panoramic paintings of grottos by reading a description of the Drury Lane theatrical production *Harlequin and the Flying Chest, or Malek and the Princess Schirine*, reviewed in the *European Magazine and London Review* in 1823. The review notes that Stanfield painted some backdrops for the show: "Among the eighteen new scenes exhibited on this occasion, we cannot help selecting for particular commendation . . . *The Grotto of Chrystals*; and, above all,

The Moving Diorama, by Clarkson Stanfield, which is 272 feet in length, and exhibits the Plymouth Breakwater."[34] It is possible that these panoramic scenes are the "fairy grottoes" for which Poe praised Stanfield in "The Philosophy of Furniture," and thus that he had read about them; his readers, in turn, would have been familiar with the panoramas, since the Drury Lane production was reviewed in numerous periodicals. Yet these panoramas were destroyed after the production closed, explaining Burton Pollin's assertion that no "fairy grottoes" by Stanfield exist.[35]

John Gadsby Chapman (1808–1889)

John Gadsby Chapman's life, in some ways, was much like Poe's. Born a year before Poe, Chapman moved from place to place, working hard and producing many portraits and book illustrations, including several for *Harper's Illuminated and New Pictorial Bible*. He wished to use his talent and skill to create history paintings, but he received few commissions to do so and thus spent most of his career illustrating books. Chapman's most significant contribution to the arts was *The American Drawing-Book: A Manual for the Amateur*, which was first published in 1847 and reissued multiple times in England and the United States through the 1870s. However, "despite this long history of evident popularity, the *Drawing Book* cost the author more than it repaid." Chapman was never financially secure, and he suffered from "recurring illnesses—which plagued him throughout his life."[36]

Poe knew Chapman's work from seeing the books he illustrated, and Poe certainly would have seen Chapman's drawings in *Harper's Illuminated and New Pictorial Bible* and *The American Drawing-Book*. Poe also would have encountered Chapman's paintings at the Pennsylvania Academy of the Fine Arts, where they were included in the group exhibits of 1838 and 1840 and in a special exhibit in 1843. Additionally, Chapman painted the image used in Poe's plate piece "Morning on the Wissahiccon," published in 1844. However, Poe's first acquaintance with Chapman's work may have been his 1825 fire screen painting *The Lake of the Dismal Swamp* (fig. 17); Chapman later used this image to create a large oil painting by the same title. Chapman's aunt, Mrs. A. Newton of Richmond, owned the fire screen, and since Poe lived in Richmond in 1825 until February 1826, he would have seen it in her home.[37] Poe's early

Fig. 17 John Gadsby Chapman, *The Lake of the Dismal Swamp*, 1825. Painted fire screen. Virginia Historical Society, Richmond. Lora Robins Collection of Virginia Art, 1995.120.

poem "The Lake," published in 1827, suggests that he was aware of the fire screen. However, T. O. Mabbott argues that Poe visited the actual Dismal Swamp near Norfolk, Virginia, basing this conclusion on an article written by "Professor Robert Morrison in the *Explicator*, December 1948, after he had visited the spot. It may be firmly accepted, for no other lake Poe is likely to have known, so closely fitting his description, has been discovered by commentators" (*Poems*, 82). To avoid completely contradicting Mabbott's and Morrison's

Fig. 18 John Gadsby Chapman, *The Lake of the Dismal Swamp*, in *The Magnolia for 1837* (New York: Bancroft and Holley, ca. 1836). Courtesy the American Antiquarian Society, 444285.

assumption, I would argue that a combination of Poe's visiting the swamp and seeing the fire screen could have prompted his youthful poem, which reads as follows:

> In youth's spring, it was my lot
> To haunt of the wide earth a spot
> The which I could not love the less;
> So lovely was the loneliness
> Of a wild lake, with black rock bound,
> And the tall trees that tower'd around.
> But when the night had thrown her pall
> Upon that spot—as upon all,
> And the wind would pass me by

In its stilly melody,
My infant spirit would awake
To the terror of the lone lake.
Yet that terror was not fright—
But a tremulous delight,
And a feeling undefin'd,
Springing from a darken'd mind.
Death was in that poison'd wave
And in its gulf a fitting grave
For him who thence could solace bring
To his dark imagining;
Whose wild'ring thought could even make
An Eden of that dim lake.

(*Poems*, 84–85)

The oil painting *The Lake of the Dismal Swamp*, which Chapman composed years later, hung in the National Academy of Design's 1836 exhibition along with fifteen of his other paintings and five engravings of his work. The painting measures 36 × 48 inches and, therefore, would have been the right size to adorn the wall of Poe's ideal parlor, since he believed that only large paintings were aesthetically appropriate. At the time of the 1836 exhibit, the painting was owned by "Bancroft," according to the *National Academy of Design Exhibition Record, 1826–1860*. This "Bancroft" was George Bancroft, author of *History of the United States of America, from the Discovery of the American Continent*, who lived in both Washington, D.C., and Newport, Rhode Island. According to John McGuigan, *The Lake of the Dismal Swamp* was sold to Bancroft for $200 on August 28, 1835.[38]

Poe was introduced to Bancroft by publisher and editor Thomas Willis White in Richmond in April 1836, at Bancroft's request. Bancroft desired to meet Poe, who had "unintentionally done him some injustice" in a review of Francis L. Hawks's *Ecclesiastical History* in the March issue of the *Southern Literary Messenger*. Poe subsequently apologized to Bancroft in an editorial in the April issue for the "injustice (of course, unintentional) [that] has been done that gentleman, not only by ourselves, but by Dr. Hawks and others" (*Poe Log*, 196). When Poe and Bancroft met in April, did Chapman's painting *The Lake of the*

Dismal Swamp come up in conversation? Did Bancroft know of Poe's poem "The Lake" and think that Chapman's painting of a lake in Virginia might be of interest to Poe? Since Bancroft had purchased the painting only eight months prior to meeting Poe, would he have mentioned the painting or described it to Poe? These are all conjectures, of course, but clearly Poe chose this particular painting to include in "The Philosophy of Furniture," when he could have chosen any other landscape as appropriate for his ideal parlor. Burton Pollin points out that Poe was not in New York for the National Academy of Design's 1836 exhibition, which included Chapman's painting *The Lake of the Dismal Swamp*: "It is likely that he saw only the engraving which was made by the highly skilled and well known artist James Smillie." This engraving was published in the gift book *The Magnolia for 1837* as a plate illustrating William Gilmore Simms's poem "The War-Eagle of the Dismal Swamp" (fig. 18). Pollin notes that "from the *Magnolia* caption in the preliminary 'List of Embellishments' Poe could have learned about the 'original painting by J. G. Chapman, N. A.' But he probably derived it from the leading monthly of New York, the *Knickerbocker*, which he read assiduously. Chapman's picture, engraved, appears as the frontispiece in the May 1839 issue."[39]

Pollin interprets Poe's choice of this painting for "The Philosophy of Furniture" as a reflection of his "general attitude toward lake scenery in his creative work," where lakes are used as "sources and symbols of disaster to man."[40] In addition, Pollin believes that Poe chose this painting for "the contrast of the magical and charming" (embodied by Stanfield's grottoes) with "the grim and melancholy that Poe is seeking in his two scenes for the walls of his drawing-room."[41] This seems a curious interpretation, since the narrator of "The Philosophy of Furniture" asserts quite openly that the paintings in his ideal room would be chosen because of the "repose" they express—rather than as reminders of gloom and destruction. However, David C. Miller draws a connection between this desire for repose and the "mystic aura" of Lake Drummond, which lies in the heart of the Dismal Swamp and "[calls] to mind both the exotic and the dead." "The great value placed on repose by Poe . . . bespeaks a compelling desire for return to a former state of stability and contentment that could take on overtones of death," Miller explains. "Pervaded by gloom, the image of Lake Drummond prodded the sentimentalist's pleasure in its charms with the gentle reminder of pain. . . . The almost palpable silence and repose gave rise to a brooding suggestiveness."[42]

"The Landscape Garden" (1842)

Poe's fascination with landscape gardening during the early 1840s was timely, as T. O. Mabbott and many other critics have pointed out. In 1841, a year before Poe published "The Landscape Garden," Andrew Jackson Downing's popular *Treatise on the Theory and Practice of Landscape Gardening* was published and reviewed numerous times. Poe was quite familiar with Downing's book and its reviews, as evidenced by the fact that in his story he quotes from a review of Downing's book entitled "American Landscape Gardening," which appeared in the New York magazine *Arcturus* in June 1841 (*Tales*, 1:701). Poe's concern with landscape gardening, however, takes a turn from the practical nature of Downing's book by giving Poe an opportunity to express, yet again, his visual aesthetics. In "The Landscape Garden," Poe voices his view that "the world will *never* behold that full extent of triumphant execution, in the richer productions of Art, of which the human nature is absolutely capable" (1:706). That said, he nonetheless describes the character of Ellison as someone who, through good fortune and a thoughtfully grounded philosophy of life, has achieved a magnificent expression of the "poetic spirit" in a medium that others have ignored as a potential vehicle for that expression: landscape gardening.

In this sketch, the first incarnation of Ellison is that of the idealized artistic persona. Here Poe developed a figure of the artist who is capable of manifesting "the true character, the august aims, the supreme majesty and dignity of the poetic sentiment. The proper gratification of the sentiment [Ellison] instinctively felt to lie in the *creation of novel forms of Beauty*. . . . [It] was to be found in the creation of novel moods of purely *physical* loveliness" (*Tales*, 1:706). For Ellison, this "physical loveliness" is found in "the endless combining of forms of novel Beauty; the elements which should enter into combination being, at all times, and by a vast superiority, the most glorious which the earth could afford." As the narrator admits, manipulating the natural landscape at first appears counter to the universal mandate to consider "Nature as supreme." He concedes, nonetheless, that the landscape gardener exceeds nature, creating "novel forms of Beauty" that transform "excesses and defects" of nature (1:707–8). Said in another way, the narrator reinforces the idea that nature can be improved: "The original beauty is never so great as that which may be introduced" (1:710).

To make his point even clearer, the narrator refers to the paintings of Claude Lorrain: "No such Paradises are to be found in reality as have glowed upon the canvass of Claude" (*Tales*, 1:707). Art historian Helen Langdon describes Claude's work in this way: "The landscapes of Claude Lorrain create an intensely imagined and flawlessly consistent poetical world. His vision is based first of all on a passionate study of nature. . . . Claude created an ideal world, classically structured and balanced, ordered and harmonious. His landscape evokes a dream of pastoral peace."[43] Joshua Taylor further explains, "Claude Lorrain's paintings proved that nature could smile on man and make him feel . . . a welcome part of a well-ordered natural world. Claude's open vistas, clumps of trees that had grown without need to struggle, and clear untroubled light, produced that sense of uninterrupted harmony and spiritual calm that man has traditionally associated with the term 'beauty.'"[44] Claude was considered by many to be the father of landscape painting and one of three painters, along with Annibale Carracci and Nicolas Poussin, whose paintings "were ultimately subsumed under the common label of 'ideal landscapes' . . . created according to the laws of aesthetic harmony rather than the exact appearance of the model."[45] The reference to Claude, then, makes perfect sense in Poe's sketch of the ideal artist.

Here, again, it is useful to recall that Poe's Ellison, like the painter Claude Lorrain, transforms the natural landscape to create beauty that, according to the narrator, surpasses the original. Although the reference to Claude is fleeting, it is curious that Poe chooses to mention his landscape paintings over Thomas Cole's or Asher Durand's. In doing so, Poe overlooks the growing prominence of American landscape painting. American landscape painters strove to distinguish themselves from their European forebears, whose work, nonetheless, exercised great influence. The American landscape, of course, differs substantially from Europe's, and American landscape paintings reveal that difference. Public regard for these paintings in the United States began to grow in the mid-1820s and by midcentury the paintings by the Hudson River school gained high esteem. Thomas Cole's work was especially popular, as evidenced by the numerous positive reviews of it in the *New-York Mirror* from the mid- to late 1830s to the early 1840s.[46] His work was the inspiration for the American landscape aesthetic. Art critic Barbara Gallanti notes that "Cole's works invoked the widespread sensibility that endowed rural scenery with the power of Divine presence."[47] His paintings gained widespread attention, especially his popular series *The Course of Empire* (1834), which was shown numerous times in many venues, including a special exhibit at the Pennsylvania Academy of the Fine Arts in 1844. Even with Cole's popular renown, however, Poe chose to ignore him both in "The Landscape Garden" and in its extended version, "The Domain of Arnheim," preferring the French painter Claude Lorrain, whose reputation was well established abroad and in the United States.

"Morning on the Wissahiccon" (Written in 1843; Published in 1844)

In "Morning on the Wissahiccon," Poe makes brief note of the painter Salvator Rosa, signifying, yet again, his preference for European painters over American painters. If, as Louis Renza claims, Poe's intent in this sketch is for his narrator to "imagine discovering the radical meaning of a truly original American literature—one of the 'most unspeakable glories of the land'—a primordial 'Wissahiccon' literature of the 'red man,'"[48] then it would seem more likely that Poe would cite an American painter than a European one. Had he been seeking to valorize American creativity in this sketch, he likely would have mentioned Thomas Cole, whose paintings, like those of Rosa (whom Cole not only admired but emulated), depicted rugged terrain. However, Poe chose to highlight Rosa instead of Cole in his narrator's description of a lofty promontory encountered along the Wissahiccon: "It was a steep rocky cliff, abutting far into the stream, and presenting much more of the Salvator character than any portion of the shore hitherto passed" (*Tales*, 2:865).

On this rocky cliff, the narrator sees a magnificent elk, a manifestation of his dreamlike reveries about what the land was like before the "stern hand of the utilitarian" transformed its natural, sublime state (*Tales*, 2:866). Here the narrator distinguishes the scenery of the Wissahiccon from that of Louisiana, which he describes at the beginning of the sketch as a place of "exuberant beauty": "And *beauty* is, indeed, its sole character. It has little, or rather nothing, of the sublime" (2:862). The banks of the Wissahiccon, on the other hand, "are generally, indeed almost universally, precipitous, and consist of high hills, clothed with noble shrubbery near the water, and crowned at a greater elevation, with some of the most magnificent forest trees of America, among which stands conspicuous the *liriodendron tulipiferum*. The immediate shores, however, are of granite, sharply-defined or moss-covered. . . . The windings of the stream are many and abrupt." Because the dramatic nature of this scenery enhanced the height of the banks of the Wissahiccon, the narrator makes it known that it can only be appreciated if seen in "the brightest glare of a noonday sun"; otherwise the viewer will experience "an absolute dreariness of effect" (2:864–65).

Rosa's paintings do feature landscapes with similarly treacherous cliffs. However, they do not employ the bright light the narrator believes to be essential; instead, a "dreariness of effect" is felt from the dark, foreboding grays and blacks of Rosa's palette. Cole's paintings of steep terrain, on the other hand, are lit with bright light. This is the case in his *Mountain Sunrise* (1826), an image of mountainous terrain with two rocky precipices lit by the bright white light coming from the sunrise in the middle of the composition. This light illuminates the dead, broken tree trunks that cling to the edge of the bare, rocky embankments. The land is pictured as if it were before the beginning of human life, yet the feeling evoked is not desolation but a sublime awe and regard—a seeming contradiction. Another "trackless wilderness"[49] is depicted in Cole's *Landscape with Tree Trunks* (1828). This time the bright light shines from the upper-left corner of the composition, lighting a mountainous pass and landing on a dead tree with one branch ravaged by lightning and lichen. In both of these paintings, bright light is essential, as it is in Poe's sketch of the Pennsylvania landscape.

"The Assignation" (Written in 1833; Revised in 1845)

Poe's relatively early tale "The Assignation" was written in late 1833 and published first in the *Lady's Book* for January 1834, then in the *Southern Literary Messenger* (1835), in *Tales of the Grotesque and Arabesque* (1840), and finally—in revised form—in the June 7, 1845, issue of the *Broadway Journal* when Poe was editor. Not only is this story replete with references to painters and artwork, but it also embodies Poe's visual aesthetics, which are expressed in his art criticism and in his sketches "The Philosophy of Furniture" and "Landor's Cottage."[50]

"The Assignation" is the tale of a Marchesa and her lover, a wealthy young man who invites the narrator to visit his extravagantly furnished apartment. When the narrator enters the apartment, he is struck by the lack of "keeping" in its overall design. In the 1834 version of the story, entitled "The Visionary," the Marchesa's lover notes that aside from the narrator and one other unnamed person, his valet is the only one who has been in his apartment. And, in the 1845 version, he remarks that the valet was just as amazed as the narrator at its "bedizzened" state (*Tales*, 1:159). The word "bedizzened" only appears in the final version of the story, which is particularly curious since in "The Philosophy of Furniture" it is used in a pejorative way. However, in "The Visionary," the Marchesa's lover has nothing but praise for his own decorative ability and the wealth and splendor of his apartment.

In the 1845 version, the young lover's first response to the narrator's amazement is to laugh, but when that emotional response subsides, he wastes no time in boasting about his design choices. Though it fits no pattern or sense of compatibility, he claims that his decor is "better than fashion. . . . This has but to be seen to become the rage—that is, with those who could afford it at the cost of their entire patrimony" (*Tales*, 1:159). Despite the lack of "keeping," the narrator is impressed by the choice of paintings in the lover's apartment. They span centuries and reflect his passionate nature. "Here are paintings from the Greeks to Cimabue, and from Cimabue to the present hour," the lover says. "Many are chosen, as you see, with little deference to the opinions of Virtu." He is aware that some might call his art scandalous, but he is more concerned with the allure of the works than moral censure. He even goes so far as to say that he prefers Antonio Canova's *Venus* to the restored *Venus de Medici*, calling the restoration of her arms "the quintessence of all affectation" (1:160). The French painter Jacques-Louis David referred to Canova as the "seductive worker in marble."[51] None of Canova's marble sculptures—such as *Psyche Revived by Cupid's Kiss* (with Cupid's hand caressing Psyche's breast), *Cupid and Psyche Standing* (with Psyche holding a delicate butterfly between her breasts as she offers it to Cupid, who leans his head against her shoulder), or *Venus* (with her fingers touching her erect nipples)—would have suited a "moralistic" American viewer of the mid-nineteenth century.

The young lover's regard for allure over "decency" in art reflects the same values that Poe proclaimed were important in his 1845 reviews in the *Broadway Journal* of Titian's painting of Venus and Jean-Baptiste De Cuyper's *La sortie du bain*, on display in "rooms at Broadway." "The Assignation" and Poe's reviews of Titian's work are also similar in that they express Poe's concern about whether a work is an original or a copy. In the reviews, he eventually determines that such concern is unnecessary if the object, whether the original or a copy, provides pleasure to the viewer. However, this directly conflicts with the sentiment expressed in both versions of "The Assignation." In "The Visionary," the lover is disgusted by those who cannot distinguish between a copy and the original, and he exempts himself from their company: "Apollo too! . . . It is a copy; there can be no reasonable doubt of it. Sir, I will not bow to falsity, although begrimed with age—there is *no* inspiration in the boasted Apollo." In the revised version of the tale, the latter sentence is excised, but the insistence that a copy is not a work of art remains. After disparaging the Venus of the Medici, the lover remarks, "The Apollo, too, is a copy—there can be no doubt of it—blind fool that I am, who cannot behold the boasted inspiration of the Apollo!" He quotes Socrates and then Michelangelo, remarking that "the statuary found his statue in the block of marble" (*Tales*, 1:160–61).[52] He prefers, instead, the figure of Hadrian's lover, Antinous, represented many times in marble or bronze, either as a bust or full body, and always as a sensual representation. Curiously, these statues were often copies of original Roman representations of Hadrian's favorite. Nonetheless, Poe is clearly taken by this conundrum of copy versus original, since he engaged with this problem in a number of venues.

"The Domain of Arnheim" (1846)

In "The Domain of Arnheim," an extension of "The Landscape Garden," Poe's narrator reintroduces Ellison in this way: had Ellison been born "under other circumstances than those which invested him, it is not impossible that he would have become a painter." He would not have been a sculptor, according to the narrator, since sculpture is "too limited in its extent and consequences" (*Tales*, 2:1271). Poe's representation of the ideal artist in this sketch is the landscape gardener. Ellison's incredible inheritance affords him the leisure to indulge his artistic penchant, and he uses this opportunity and his innate ability to arrange vast areas of color and concrete forms, thereby creating a grand canvas in three-dimensional space. It would seem that landscape gardening, then, is more akin to sculpture than painting. Nonetheless, the narrator claims Ellison's affinity to painting, not sculpture. As in "The Landscape Garden," only one painter, Claude Lorrain, is mentioned in this narrative.

In coming to understand Ellison's intuitions regarding landscape gardening and the philosophy that underpins the need for such creative rearrangement of the natural environment, the narrator concludes that he finally grasped what had been an enigma to him: "I mean the fact (which none but the ignorant dispute) that no such combination of scenery exists in nature as the painter of genius may produce. No such Paradises are to be found in reality as have glowed on the canvass of Claude" (*Tales*, 2:1272). Poe had an opportunity to see Claude's *Marine View and Sea Port* in a special exhibit at the Pennsylvania Academy of the Fine Arts in 1844. That, along with the fact that it was commonplace in articles on landscape painting to cite Claude as the master to be emulated, must have influenced Poe's choice to mention Claude in this sketch.

Ellison explains that God's creation of the perfect, beautiful landscape reflects His initial conception that man would have eternal life. However, this changed when God prefigured death as necessary for man. As a consequence, "geological disturbances—disturbances of form and color-grouping"—occurred. Ellison challenges the narrator to "admit the earthly immortality of man to have been the first intention [of God]. We have then the primitive arrangement of the earth's surface adapted to his blissful estate, as not existent but designed. The disturbances were the preparations for his subsequently conceived deathful condition" (*Tales*, 2:1273–74). These disturbances also created the opening for man's ability to correct the flaws resulting from such natural disruptions. Ellison explains that in this process of "correction" lies the "soul of art." "Allaying" and "correction" become man's creative objective (2:1273). And, thus, rearranging the natural but flawed environment through landscape gardening becomes his goal and artistic pursuit. Ellison furthers this notion when he proclaims, "You will understand that I reject the idea . . . of recalling the original beauty of the country. The original beauty is never so great as that which may be introduced" (2:1275).

Claude Lorrain's paintings reflect Ellison's aesthetic philosophy about art's ascendance over nature's ability to create compositionally striking form, light, and color. His landscape paintings were most often made in pairs, each picturing a similar scene in different light. In particular, *Pastoral Landscape* (1648) exemplifies Claude's purposeful organization of nature: "The composition is arranged primarily in horizontal planes, punctuated by the verticals of the monumental tress, and the scene is illumined by a soft, clear light. . . . One can observe the influence of Poussin's penchant for spatial clarity and a geometrical ordering of nature."[53]

"Landor's Cottage" (1849)

When the narrator of "Landor's Cottage" reaches his destination, he is met at the cottage door by a young woman named Annie. He immediately comes under the sway of her "womanliness": "So intense an expression of *romance*, perhaps I should call it, or of unworldliness, as that which gleamed from her deep-set eyes, had never so sunk into my heart of hearts before. I know not how it is, but this peculiar expression of the eye, wreathing itself occasionally into the lips, is the most powerful, if not absolutely the *sole* spell, which rivets my interest in woman. . . . 'Romance' and 'womanliness' seem to me convertible terms" (*Tales*, 2:1338–39). Still under Annie's spell, the narrator begins to look around inside the cottage. In describing the interior, he names only one artist, "Julien," whose three unframed lithographs hang on the parlor wall. T. O. Mabbott takes this reference to Julien to mean the French painter and lithographer Bernard-Romain Julien, who was known for his beautifully rendered portraits. The narrator describes each of the three lithographs explicitly: "One of these drawings was a scene of Oriental luxury, or rather voluptuousness; another was a 'carnival piece,' spirited beyond compare; the third was a Greek female head—a face so divinely beautiful, and yet of an expression so provokingly indeterminate, never before arrested my attention" (2:1340). Julien's work "achieved a popularity which never after abandoned him"[54] following the publication of his drawing book *Étude à deux crayons* in 1840. Here again, then, Poe resists mentioning an American artist, instead referring to a European artist. He could have just as easily named John Gadsby Chapman, whose *The American Drawing-Book: A Manual for the Amateur* (1847) was also widely known.

"Landor's Cottage" could be read as the culmination of Poe's esteem for "graphicality" and for landscape painting in particular. The sketch begins with the narrator's extended and very specific descriptions of what he sees as he nears the cottage and winds down his day's trek in the countryside. These scenic descriptions can easily be read as a series of landscape paintings that obliquely refer to the Hudson River school painters Thomas Cole, Frederic Church, and Asher Durand. Instead of critiquing individual paintings or painters in this sketch, Poe creates the following three "paintings" with words.

Imaginary painting 1:

> A smoky mist, resembling that of the Indian summer, enveloped all things. . . . The tall shrubberies and overgrown undergrowth met overhead [along the path], [and] there was no obstruction whatever below. . . . [The grass] looked more like green Genoese velvet than anything else . . . so short, so thick, so even, and so vivid in color. . . . The stones that once

obstructed the way had been carefully *placed*—not thrown—along the sides of the lane, so as to define its boundaries at bottom with a kind of half-precise, half-negligent, and wholly picturesque definition. Clumps of wild flowers grew everywhere, luxuriantly, in the interspaces.

. . . [A figure sits] on one of the blossomy stones and gaz[es] up and down this fairy-like avenue. (*Tales*, 2:1328–30)

Imaginary painting 2:

The fog had thoroughly disappeared, [and] the sun . . . had come again fully into sight; glaring with a purplish lustre through a chasm that entered the valley from the west. . . . This whole valley and everything in it became brilliantly visible.

. . . The sunlight came out through the chasm, tinted all orange and purple; while the vivid green of the grass in the valley was reflected more or less upon all objects, from the curtain of vapor that still hung overhead, as if loth to take its total departure from a scene so enchantingly beautiful. (*Tales*, 2:1330–31)

Imaginary painting 3:

The little vale . . . could not have been more than four hundred yards long; while in breadth it varied from fifty to one hundred and fifty, or perhaps two hundred. It was most narrow at its northern extremity, opening out as it tended southwardly, but with no very precise regularity. The widest portion was within eighty yards of the southern extreme. The slopes which encompassed the vale could not fairly be called hills, unless at their northern face. Here a precipitous ledge of granite arose to a height of some ninety feet. . . . The whole vale was engirdled by eminences, more or less high, except at two points. . . . As regards vegetation, as well as in respect to everything else, the scene *softened* and *sloped* to the south. (*Tales*, 2:1331–32)

Immediately following one of these "paintings," the narrator reflects on the compositional aesthetics of the landscape. The descriptors and aesthetic rules are similar to those in "The Philosophy of Furniture." The narrator of "Landor's Cottage" emphasizes the curved, repeating lines and the colors in the landscape, noting that there are few straight lines and "no long uninterrupted lines. . . . Everywhere was variety in uniformity. It was a piece of 'composition'" (*Tales*, 2:1330). As the fog lifts and the valley is lit by the setting sun, which reappears through the chasm between the mountains, a panorama is created; it reminds the narrator of a backdrop for "some well-arranged theatrical spectacle" he had seen as a boy (2:1331). Here he could have easily been referring to the huge panoramas of Clarkson Stanfield. These gestures toward the artificial as more prominent in the mind's eye than the immediate scene before him reinforce the idea that the narrator's descriptions of nature elicit painterly analogues—images that improve upon nature.

As in earlier works, Poe's narrator only alludes to one painter of nature, Salvator Rosa, and completely avoids mentioning the Hudson River school painters who would have created the scenes he composes with words. Unlike these painters—with the exception of some of Thomas Cole's paintings—Rosa often depicted rugged, dark, rocky landscapes that epitomize the sublime. Poe would have known about Rosa's work from the frequent references to the artist in contemporary periodicals. He also had the opportunity to see Rosa's paintings, or those attributed to him, at the Pennsylvania Academy of the Fine Arts. According to Richard Wallace in *Salvator Rosa in America*, "Exhibition records reveal that pictures by or attributed to Salvator Rosa were shown more frequently in the Pennsylvania Academy's annual exhibitions of the nineteenth century than the work of almost any other old master."[55] One such work, *Landscape with Mercury and Argus*, was part of a gift of four paintings that "led to the establishment of the Academy. . . . It is quite typical of the pattern of Rosa's influence that the *Landscape with Mercury and Argus* is not in fact a genuine Rosa, but a close imitation, [perhaps] done . . . after a lost original."[56] As Wallace describes them, Rosa's paintings typically "produce the sublime—rugged, irregular forms, obscurity, power, privation, and strong contrasts of light and dark."[57]

Poe creates a few more written "paintings" before his narrator finally comes upon Landor's cottage. The narrator is greatly awed by it: "Its *tout ensemble* struck me with the keenest sense of combined novelty and propriety—in a word, of *poetry*. . . . Its marvellous *effect* lay altogether in its artistic arrangement *as a picture.* I could have fancied, while I looked at it, that some eminent landscape-painter had built it with his brush" (*Tales*, 2:1335). In this description, Poe reveals a possible undercurrent of meaning that elevates the sketch, with its "paintings," to a level of importance that significantly surpasses that of a lengthy piece of "travel writing." Considering the "paintings" listed above, this is a credible deduction. Thus, Poe's penchant for "graphicality" is explicitly manifested in this sketch, which, it would turn out, was the last of his publications during his lifetime.

"Landor's Cottage" signals an obvious change in Poe's visual sensibility—a move away from the sublime to an appreciation and regard for the beautiful, a return to the youthful idealism expressed in his early poetry. T. O. Mabbott believes that Poe imagined this sketch as one of a set of three, the other two being "The Domain of Arnheim" and an unwritten but proposed piece. "In the last paragraph of 'Landor's Cottage' as first published, Poe mentioned that he had some idea of writing a sequel," Mabbott explains. "It is practically sure that he did not compose it, but there is some reason to believe he made some plans for it" (*Tales*, 2:1327). The proposed triptych suggests a new direction in Poe's writing career—a direction cut short by his death. "Landor's Cottage" reclaims the aesthetics of beauty and signals a renewed desire to move closer to the sensibility of the Romantic poet rather than the magazinist. This sensibility is expressed in the epigraph to Poe's youthful poem "Stanzas":

> How often we forget all time, when lone
> Admiring Nature's universal throne;
> Her woods—her wilds—her mountains—the intense
> Reply of HERS to OUR intelligence!
>
> (Poems, 77)

This timelessness might exist in a painting of nature that serves as "a symbol and a token, / Of what in other worlds shall be—and given / In beauty by our God" (78).

It is worth mentioning here that Mabbott's introduction to the poem quotes from a letter Poe wrote to James Russell Lowell on July 2, 1844: "There are epochs when . . . nothing yields me pleasure but solitary communion with the 'mountains and the woods'—the 'altars' of Byron." Poe had recently left

Philadelphia and was living in Manhattan, in what was then the countryside (now the Upper West Side). In his introduction, Mabbott also cites Poe's friend Thomas M. Alfriend, who recalled that Poe told him "probably in the summer of 1849" that "Nature rests me. . . . She never fails to bring me peace" (*Poems*, 76).

3

POE'S HOMELY INTERIORS

In a letter to George Eveleth dated October 1, 1878, Helen Whitman reveals that Poe told her he was intent on "writing a pendant to 'The Domain of Arnheim' in which the most charming effects should be attained by artistic combinations of familiar and unvalued materials" (*Tales*, 2:1326). This chapter explores these ordinary and undervalued objects in the stories, sketches, and essays that Poe did write. Such homely details can be read as vehicles for undercurrent themes, nuanced complications of plot, and/or satirical and critical responses to cultural norms. Scholars such as Nina Baym, David Ketterer, Richard Wilbur, and Joan Dayan, to name just a few, have interpreted the phantasmagoric interiors in Poe's more popular stories from the late 1830s and 1840s (including "The Fall of the House of Usher," "Ligeia," "The Black Cat," and "The Masque of the Red Death"). However, the homely decorative objects and interior design in the domestic settings that Poe creates for his characters in the tales and sketches of this period have received little critical attention. Specifically, this chapter examines the visual cues found in the homely details (or the material culture) of "The Devil in the Belfry," "William Wilson," "The Philosophy of Furniture," "The Domain of Arnheim," and "Landor's Cottage."

"The Devil in the Belfry" (1839)

A year after Poe moved to Philadelphia, "The Devil in the Belfry" was published in the May 1839 issue of the *Philadelphia Saturday Chronicle and Mirror of the*

Times. The story includes a detailed description of the interior of a burgher home that, according to the narrator, mirrors all of the other homes in the city of Vondervotteimittiss. This description reinforces the narrator's satiric overview of the townspeople, who thrive on uniformity, conformity, and punctuality. The ostensible intent of his story is to reveal the terrible chaos that erupted one day after the town clock struck thirteen, in hopes of prompting his auditors to come to the aid of the villagers whose lives were torn asunder. However, this overt purpose is complicated by the implications of the narrator's focus on the interior decoration of the cottages. When this is taken into consideration, his underlying intent seems altogether less like a call for help in restoring the villagers' disrupted routines and more like a scathing critique of their systematic lives.

The narrator carefully describes the typical burgher home as follows:

> The dwellings are as much alike inside as out, and the furniture is all upon one plan. The floors are of square tiles, the chairs and tables of black-looking wood with thin crooked legs and puppy feet. The mantel-pieces are wide and high, and have not only time-pieces and cabbages sculptured over the front, but a real time-piece, which makes a prodigious ticking, on the top in the middle, with a flower-pot containing a cabbage standing on each extremity by way of outrider. Between each cabbage and the time-piece, again, is a little China man having a large stomach with a great round hole in it, through which is seen the dial-plate of a watch. (*Tales,* 1:367)

The Chinese object on the hearth might seem innocuous and could easily be overlooked despite being in plain sight—just like the letter openly displayed on the "trumpery fillagree card-rack of pasteboard . . . just beneath the middle of the mantel-piece" in Minister D——'s apartment in "The Purloined Letter" (1844; *Tales,* 2:990–91). In addition, the narrator of "The Devil in the Belfry" makes note of the "fierce, crooked-looking fire-dogs" in front of the fireplace (1:367–68)—andirons that call to mind the crooked, fierce-looking lions that guard Chinese tombs. Poe's attention to detail and his philosophy of overall effect make these objects, which seem out of place in a Pennsylvania Dutch home, stand out and beg interpretation. How a Chinese object, such as the "little China man having a large stomach," found its way into the homes of ordinary Pennsylvanians—here, in the "Dutch borough of Vondervotteimittiss"

(1:365)—is an engaging story of its own. It circles back to the explicit reference to history in the very first paragraph of "The Devil in the Belfry."

Initially, the narrator claims to tell his tale like a historian: "No one who knows me will doubt that the duty thus self-imposed will be executed to the best of my ability, with all that rigid impartiality, all that cautious examination into facts, and diligent collation of authorities, which should ever distinguish him who aspires to the title of historian" (*Tales*, 1:365). However, the tone of his overly self-conscious claim of "rigid impartiality" brings to mind Poe's other neurotic narrators. Although lacking the rhetorical frenzy of the narrator of "The Black Cat" or "The Tell-Tale Heart," the narrator of "The Devil in the Belfry" insists emphatically on the value of such impartiality and historical perspective. However, this claim is undermined when, instead of giving a date or time of origin for the "ancient village" where his story takes place—the most basic detail a historian might provide—the narrator makes only a vague mathematical allusion: "The date, I may thus say, in regard to the remoteness of its antiquity, cannot be less than any assignable quantity whatsoever" (1:365–66). Exactly what does that mean?

Despite this purposeful and meaningless ambiguity, the reference to history is quite useful to the reader. The "little China man having a large stomach"— the central decorative object on the mantelpieces in the burgher homes in Vondervotteimittiss—is a clue that helps reveal an undercurrent theme. This object directly alludes to the decorative choices made by wealthy Philadelphians and their imitators in the early to mid-nineteenth century. At this time, the China trade was flourishing in Philadelphia, and the Chinese objects that appeared in the homes of the wealthy had an influence on fashion throughout the United States until about 1844. Poe's disdain for country burghers who chose to imitate the wealthy is obliquely expressed in his May 1836 *Southern Literary Messenger* review of Frances Trollope's *Paris and the Parisians in 1835*. Poe claims that the book "appeared to us (we speak in all candor, and in sober earnest) an unusually well-written performance, in which, upon a basis of downright and positive truth, was erected, after the fashion of a porcelain pagoda, a very brilliant, although a very brittle fabric of mingled banter, philosophy, and spleen" (*Works*, 9:16). Poe's use of the porcelain pagoda as a metaphor for Trollope's "brilliant" yet "brittle" diatribes reveals a subtle but nonetheless negative response to the impact of the China trade on good taste.

This disdain is also evident in the narrator's satiric discussion of the decora-tive choices made by the homeowners in Vondervotteimittiss. This would-be bourgeoisie presumably deems Chinese-influenced items "fashionable" because they are like the objects—Chinese tea sets, sculptures, furniture, screens, and paintings—found in the wealthiest homes in Philadelphia. As Poe pointed out directly a year later in "The Philosophy of Furniture," "The populace, looking always upward for models, are insensibly led to confound the two entirely sepa-rate ideas of magnificence and beauty. In short, the cost of an article of furniture has at length come to be, with us, nearly the sole test of its merit in a decorative point of view" (*Tales*, 1:496–97). In modeling their decor after what the rich deem fashionable—including Chinese items—the burghers of Vondervotteim-ittiss are simply following the decorative rage of the time.

In *Philadelphians and the China Trade, 1784–1844*, Jean Gordon Lee notes that "almost all of the 'old families' of [Philadelphia] had interests in China."[1] She focuses her overview of the China trade in this period on one Philadelphia businessman: Nathan Dunn. His collection of objects from China, worth over half a million dollars, prompted him to open a Chinese museum (fig. 19) on Ninth and George (now Sansom) Streets, only a few short blocks from Poe's home on North Eighth Street. An opening reception was held on December 22, 1838, and a catalog accompanied the exhibit: *"Ten Thousand Chinese Things": A Descriptive Catalogue of the Chinese Collection, in Philadelphia, with Miscellaneous Remarks upon the Manners, Customs, Trade, and Government of the Celestial Empire.* An ad in *A. M'Elroy's Philadelphia Directory, for 1839* features an image of the pagoda in the labyrinth garden located on the 2400 block of Fairmount Avenue (erroneously depicted as the site of the Chinese Collection) and reports that the museum has attracted "many thousand Visitors," who have found the collection to be "the most striking illustration of the Manners, Customs, and peculiarities of this interesting portion of the East, than any work that has here-tofore appeared."[2]

E. C. Wines describes the opening night reception, where Nathan Dunn entertained "a select party of his friends, . . . over a hundred gentlemen"; they included "artists, mechanics, editors, and . . . a goodly representation from all the learned professions."[3] Was Poe among them? Possibly. If not, he was sure to have visited the museum, since it was a "tremendous success, reportedly visited by 100,000 people over a period of three years."[4] In 1840, Dr. John Kearsley Mitchell, Poe's friend and physician, donated Maelzel's "automaton chess

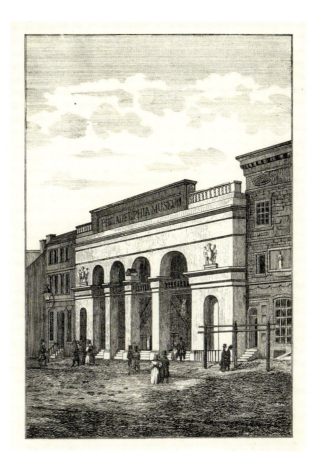

Fig. 19   Museu de Filadelphia, ca. 1845. The Library Company of Philadelphia. Gift of S. Marguerite Brenner, P.9057.33.

player" (an item Mitchell had purchased at an auction in 1838) to the museum. Certainly, if Poe had not already been to see the collection, he would have been inclined to do so because of this new addition.[5]

Given this history, it becomes clear that decorating a living room or parlor with a "little China man having a large stomach" would have been commonplace, if not cliché. Jonathan Goldstein, in *Philadelphia and the China Trade, 1682–1846*, verifies the observation that Poe so aptly makes in his satirical story: "Chinese influence in the Philadelphia region . . . was not confined to the posh houses of the inner city. The majority of Chinese articles shipped to early Pennsylvania were found in poorer homes."[6] The burghers of Vondervotteimittiss were taken by the impulse to mimic the rich in their home decoration. The Chinaman on the mantelpiece and the "huge pot . . . full of sauer-kraut and pork" cooking over the blazing fire (*Tales*, 1:368) suggest the townspeople's complete conformity to fashion as well as their adherence to ethnic customs.

The narrator's stated motive for telling the story of how Vondervotteimittiss was catapulted into chaos by a "devil in the belfry"—specifically, in order to encourage his auditors, the "lovers of correct time and fine kraut," to "restore the ancient order of things" in the town—is suspect, as the end of the tale reveals (*Tales*, 1:374). Clearly, the narrator is far more disgusted with the whole scene than bent on righting a wrong. He realizes that the "ancient order of things" cannot be restored by the townspeople themselves because they have become too caught up in adhering to what fashion demands and the clock indicates. They do not consider the striking of thirteen to be an aberration; when they hear the bell's peal, the men and boys harangue their wives and mothers because their lunches are "late." They believe that the noon hour has passed without their meals and afternoon smoke, and therefore nothing is as it should be: their bellies feel hungry and their pipes need to be stuffed. In fact, however, nothing has changed materially; the townspeople simply believe that they have missed the hour when they would normally eat and smoke their pipes. Their lives, determined by imitation and rigid patterns—whether prescribed by the clock or by fashion—do not allow them the capacity for critical evaluation or truly felt perceptions. The narrator's disgust with the town's demise, then, relates not only to the devil's shenanigans but also to the townspeople's inability to recognize that the appearance that something is awry is just that: appearance. Their adherence to conformity makes them effete as well as numb to real feelings.

Not only can "The Devil in the Belfry" be read as an expression of Poe's disdain for "the weighty German scholarship of the time," as T. O. Mabbott suggests (*Tales*, 1:362), but in its detailed descriptions of interior decoration, it can also be seen as a critique of the American propensity to fall prey to the whims of fashion. It satirizes Americans who choose to decorate their homes with the newest "exotic" objects not because these help achieve repose or aesthetic harmony but because they want to mimic the rich. In doing so, they become unthinking slaves to fashion and blind and numb to their own desires and aesthetic sensibilities.

"William Wilson" (1839)

"William Wilson," a short story published around the same time as "The Devil in the Belfry," also features a narrator who admits a strong attachment to homely details. As he begins to tell the story of his miserable life, he states quite openly that the only solace he can find is in remembering the homely details of the boarding school of his youth: "It gives me, perhaps, as much of pleasure as I can now in any manner experience, to dwell upon minute recollections of the school and its concerns. . . . These, moreover, utterly trivial, and even ridiculous in themselves, assume, to my fancy, adventitious importance" (*Tales*, 1:428). Such "adventitious importance" also applies quite profoundly to a homely detail described at the end of his tale, which is often overlooked.

Initially, as the narrator speaks of the school that affords him his only pleasure, he focuses on the exterior of the "excessively ancient" house (*Tales*, 1:428). Then he begins to recall specific details of the interior of the schoolroom: "The school-room was the largest in the house—I could not help thinking, in the world. It was very long, narrow, and dismally low, with pointed Gothic windows and a ceiling of oak. In a remote and terror-inspiring angle was a square enclosure of eight or ten feet. . . . It was a solid structure, with massy door" (1:429–30). This "solid structure" was the office of the principal, Dr. Bransby. In addition to this enclosure, there were two other small "boxes" for the ushers: "One of these was the pulpit of the 'classical' usher, one of the 'English and mathematical.'" All three "boxes" inspired terror in the students, according to the narrator. Curiously, the only objects in the large schoolroom aside from chairs, desks, and books were a "huge bucket with water . . . and a clock of stupendous dimensions" (1:430). The narrator's claim that these details have "adventitious importance" is not an idle one. A simple homely detail becomes a crucial clue in interpreting the purposefully puzzling outcome of the story: a dramatic, bloody "death."

The narrator takes many pages to reveal his moral downfall, retracing his steps from the time he left Dr. Bransby's school to the "instant [when] all virtue dropped bodily as a mantle" (*Tales*, 1:426). He provides a "blow-by-blow" account of his disastrous encounter with the man who shares his name, William Wilson, at a masquerade in Rome, the event that leads to his need to reveal his life's demise. The narrator claims that this encounter with the other Wilson was the "final straw"; he could no longer abide this Wilson's persistent interference in his life. The narrator challenged him to a duel and dragged him off to an antechamber, where they began to fight. He claims to have been "frantic with every species of wild excitement": "I forced [Wilson] by sheer strength against the wainscoting, and thus, getting him at mercy, plunged my sword, with brute ferocity, repeatedly through and through his bosom." He then recalls having heard someone approaching the antechamber and, running to the door to prevent the intruder from entering the murder scene, successfully locked it. He returned to the scene of the crime, finding that Wilson was no longer slumped against the wainscoting, dying from multiple stab wounds to the chest. Instead, a homely detail emerged that hadn't been there before: "The brief moment in which I averted my eyes had been sufficient to produce, apparently, a material change in the arrangements at the upper or farther end of the room. A large mirror,—so at first it seemed to me in my confusion—now stood where none had been perceptible before; and, as I stepped up to it in extremity of terror, mine own image, but with features all pale and dabbled in blood, advanced to meet me with a feeble and tottering gait" (1:447–48).

At first, this homely detail—a mirror that wasn't there before—encourages readers to think that the figure of William Wilson in the "mirror" is, in fact, the narrator himself or a manifestation of the narrator's conscience. Consequently, it would be deduced either that the narrator had stabbed himself and now stands at death's door or that he had effectively killed off his conscience. In the latter case, the "death" would be a spiritual or psychological one, reinforcing the epigraph preceding the tale: "What say of it? What say of CONSCIENCE grim, / That spectre in my path?" However, two facts negate these conclusions: the narrator is writing his life's story on "the fair page now lying before me" (*Tales*, 1:426), and it would be impossible for a man bleeding to death from stab wounds made "with brute ferocity" to pen such a lengthy narrative. Indeed, the mirror does not reflect the narrator's own image, as he himself initially believed: "Thus it appeared, I say, but was not. It was my antagonist—it was Wilson, who then stood before me in the agonies of his dissolution" (1:448).

Thus, the narrator's claim at the start of the tale—that "death approaches"—is referring not to his suicide or to the destruction of his conscience, but rather to the impending death at the gallows that he faces for murdering William Wilson. The narrator therefore appeals to his readers for understanding:

> Death approaches; and the shadow which foreruns him has thrown a softening influence over my spirit. I long, in passing through the dim valley, for the sympathy—I had nearly said for the pity—of my fellow men. I would fain have them believe that I have been, in some measure, the slave of circumstances beyond human control. I would wish them to seek out

for me, in the details I am about to give, some little oasis of *fatality* amid a wilderness of error. I would have them allow—what they cannot refrain from allowing—that, although temptation may have ere-while existed as great, man was never *thus*, at least, tempted before. (*Tales*, 1:427–28)

The narrator, like so many of Poe's murderers, is not writing a suicide note. No; like the others—the narrators of "The Black Cat," "The Imp of the Perverse," and "The Tell-Tale Heart"—he awaits his punishment and, while doing so, pens his apologia. In recording the details of his life, he hopes to garner "the sympathy . . . of my fellow men." It is not insignificant that he begins his tale by recalling the homely details of the "large, rambling, Elizabethan house" of his youth. Such "recollections of the school and its concerns," being the only pleasure afforded him as he faces execution, reinforce the importance of homely details and interior decoration in his tale (*Tales*, 1:427–28). These homely details that still give him a modicum of pleasure to recall, ironically, point to the one homely detail that transforms his ostensible self-mutilation and suicide (whether real or psychological) into what it really is: the horrific murder of an innocent guest at a masquerade.

"The Philosophy of Furniture" (1840)

In chapter 5, I will read "The Philosophy of Furniture" as a way of understanding Poe's visual aesthetics, arguing that the judgments he uses to evaluate interior decoration apply to all visual art. Here, however, I focus on the specific furniture and accoutrements described in this sketch to better understand Poe's "ideal" homely interior and his aversion to popular fashion. "The Philosophy of Furniture" was first published in 1840; its opening paragraph was omitted when it was revised for publication in the *Broadway Journal* five years later. In the original version, the narrator begins by expressing his disdain for Americans' crassness and their penchant for following fashion: "There is philosophy even in furniture—a philosophy nevertheless which seems to be more imperfectly understood by Americans than by any civilized nation upon the face of the earth" (*Tales*, 1:495). This scorn for American taste finds full expression as an undercurrent of meaning in "The Devil in the Belfry." The connection between "The Devil in the Belfry" and "The Philosophy of Furniture" is reinforced by the conjunction of two judgments found in the revised version of the latter. Here the narrator simply states, "The Dutch have, perhaps, an indeterminate idea that a curtain is not a cabbage. . . . The Yankees alone are preposterous" (1:496). Poe's disdain for the Dutch—and, by inference, the Pennsylvania Dutch—is clear in this dismissive statement, although it remains implied in "The Devil in the Belfry." The narrator of that tale emphasizes the numerous ways in which cabbages are used as a central element of interior decoration in the burghers' parlors—whether they are engraved on the mantelpiece or placed in flowerpots atop each end.

In both versions of "The Philosophy of Furniture," Poe pays particular attention to light. He praises the astral lamp invented by Ami Argand as the only satisfying way to illuminate a parlor. Poe would have been familiar with this invention not only by visiting wealthy acquaintances but also by reading about it in Abraham Rees's 1819 *Cyclopaedia; or, Universal Dictionary of Arts, Sciences, and Literature*. On the problem of glare, Rees writes, "The public have long been in possession of a complete remedy for this, and several other disadvantages in lamps, by the invention of the Argand lamp."[7] However, the narrator of "The Philosophy of Furniture" is quite adamant that such concerns are not important to Americans, and he is critical of their preference for flashiness over repose. "*Glare* is a leading error in the philosophy of American household decoration," he opines. "We are violently enamored of gas and of glass. . . . It is not too much to say, that the deliberate employer of a cut-glass shade, is either radically deficient in taste, or blindly subservient to the caprices of fashion" (*Tales*, 1:498–99). Softer light, he claims, is preferable: "A mild, or what artists term a cool light, with its consequent warm shadows, will do wonders for even an ill-furnished apartment. Never was a more lovely thought than that of the astral lamp. We mean, of course, the astral lamp proper—the lamp of Argand, with its original plain ground-glass shade, and its tempered and uniform moonlight rays." According to the narrator, this kind of lamp is quite the opposite of the more popular cut-glass shade preferred by most Americans. The latter emits light in "unequal, broken, and painful" rays, completely removing the possibility of repose (1:499).

In the first biography of Ami Argand, *Brandy, Balloons, and Lamps*, John J. Wolfe notes that Argand's lamp transformed the way people lived; before it became popular, "most of the world just went to bed shortly after dark."[8] Wolfe elaborates on Argand's various inventions, and it is interesting to note that three of these are subjects Poe popularized in "The Balloon Hoax," "King Pest," and, of course, "The Philosophy of Furniture." Prior to patenting his lamp, Argand became known for discovering a new way to distill brandy, making its production more efficient and, thus, making brandy more available. Argand was also instrumental in improving the technology for the first balloon to fly over Paris, which made a safe landing on September 19, 1783, with sheep, cock, and duck aboard—providing inspiration for Poe's "The Balloon Hoax." Jean-Pierre Blanchard, the first balloonist to cross the English Channel, wrote in the *Courrier de l'Europe* in 1785, "It is not for me to make known Mr. Argand, friend and collaborator of Montgolfier, who helped in all of his research. It is to him that Mssrs. Charles and Robert [the first to launch a hydrogen balloon] owe the ingenious and simple idea of using a barrel to produce large amounts of hydrogen gas; but because of his modesty, [Argand] has hardly been named in all these experiments to which he so eminently contributed to their success."[9]

Shortly after the Paris balloon launch, Argand did share his invention of the astral lamp with friends, who encouraged him to reveal all of the details of his mechanism. Eventually, between December 1783 and February 1874, Argand received a patent and partnered with William Parker to form Argand's Patent Lamp and Company.[10] The astral lamp became popular among the wealthy in the United States during the first quarter of the nineteenth century; it was only in the 1830s that it became available to others: "By 1830, the number and variety of lamps employing Argand technology reached well down the economic ladder. Expensive lamps continued to be manufactured, but painted tin or japanned variations also sold well. On the expensive end were the heavy mantel lamps popular in the 1830s and 1840s, many of them weighing upwards of twenty pounds. A growing variety of expensive, free-standing table lamps was also introduced at this time. . . . A good many evidences of the use of these lamps in American homes survives in the form of drawings, paintings, and prints."[11] The narrator of Poe's "Philosophy of Furniture" lauds Argand's lamp, "with its original plain ground-glass shade," but specifically damns the "huge and unmeaning glass chandeliers, prism-cut, gas-lighted, and without shade, which dangle in our most fashionable drawing-rooms" (*Tales*, 1:499). These, in combination with mirrors, are the quintessence of American gaudiness and bad taste. Here, without the subtle satire of "The Devil in the Belfry," Poe connects such interior decoration choices with American materialism: "The corruption of taste is a portion or a pendant of the dollar-manufacture. As we grow rich, our ideas grow rusty" (1:500).

Having thoroughly dismissed these poor choices and concluded his diatribe against gaudiness and "glitter," the narrator describes what he believes to be an ideal interior setting. He sees in his mind's eye "a small and not ostentatious chamber with whose decorations no fault can be found" (*Tales*, 1:500). However, much of his description can be questioned. In the next paragraph, the adjective "small," in relation to the size of the chamber, seems to have been forgotten. Instead, the narrator speaks of a room "some thirty feet in length and twenty-five in breadth"—hardly a small chamber. Despite its breadth, the room has only two windows "reaching down to the floor," not with clear panes to let in light, but with crimson-colored panes. The window frames are "more massive than usual," and "thick silver tissue" hangs loosely over the crimson panes. Thus, this almost thirty-square-foot room is dimly lit during the day, even when the sun is shining brightly. The narrator goes on to say that curtains of an "exceedingly rich crimson silk, fringed with a deep network of gold, and lined with the silver tissue," have "an airy appearance" (1:501). However, it is difficult to imagine the windows having an "airy appearance" in light of the red panes, their coverings, and the "massive" window frames.

Gold, silver, and crimson color the whole room—yet the narrator ostensibly prefers repose to glitter. The thick crimson carpet (which is the "soul" of the apartment) is patterned with a "gold cord" forming a "succession of short irregular curves" (*Tales*, 1:501; see also 497). The walls are covered with "a glossy paper of a silver gray tint, spotted with small Arabesque devices of a fainter hue of the prevalent crimson." The walls are hung with "landscapes of an imaginative cast—such as the fairy grottoes of Stanfield, or the lake of the Dismal Swamp of Chapman." These paintings must be large, the narrator asserts, since "diminutive paintings give that *spotty* look to a room, which is the blemish of so many a fine work of Art overtouched." In addition, he specifies how the paintings should be framed and hung. They must "lie flat on the walls," since the overall "keeping" of the room—the most important compositional concern—would be marred if they were hung from wires (1:502). Wires distract the eye and ruin the flow of the wall covering.

The rest of the decor includes furniture made of rosewood—two sofas, two chairs, and a pianoforte—and an octagonal table made of "gold-threaded marble." The only other "furniture" consists of "light and graceful hanging shelves, with golden edges and crimson silk cords and gold tassels," which hold hundreds of books. Again, "gold-threaded marble" and "golden edges and crimson silk cord and gold tassels" hardly lack glitter. The furniture, rugs, and curtains are additionally complemented by "four large and gorgeous Sèvres vases, in which bloom a profusion of sweet and vivid flowers" (1:502–3). These vases would most probably include gold in their designs and have a Gothic feel. As Jeffrey Munger explains, "Interest in the Gothic style emerged [in the 1820s] at Sèvres and remained popular for much of the nineteenth century. Strict adherence to Gothic motifs was rarely observed, however, and the Gothic style was more evoked than faithfully copied."[12] Finally, the room is lit by a "tall candelabrum, bearing a small antique lamp with highly perfumed oil," and by "an Argand lamp, with a plain crimson-tinted ground-glass shade, which . . . throws a tranquil but magical radiance over all" (1:503).

All in all, Poe's ideal room hardly lacks ostentatiousness. It is neither small nor simply decorated. Poe's intention to depict a room that avoids glitter and creates repose is only reflected in the narrator's choice of the Argand lamp with its bright but steady glow, but even that is covered with a crimson shade. The overall color scheme and the four large Sèvres vases betray the stated purpose of avoiding glitter and drama. Nonetheless, this sketch does project a picture of wealth and comfort, a place of refuge and luxury that does not fall prey to the whims of fashion—we find here no Chinese decorations, no cut-glass chandeliers, no multicolored carpet. The overall sensibility adheres to the aesthetics of beauty as portrayed by Sully, Chapman, and Stanfield—two American painters and one British—whose works Poe mentions and whom he admired for their Romantic landscapes, portraiture, and seascapes. Though not quite true to his promise to depict a humble room dedicated to repose, the narrator of this sketch does provide the reader with an alternative to what he describes as the Yankee penchant for "preposterous" home decoration: "There could be nothing more directly offensive to the eye of an artist than the interior of what is termed in the United States . . . a well-furnished apartment" (*Tales*, 1:497).

"The Domain of Arnheim" (1846) and "Landor's Cottage" (1849)

Many years after Poe wrote "The Philosophy of Furniture" and "The Landscape Garden" and just having moved from Manhattan to a cottage in Fordham, he published "The Domain of Arnheim" and "Landor's Cottage." T. O. Mabbott notes that a "comparison of the earlier sketch, 'The Landscape Garden,' with its paragraphs incorporated in 'The Domain of Arnheim' shows that Poe did a thorough job of tightening up, eliminating adjectives and using more specific phrases in the later version" (*Tales*, 2:1267). Like "The Landscape Garden," "The Domain of Arnheim" omits any references to interiors. Nonetheless, this story signals a move away from the aesthetic of the sublime and toward a regard for the harmony of the beautiful and the value of "seclusion." This aesthetic turn is revealed when Ellison explains to the narrator why he rejects a vast, sublime plateau as the site of his new home:

> This panorama is indeed glorious, and I should rejoice in it but for the excess of its glory. . . . Grandeur in any of its moods, but especially in that of extent, startles, excites—and then fatigues, depresses. For the occasional scene nothing can be better—for the constant view nothing worse. And, in the constant view, the most objectionable phase of grandeur is that of extent; the worst phase of extent, that of distance. It is at war with the sentiment and with the sense of *seclusion*—the sentiment and sense which we seek to humor in 'retiring to the country.'" (2:1278)

Such seclusion signals a desire for privacy and repose, a direct correlative to the privacy found in a home's interior. The magnificent venue fails to satisfy Ellison because it projects the sublime, not the beautiful; excitement, not repose.

Ellison chooses, instead, the domain of Arnheim, reached only after a canoe ride down a winding river between "shores of a tranquil and domestic beauty" (*Tales*, 2:1278). At the end, "the whole Paradise of Arnheim bursts upon the view. . . . There is a dream-like intermingling to the eye of tall slender Eastern trees—bosky shrubberies—flocks of golden and crimson birds—lily-fringed lakes—meadows of violets, tulips, poppies, hyacinths and tuberoses" (2:1283). The more domestic flowers and "Eastern trees" in Arnheim trump the sublime effect of the grand prospect with its mountainous, wild vegetation. Notably, as Sydney Kurland has observed, "the description of the day-long river journey calls to mind nothing so much as Thomas Cole's four-painting series, *The Voyage of Life*. . . . Poe describes a phenomenon which the painter has also depicted in the left-hand foreground of his work—the boat's reflection: 'the keel balancing itself with admirable nicety on that of a phantom bark which, by some accident having been turned upside down, floated in constant company with the substantial one, for the purpose of sustaining it.'"[13] This connection between Poe's story and Cole's *Voyage of Life* is more than just conjecture, since the four-painting series was shown in a special exhibit at the Pennsylvania Academy of the Fine Arts in 1844, before Poe left Philadelphia for Manhattan.

Only when we turn to "Landor's Cottage," the last story published before Poe's death, do we find the interior, homely details that mirror the exterior love-liness of Ellison's secluded landscape. "Landor's Cottage," written in late 1848 as a sequel to "The Domain of Arnheim," is replete with descriptions of interior decoration. After the narrator relates his travels through the mountains, he finds his way to the front door of Landor's cottage. Annie, the mistress of the cottage, invites him in. Despite his initial enchantment with Annie's beauty, he immediately becomes "more intent on observing the arrangements of the dwelling which had so much interested me, than the personal appearance of the tenant" (*Tales*, 2:1339).

The narrator notes the simplicity of the furniture in the parlor and the "ingrain carpet, of excellent texture—a white ground, spotted with small circular green figures." How different the carpet is in this picture of domestic bliss than the crimson and gold carpet described in "The Philosophy of Furniture." The curtains on the cottage windows, too, stand in stark contrast to the rich silk draperies in Poe's ideal parlor; here they are made of "snowy white jaconet muslin"—a simple, light cotton fabric devoid of color. The cottage walls are papered—but with "a French paper of great delicacy." The silver background is simply patterned with a "faint green cord running zig-zag throughout" (*Tales*, 2:1339), rather than with "small Arabesque devices of a fainter hue of the prevalent crimson" (1:502).

Three lithographs by Bernard-Romain Julien, not of large dimension, have been hung on the wall of Landor's parlor using the method required for hanging paintings in Poe's ideal parlor: they do not hang from wires but are simply "fastened to the wall without frames" (*Tales*, 2:1340). This is an important detail in "The Philosophy of Furniture," because although paintings may be "seen to better advantage" when hung by wires, "the general appearance of the chamber is injured" when this is done. One rule, however, is completely ignored in Landor's cottage: the avoidance of "diminutive paintings [that] give that *spotty* look to a room" (1:502). The three lithographs by Julien could not be large. Moreover, unlike Chapman's painting *The Lake of the Dismal Swamp*, which is explicitly named in "The Philosophy of Furniture," the lithographs described by the narrator do not fit any of Julien's extant images. Nowhere has there been found a "scene of Oriental luxury" or a "carnival piece" or a "Greek female head" by this artist (2:1340).

The first sentence of the penultimate paragraph, however, curiously evokes a still-life image: "On the table were a few books; a large, square, crystal bottle of some novel perfume; a plain, ground-glass *astral* (not solar) lamp, with an Italian shade; and a large vase of resplendently-blooming flowers." The rest of the paragraph bursts with a profusion of flowers: "Flowers indeed of gorgeous colors and delicate odor, formed the sole mere *decoration* of the apartment. The fire-place was nearly filled with a vase of brilliant geranium. On a triangular shelf in each angle of the room stood also a similar vase, varied only as to its lovely contents. One or two smaller *bouquets* adorned the mantel; and late violets clustered about the open windows" (*Tales*, 2:1340). This lush floral beauty reminds the reader of the narrator's claim in "The Domain of Arnheim" that there is nothing in nature that can't be transformed into an even greater beauty. The clustering of flowers throughout the apartment gives a nod to the value of creating the repose of domesticity with the colors and forms of nature's gifts. However, not one of these conclusions is drawn explicitly in "Landor's Cottage," as they were in "The Domain of Arnheim." "Landor's Cottage" ends abruptly with the narrator's pronouncement that his purpose was not to do more "than give, in detail, a picture of Mr. Landor's residence—*as I found it*. How he made it what it was—and *why*, with some particulars of Mr. Landon [*sic*] himself—may, *possibly* form the subject of another article" (2:1340).[14]

4

POE'S VISUAL TRICKS

Not only was Poe attracted to the art he saw, but he was also intrigued by the very act of seeing. The act of seeing plays a pivotal role in many of his tales, including "The Sphinx," "The Purloined Letter," and "The Spectacles," but especially in "Ligeia" and in his only published novel, *The Narrative of Arthur Gordon Pym*. Poe was keenly aware of the public's fascination with extraordinary visual phenomena. He also understood people's willingness to see otherworldly visual occurrences as real, despite the fact that David Brewster's popular *Letters on Natural Magic* revealed the mechanical underpinnings of many such "miraculous events." Brewster's book is a series of letters addressed to Sir Walter Scott; it was first published in London by John Murray in 1832 and was reprinted numerous times in the United States, beginning with the *Harper's* reprint in 1835. *Letters on Natural Magic* served as a rich resource for Poe's narratives. Laura Saltz suggests that "Poe's debt to Brewster extends from 1833, with 'Manuscript Found in a Bottle,' till the end of his career, with the publication of *Eureka*."[1] Saltz provides an overview of the ways in which Poe used *Letters on Natural Magic*: "These include the mysterious appearance of the word 'DISCOVERY' on the ship's sail in 'Manuscript Found in a Bottle,' William Wilson's death-duel with his mirror image . . . , the specter images of ships in *The Narrative of Arthur Gordon Pym*, and the mysterious handwriting in 'A Tale of the Ragged Mountains.' What's more, 'Maelzel's Chess-Player' is based entirely on Brewster's letter on automata."[2]

Poe openly criticized other writers and dramatists for not taking advantage of such visual tricks. In Marginalia 54, he disparaged American theater directors for their unwillingness to use optical devices in their staging: "Enslen, a German optician, conceived the idea of throwing a shadowy figure, by optical means, into the chair of Banquo; and that thing was readily done. Intense effect was produced; and I do not doubt that an American audience might be electrified by the feat. But our managers not only have no invention of their own, but no energy to avail themselves of that of others."[3] The popularity of *Letters on Natural Magic* was preceded by a public fascination with optical toys such as the kaleidoscope (1815), the diorama (1820s), the thaumatrope (1825), the phenakistoscope (1830s), the zoetrope and the stroboscope (mid-1830s), and the stereoscope (late 1830s). Not only were these visual toys highly entertaining, but they also marked the "reorganization of vision in the first half of the nineteenth century . . . especially in the 1820s and 1830s."[4]

Poe incorporated visual trickery in various ways in many of his tales. The last chapter of *The Narrative of Arthur Gordon Pym*, for example, includes striking descriptions of the narrator's surroundings that invite the reader to prepare for images beyond the real:

> Many unusual phenomena now indicated that we were entering upon a region of novelty and wonder. A high range of light gray vapor appeared constantly in the southern horizon, flaring up occasionally in lofty streaks, now darting from east to west, and again presenting a level and uniform summit. . . . The heat of the water was now truly remarkable, and in color was undergoing a rapid change, being no longer transparent, but of a milky consistency and hue . . . [with] sudden and extensive agitations of the surface—these, we at length noticed, were always preceded by wild flickerings in the region of vapor to the southward. . . . A fine white powder, resembling ashes—but certainly not such—fell over the canoe and over a large surface of the water, as the flickering died away among the vapor and the commotion subsided in the sea. . . . The whole [white] ashy material fell now continually around us, and in vast quantities. The range of vapor to the southward had arisen prodigiously in the horizon, and began to assume more distinctness of form. I can liken it to nothing but a limitless cataract, rolling silently into the sea from some immense and far-distant rampart in the heaven. The gigantic curtain ranged along the whole extent of the southern horizon. It emitted no sound. . . . A sullen darkness now

hovered above us—but from out the milky depths of the ocean a luminous glare arose.[5]

The novel ends with the vision of "a shrouded human figure, very large in proportions than any dweller among men. And the hue of the skin of the figure was of a perfect whiteness of snow."[6] This ending has intrigued many scholars, including Richard Kopley, Kent Ljungquist, Carol Peirce, and Richard Wilbur, among others.[7]

In addition to puzzling readers, visual phenomena in Poe's works prove to be more than confounding for some of his characters. For instance, the narrator of "The Sphinx" almost loses his mind as the result of an optical illusion. "The Sphinx" was first published in the January 1846 issue of *Arthur's Ladies' Magazine*. During this time—and this is a detail not to be overlooked—Poe was working on revisions to his favorite tale, "Ligeia," which was first published in 1838. The final, revised version appeared in the September 27, 1845, issue of the *Broadway Journal*, while Poe was its editor. According to T. O. Mabbott, "On August 9, 1846, Poe wrote Cooke that he had improved the story" (*Tales*, 1:307). That Poe improved "Ligeia" and then wrote the seemingly insignificant "Sphinx" is worth noting, since a fantastic visual occurrence is central to both stories, linking passivity with apparent madness and subsequent horror.

In "The Sphinx," the narrator's horror and fear result from seeing something frighteningly extraordinary through the window where he sits reading: a "living monster of hideous conformation." The narrator had gone to his friend's country home to seek refuge from the cholera epidemic in New York City, hoping to diminish his fear of dying of this plague by burying himself in books. However, he explains, the books he chose to read "force[d] into germination whatever seeds of hereditary superstition lay latent in my bosom." While absorbed in reading, he falls prey to an extraordinary visual perception that, he explains, both "appalled, and at the same time . . . confounded and bewildered me" (*Tales*, 2:1247). The intensity of this experience proves even more powerful than the fear evoked by the "dread reign of the Cholera in New-York" (2:1246). Here, again, we see Brewster's influence at work. In *Letters on Natural Magic*, he describes in detail the same visual phenomenon experienced by the narrator of Poe's tale. Brewster remarks that such hallucinations most often occur in "persons of studious habits, who are much occupied with the operations of their own minds, [and for whom] the mental pictures are much more distinct than in ordinary persons." He extends this concept by suggesting that "even ordinary men, not much addicted to speculations of any kind, often perceive in their mind's eye . . . ludicrous creations of fancy."[8] Poe's narrator fits this description of a studious man absorbed in books, thus easily explaining why he becomes obsessed with the "monster" he sees through the window.

The narrator, in fact, does fear that he has fallen prey to "ludicrous creations of fancy" and confesses that "when I describe the monster, (which I distinctly saw, and calmly surveyed through the whole period of its progress,) my readers, I fear, will feel more difficulty in being convinced of these points than even I did myself" (*Tales*, 2:1247–48). This stance is similar to the one the narrator takes in "The Black Cat"; he likewise assumes that his readers will have trouble believing his claims that he has been haunted by the cat he hung from a tree in his garden. He addresses their skepticism most notably when he describes the image of a hanged cat that mysteriously appeared on the remains of the bedroom wall left standing after his house burned to the ground. Both narrators are convinced that they did see an incredible but nonetheless real sight: the reconstituted cat and the horrific monster. And both believe that seeing these monstrosities betokens a fall into mania—the extreme outcome of their distracted visions. The narrator of "The Black Cat" blames alcohol for his mania, while the narrator of "The Sphinx" blames his excessive fear. The latter perceives the monster as a clear omen of his impending insanity and, luckily, turns to his friend for help.

In "The Sphinx," the narrator's anxiety is relieved when his friend draws a logical connection between the narrator's description of the monster and the description of an insect in a natural history book. In contrast to the horror that the reader feels at the end of "The Black Cat" when the second black cat and the narrator's murdered wife appear from behind a plaster wall—or the gripping shock and wonder that the reader ostensibly shares with the narrator in "Ligeia" at the reincarnation of his dead wife—horror and wonder are completely dissolved in "The Sphinx" by the friend's ratiocination. Instead of horror, the narrator of "The Sphinx" describes his sense of relief after his friend explains the mechanics of the narrator's visual misperception. The host's inductive reasoning relieves the narrator of his fear that he will fall into severe mania by determining that the monster is simply a bug. This use of induction occurs in other tales as well, where Poe deploys a similar method of having his characters use inductive reasoning to overcome seemingly overwhelming circumstances that threaten their lives or mental health. For example, in "A Descent into the Maelström," the narrator uses induction and his keen sense of peripheral vision to make observations that result in his survival and release from the maelstrom.

Poe also uses his characters' visual capacities or lack thereof as pivots for his tales. This is true for his comic story "The Spectacles." Here, Poe makes fun of those who will not see, with a much lighter consequence to the main character than the embarrassment felt by the prefect for his defective detection in "The Purloined Letter." These two tales demonstrate the human propensity to see what is desired and not what is actually there—a tendency not easily overcome. The narrator of "The Spectacles" provides the most obvious representation of a fool caught up in his own faulty observations. As is the case in many of Poe's tales, a bit of philosophy is entertained before the narrative proper begins. Especially ironic is the narrator's claim that "the brightest and most enduring of the psychal fetters are those which are riveted by a glance" (*Tales*, 2:887). This "philosophical" observation, however, is short-lived, and the narrator proceeds to provide the reader with an extensive (and overly detailed) overview of his family names and his own physical appearance, admitting, in the end, that he has shared "something too much of these merely personal details, which, after all, are of little importance" (2:888). However, two such details turn out to be of utmost importance: his nearsightedness and his real name. And these shape the comic plot, which depends entirely on the act of seeing; it includes such phrases as "I gazed at this queenly apparition for at least a half an hour," "I kept my eyes riveted," and "I thus feasted my eyes" (2:890, 892, 893), as well as the use of technical devices to help the narrator see, such as the "double eye-glass"—"a complex and magnificent toy, richly chased and filigreed, and gleaming with jewels" (2:906–7). The narrator ends up falling in love with a woman he sees from afar—or, rather, does not see very well—and in a complex and comic set of circumstances finds himself married to his great-great-grandmother. The story is not one of Poe's finest, as T. O. Mabbott points out, and Poe himself openly admitted that it was far too long when he republished it in the November 22, 1845, issue of the *Broadway Journal*: "We were not aware of the great length of 'The Spectacles' until too late to remedy the evil" (2:884; see also 883). Nonetheless, it is an excellent example of how Poe employs a favorite conceit: the importance of seeing what is there and not what we want to see.

This conceit is especially true in "Ligeia" because the denouement depends entirely on the reader's response to the fantastic visual occurrences described by the narrator. Even though he tries to obscure his purposeful role in the death of Rowena, his second wife, by emphasizing his opium intake as he sits in her bedchamber during her illness, it can be concluded that this "impairment" is merely a foil, if the visual cues in the tale are pieced together effectively. What the narrator describes in the denouement—Rowena's death and the transformative reincarnation of his first wife, Ligeia—becomes overwhelmingly suspect, as is his horror at Ligeia's reappearance. At first glance, the ending cannot be explained rationally, but if the potential for aerial optical illusions in the elaborately decorated bedchamber is taken into consideration as a corollary to the explicit reference to anamorphosis in the text, then Ligeia's reappearance might not be as fantastic as it first appears, and the narrator's role as an innocent bystander can be called into question. All of these tales show Poe's keen interest in demonstrating the human propensity to see what is desired and not what is actually there.

However, since no one can escape this flaw, the fact that Poe cites it as if he could escape it himself constitutes an anamorphic fiction that further complicates the reader's response to the effects of his manipulations.[9] This inability to see, or blindness to what has actually occurred, coheres with Predrag Cicovacki's definition of anamorphosis:

> As a verb, [anamorphosis] means "to form anew," and suggests that our picture of reality is not given once and forever. With new information and insights our map has to be modified and corrected, it has to be formed anew. As a noun, *anamorphosis* stands for a picture which to the naked eye is only a broken and fragmentary deformity but, when reflected in a conic mirror, shows a recognizable and "normal" form. . . . The original meaning of *anamorphosis* allows one more twist: our map of reality may be damaging and distorting not only because there is something intrinsically wrong with the map itself, but because there is something wrong with our attitude toward the map. One-sidedness may be bad in itself, but it becomes an even bigger problem when it is not recognized as such and is mistaken for completeness and comprehensiveness. Our map becomes damaging when we are not aware of the limited nature of our approach to reality, when we are not aware of our ignorance. In our ignorance, we may mistake our map of reality for reality itself. In our ignorance, we may presume that

our scientific map, which excludes values, freedom, and faith, portrays the only reality that exists.[10]

Anamorphosis, quite simply, however, is the manipulation of perspective to create a distorted image that nonetheless, when seen from a specific point of view or with a mechanical device, can be coherently read. Poe purposefully inserts this definition of anamorphosis in "Ligeia" as a means of presenting "in plain sight"—a way to read the story's seemingly fantastic ending. In effect, then, Poe creates his own anamorphosis. In the narrator's ability to repress the visual potential of the bedchamber's purposefully constructed decoration, in his subsequent innocent response to the seemingly supernatural occurrences that prompt his retelling of what he presents as a horrific experience, and in the obvious, though not initially apparent, widowed status he sustains even after the "miraculous" reappearance of Ligeia, we can detect another instance of Poe's "imp of the perverse" and a decided critique of his readers' vulnerability to fictional and visual manipulations—the same susceptibility that attracted his readers to the productions of "veiled ladies," mesmerists, and popular visual toys such as the kaleidoscope.

The narrator openly describes the mechanisms that produce the "miraculous" transformation of Rowena into Ligeia as he tells his tale. He projects doubt on his having been able to create a stage to present his "miraculous" reincarnation by claiming that he had been under the influence of "an immoderate dose of opium" (*Tales*, 1:325). This claim is meant to distract the reader from his manipulated production of awe and horror. However, like the narrator in "The Tell-Tale Heart," the narrator of "Ligeia" reveals, if covertly, his culpability in his second wife's murder—but only if the reader pays attention to the seemingly trivial detail of anamorphosis explicitly described in the tale and takes into consideration Poe's use of Brewster's *Letters on Natural Magic*.

Brewster reveals the mechanisms that produced "magical" projections when governments "were unable or unwilling to found their sovereignty on the affections and interests of their people," but instead chose to make them "obedient slave[s] of a spiritual despotism" through the use of "natural magic."[11] The science of acoustics and the principles of hydrostatics were often used, but the science of optics, Brewster suggests, is "the most fertile in marvellous expedients." In fact, he asserts that "the eye is . . . the principal seat of the supernatural. . . .

When visible bodies disappear and reappear without any intelligible cause; and when [the eye] beholds objects, whether real or imaginary, for whose presence no cause can be assigned, the conviction of supernatural agency becomes under ordinary circumstances unavoidable."[12]

Such visual tricks, of course, depend on the use of mirrors and lenses and the manipulation of perspective.[13] The devices that create these illusions fascinated first the French and then the British and Americans. As Brewster wrote to his wife, the kaleidoscope he invented in 1819 quickly became ubiquitous: "You can form no conception of the effect which the instrument excited in London; all that you have heard falls infinitely short of the reality. No book and no instrument in the memory of man ever produced such a singular effect."[14] The thaumatrope, or "wonder turner," created by London physicist Dr. John Ayrton Paris in 1825 also fascinated the general public; Brewster speculates, "Had the principle of this instrument been known to the ancients, it would doubtless have formed a powerful engine of delusion in their temples, and might have been more effective than the optical means which they seem to have employed for producing the apparitions of their gods."[15]

Another method of visual manipulation became prevalent through the science or art of anamorphosis. In *Anamorphosis: An Annotated Bibliography*, Alberto Pérez-Gómez and Louise Pelletier offer the following definition of anamorphosis:

> The word "anamorphosis" comes from the Greek: *ana-* "back," indicating a return toward, and *morphe-* "form," and is defined as a projection of forms outside their visible limits. Viewed from a precise vantage point (the convergence point of a geometrical construction) the distorted image recovers a recognizable form, and as has often been observed, the projected image seems to lift up from the actual surface of the anamorphosis itself. . . . The anamorphic distortion bears some resemblance to the technique of optical correction, mentioned by writers on architecture since Vitruvius. In fact, at its origins anamorphosis emerged from a similar consideration of transforming an image in such a way that only from a specific vantage point would the image recover its appropriate proportions. . . . In a large number of treatises on perspective drawing which contain examples of primitive anamorphosis, the relationship with optical correction is obvious. . . . The concept of optical correction aims at modifying slightly the physical reality

of the work to make it appear perfectly proportioned according to a given angle of vision, the anamorphic projection dissolves completely the subject of representation, allowing the viewer to witness the magical reappearance of a hidden image from a stationary point determined by a geometrical construction. . . . Seventeenth century anamorphic distortions were meant to be used with discernment and care, as they presupposed a magical connection between image and its source. . . . In parallel with the autonomous development of anamorphosis in the seventeenth century, the sciences of geometry and mathematics soon started to include examples of anamorphic projection as scientific "recreations," treating them as a special category of optics and mathematics. On the other hand, as part of the Cartesian process of questioning, philosophers like Descartes gave philosophical justification to anamorphic distortions. Seen as the epitome of illusion, they highlighted the philosophical distance between representation and the object itself.[16]

The use of anamorphosis in China, France, and Italy began in the seventeenth century. According to Jurgis Baltrušaitis, Jean François Niceron distinguished three types of anamorphosis "according to the viewpoint and its relation to the subject and its siting: 'optical' when one looks horizontally along a vast hall or gallery; 'anoptric' when one looks up towards the top of a very high wall, and 'catoptric' when one looks down, for example, from an open window, above a painting designed to be thus viewed."[17] Poe would have come across such depictions of anamorphosis and aerial projections by reading Brewster's letter "Science Used as an Instrument of Imposture." This letter employs the term "anamorphous drawing" and includes a description and illustrative diagrams of the process of creating an anamorphic image through catoptrics. "Among the ingenious and beautiful deceptions of the 17th century, we must enumerate that of the reformation of distorted pictures by reflexion from cylindrical and conical mirrors," Brewster writes. "In these representations the original image from which a perfect picture is produced, is often so completely distorted, that the eye cannot trace in it the resemblance to any regular figure, and the greatest degree of wonder is of course excited, whether the original image is concealed or exposed to view. These distorted pictures may be drawn by strict geometrical rules."[18] In this letter, Brewster also describes "the art of forming aërial representations" and relays Athanasius Kircher's claim that "he once exhibited in this manner a representation of the Ascension of our Saviour, and that the images were so perfect that the spectators could not be persuaded till they had attempted to handle them, that they were not real substances."[19]

Earlier, in his 1658 text *Natural Magick*, Italian scholar Giambattista della Porta wrote a whole section elaborating on "experiments concerning Catoptrick glasses": "For these shine amongst Geometrical instruments, for Ingenuity, Wonder, and Profit: For what could be invented more ingeniously, then that certain experiments should follow the imaginary conceits of the mind, and the truth of Mathematical Demonstrations should be made good by Ocular experiments? what could seem more wonderful, then that by reciprocal strokes of reflexion, Images should appear outwardly, hanging in the Air, and yet neither the visible Object nor the Glass seen? that they may seem not be to the repercussions of the Glasses but Spirits of vain Phantasms?"[20]

The self-proclaimed first manual in English on perspective—*Practical Perspective or Perspective Made Easy . . . Useful for All Painters, Engravers, Architects, &c. and All Others that Are Any Waies Inclined to Speculatory Ingenuity*, written and printed by Joseph Moxon in 1670—teaches readers how "to draw on a Quadrant a Figure seemingly confused and without Design, yet when of this Quadrant a Cone shall be made, a comely and proportional Figure shall appear."[21] It teaches, as well, how to put catoptrics to use: "Operation LIX: To Draw an Appearance seemingly confused and without design which Shall Reflect on a Cilinder Perpendicularly erected in a designed place, an intended Figure."[22] This inclusion of anamorphosis in a basic manual on perspective suggests the importance of anamorphosis in understanding the mechanisms of perspective. For example, although the position of the viewer is absolutely integral to viewing an anamorphic image, an optimal viewing of a straightforward representation likewise depends on the viewer's viewpoint. In an 1820 manual on perspective, drawing, and painting, Charles Hayter explains that "the utmost perfection perspective can give to a picture, is only to convey the true idea of a scene or object, when viewed at the viewpoint of distance the artist determined his picture by; which . . . means the measured distance of the eye (*of perspective*) from the picture."[23]

Anamorphosis plays with visual perception using the rules of perspective. It allows images to be hidden within what appears at first to be a simple representation, as in, for example, Hans Holbein's *The Ambassadors*.[24] At first glance, these "hidden images" either are not seen or look like distortions until the viewer finds the "proper" perspective or uses a mirror or anamorphic device to transform them. This geometric manipulation also helped facilitate the painting of murals on curved surfaces. Poe's inordinate fascination with word puzzles would naturally have drawn him to the manipulative potential of visual tricks. In "Ligeia," he uses this tool to effectively distract his readers into believing that occult practices and/or opium-enhanced perceptions bring Ligeia back to life at the end of the tale. However, the story provides one explicit clue that might indicate otherwise: a straightforward description of anamorphosis.

Anamorphosis suggests a purposeful manipulation of perspective by the artist, which yields a coherent picture only when the viewer positions himself at a specific perspective point. The artist, then, purposefully produces what appears—to all intents and purposes—to be a distortion, and yet he knows full well that this distortion appears so only to those who are unequipped to understand the mechanism of its production. Anamorphic images—in their ability to disguise and disrupt reality, in their seemingly monstrous yet covertly realistic depiction, in their ability to transport the viewer out of his expected realm of perception into the marvelous—occur with the mathematical *cum* "transcendentalist" beliefs of Poe's archetypal detective Dupin in "The Purloined Letter." "The material world," Dupin says, "abounds with very strict analogies to the immaterial" (*Tales*, 2:989).[25] In addition, the mathematical complexity of realizing these "poetic" images would have been attractive to Poe, especially as they derive from Euclid's geometry.

Many of Poe's stories similarly move from the material world to the fantastic or immaterial. Visual descriptions of elaborate interiors—ornate draperies, vaulted ceilings, lustrous colors, filtered light, intricate carvings, and arabesque censers—fashion environments that can easily enfold anamorphic images or create camouflage for projection devices. Like anamorphic images that "border on magic and conjuring" and insinuate symbols, portraits, or erotic figures in seemingly innocuous engravings, frescos, or paintings,[26] Poe's elaborate and complex settings can effectively hide in plain sight figures that come to clarity only by a careful positioning of the text. This visual manipulation enhances a viewer's sense of doubt, since what may be perceived, initially, as mere decor can suddenly represent something uncannily symbolic.

Such doubt is integral to "Ligeia." Here Poe creates a striking contrast between the hesitant forgetfulness with which the narrator opens his tale—his admitted inability to recall "how, when, or even precisely where" he came to know his beloved Ligeia—and his confident declaration that he could "minutely remember the details of the chamber": "There is no individual portion of the architecture and decoration of that bridal chamber which is not now visibly before me" (*Tales*, 1:310, 321). This assertion is similar to his confident claim that he could describe "the *person* of Ligeia," if not her background or the "deep moment" of their relationship (1:311, 321).

This contrast between what the narrator remembers and what he forgets highlights the ascendance of physical representations over human expression and feelings. As the narrator exclaims, "*Expression.* Ah, word of no meaning! behind whose vast latitude of mere sound we intrench our ignorance of so much of the spiritual" (*Tales*, 1:313). The astute clarity of his descriptions of Ligeia's physical attributes contrasts sharply with his tenuous ability to remember the emotional aspects of their relationship. Furthermore, the narrator rationalizes his forgetfulness by deferring to a supposed social truism: "In our endeavors to recall to memory something long forgotten, we often find ourselves *upon the very verge* of remembrance, without being able, in the end, to remember" (1:313–14). This defensive justification suggests more than the narrator's passive fall into forgetfulness. The contrast between his inability to recall "topics of deep moment" in his relationship with Ligeia and his ability to "minutely remember the details of the chamber" foreshadows, quite distinctly, his obsessive preoccupation with the chamber's decor (1:321).

David Ketterer points out that in other Poe stories, including "The Assignation," "Shadow," "The Masque of the Red Death," and "The Fall of the House of Usher," decor takes on an important role in unraveling the thematic concerns of the tale. Decor almost becomes a character or, at the very least, an active element in the denouement. Joan Dayan, a critic who takes particular note of this phenomenon in her analysis of "Ligeia," goes beyond Ketterer's analysis of arabesque environments. Ketterer argues that "the distinction between the literal narrative surface and the symbolic meaning disappears. . . . Arabesques exhibit not only a concern with mind-expanding arabesque decor but also a fluidity of form, technique, or structure that seeks to approximate the arabesque condition." The "arabesque condition" here means fluidity—a fluidity that cannot be controlled but that forces or allows, as the case may be, the observer to succumb to the "supernal" or, as Ketterer suggests, to "the attainment of arabesque vision."[27] However, Dayan suggests that the bridal chamber is "more than a locus for arabesque vision."[28] She argues that "the phantasmagoric chamber stages a pathological optics" and defines this as Poe's attempt "to make this room as indeterminate as the half-shut eye sustaining its either/or mental oscillation." At a crucial point in her argument, Dayan notes that the tapestry of the bedchamber is "spotted all over, at irregular intervals, with arabesque figures." This, she contends, "dares our perspectival skill," as does Poe's description of the weave of the tapestry, which was "made changeable in aspect." Dayan suggests that the designs in the tapestry change "according to our point of view."[29]

Yet Dayan's own perspective here erases the explicit description of anamorphosis in Poe's text. His full description of the tapestry reads, "These figures partook of the true character of the arabesque only when regarded from *a single point of view*. By *a contrivance* now common, and indeed traceable to a very remote period of antiquity, they were made changeable in aspect" (*Tales*, 1:322; emphasis added). In fact, it is not "our point of view" that makes the arabesque figures "changeable in aspect," as Dayan contends, but rather, as the narrator specifically notes, this variance is caused by an anamorphic device—"a contrivance now common." The narrator argues for a "single point of view," not just any point of view chosen by the viewer. In other words, Poe's text describes an anamorphosis. Dayan's observation that our "perspectival skill" is challenged in circumstances such as the one described in "Ligeia" is true, but the challenge is not born of indeterminacy, oscillation, or personal choice. Rather, the viewer of an anamorphic image (the kind described in Poe's text) must move through visual distortions in order to discern a recognizable image—or, in Poe's words, "the true character of the arabesque"—by positioning herself at a determined point or by using an anamorphic device, "a contrivance now common."

Jurgis Baltrušaitis refers directly to the anamorphic quality of Poe's "Ligeia" in his *Anamorphic Art*, concluding that "the whole story takes place in an anamorphic setting and background at a time when the system had reached its pinnacle of extravagance."[30] Citing the origins of anamorphosis in "Chinese prestidigitation [that] was grafted onto the 'catoptrics' (mirror anamorphoses) of Antiquity and the Middle Ages," Baltrušaitis describes anamorphosis in the following way:

> Anamorphosis—a word that makes its appearance in the seventeenth century but for a device already known—plays havoc with elements and principles; instead of reducing forms to their visible limits, it projects them outside themselves and distorts them so that when viewed from a certain

point they return to normal. The system was established as a technical curiosity, but it embraces a poetry of abstraction, an effective mechanism for producing optical illusion and a philosophy of false reality. . . . Anamorphosis renewed contact with the occult and at the same time with theories concerning the nature of doubt.[31]

Anamorphosis purposely toys with the viewer's sense of perception, requiring her to decipher what appears, at first, to be muddled chaos. The first response to a completely anamorphic image is to question its "true nature." Can the whirls be made representational? In a partial anamorphosis, the viewer remains at a loss as to whether something is hidden within what appears, at first, to be a representational image. Has the artist played a trick on the viewer? Can any representation be trusted? The viewer is left doubting her ability to see what can be seen.

"Ligeia" produces such doubt with a vengeance. The narrator's hesitations and his opium-induced reveries force the reader to question what actually occurs in the tale. Doubt and amazement characterize the denouement, reflected both in the narrator's startled response to Ligeia's return and in the reader's dismay at being unable to rationally untangle the means of Rowena's death or Ligeia's rebirth. One possible explanation is linked to the story's epigraph, attributed to Joseph Glanvill, which would suggest witchcraft: "Man doth not yield himself to the angels, nor unto death utterly, save only through the weakness of his feeble will" (*Tales*, 1:310). Although critics have been unsuccessful in confirming that the source of the quote is indeed Glanvill, his *Saducismus Triumphatus*, first published in 1689 and revived in 1834 as a sixpenny pamphlet entitled *Plain Evidence of the Actual Existence of Witches*, relates the testimonials of people who have witnessed spiritual possessions, and his name would have been associated not only with occult practices but also with the nature of doubt. Stuart Levine and Susan Levine note Glanvill's importance to the tale despite scholars' inability to locate the source of the epigraph: "Poe's choice of Glanvill is apt. . . . He is best-remembered in the literary histories for his philosophical skepticism."[32] In "Ligeia," the narrator concludes his tale by recalling how he witnessed the spiritual possession and transformation of Rowena's body. However, as we have seen, one can question the narrator's role in this event. Does the transformation actually occur through "witchcraft"—that is, "the goal of a wisdom too divinely precious not to be forbidden" (1:316)—or is it the result of an aerial projection put in place by the narrator himself but "forgotten" due to his opium-enhanced state?

Anamorphosis, with its occult associations and manipulated perspective—here operating through the device of aerial projection—provides another lens for viewing not only the occurrences in the bridal chamber but also the nature of the narrator's need to write a testimony of his extraordinary experience. As Charles Baudelaire conjectured, "Ligeia" is not a love story: "The principal idea on which the work pivots is something quite different."[33] Other contemporary critics pointed to qualities other than the pain of love lost in characterizing the tale. N. P. Willis noted in December 1838 that "there is a fine march of description [in "Ligeia"], which has a touch of D'Israeli's quality." In February 1845, Charles Eames, the editor of the *New World*, praised the "exquisite art . . . [that] maintains ["Ligeia's"] vigor as an exposition of the mystical *thesis* which the tale is designed to illustrate and enforce." And Thomas Dunn English, in November 1845, compared "The Gold Bug" with "Ligeia," proclaiming that the former "is the most *ingenious* story Mr. POE has written; but in the higher attributes—the great invention—an invention proper—it is not at all comparable . . . to 'Ligeia'" (*Poe Log*, 259, 503, 587). Similarly, Jeanine Plottel has identified "Ligeia" and "The Gold Bug" as examples of how Poe engaged the popular response to anamorphosis. According to Plottel, "'The Gold Bug' . . . unfolds according to an anamorphic scheme" that merely engages a playful gamesmanship, whereas "Ligeia" projects its anamorphosis as a philosophical trope: "Its secret is that of vision itself."[34]

The references to "the great invention," "the mystical thesis," and "a touch of D'Israeli's quality" draw attention to a possible pivot of the tale: a point of artificial perspective that pushes representation beyond its charge to depict reality and, in so doing, "embraces a poetry of abstraction . . . a philosophy of false reality"[35]—that is, anamorphosis. Anamorphosis, in this regard, serves as a metaphor, indicating the narrator's purposeful forgetting and consequent self-deception. In trying to relieve his grief over Ligeia's death and to overcome her failure to "will" death away—an ability mentioned in the story's epigraph, which clearly purports that man might thwart death through the power of his own will—the narrator sets out to recover and possibly to surpass Ligeia's skills by creating a false reality that pictures her triumph over death. Most importantly, this is a product of his own knowledge and practice. The narrator accomplishes his goal not by rehearsing Ligeia's occult methods but by a more powerful means: reimaging her triumph using a device of "natural magic," as per Brewster.

In the beginning of his narrative, the narrator makes a distinct point of mentioning the wealth that Ligeia's death afforded him: "I had no lack of what the world calls wealth. Ligeia had brought me far more, very far more than ordinarily falls to the lot of mortals." He also recalls the time and dedication he gave to decorating the interior of the decaying abbey that he purchased after her death: "I gave way, with a child-like perversity, and perchance with a faint hope of alleviating my sorrows, to a display of *more than* regal magnificence within. For such follies, even in childhood, I had imbibed a taste" (*Tales*, 1:320; emphasis added). "Such follies," he continues, allow for the possibility of "discovering" an "incipient madness" in the "Bedlam patterns" and "gorgeous draperies," even though they afford no visible "system, no keeping, in the fantastic display, to take hold upon the memory" (1:320–21). Yet why, then, can the narrator remember all the details of the bridal chamber? What are the "follies" that he cites? Has he used "such follies" to create the bridal chamber—or, in Dayan's words, "the phantasmagoric chamber that stages a pathological optics"[36]—with a purpose in mind?

The narrator reflects with disdain on the lack of circumspection shown by Rowena's parents in allowing her to "pass the threshold of an apartment *so* bedecked." He does not love Rowena when he marries her; in fact, he grows to hate her. She is as much a prop in his created environment as the "ceiling, of gloomy-looking oak . . . fretted with the wildest and most grotesque specimens of a semi-Gothic, semi-Druidical device" (*Tales*, 1:321). J. Gerald Kennedy believes that there is a deadly motivation behind the narrator's purposeful interior decoration and marriage to Rowena: "Even before he sets eyes on the unfortunate Rowena, he has launched his deadly plot by purchasing the abbey and filling it with 'gorgeous and fantastic draperies' and 'solemn carvings.' . . . By evoking terror, the morbid decor also partakes of a scheme of symbolic retribution. . . . The fact that he readies his chamber of horror and *then* goes looking for a bride suggests that Rowena is from the outset a sacrificial figure."[37]

The anamorphic room that the narrator designs becomes the means to "recover" his lost Ligeia, whose erudition he had absorbed: "I was sufficiently aware of her infinite supremacy to resign myself, with a child-like confidence, to her guidance through the chaotic world of metaphysical investigation." He alludes here to the potentially dangerous knowledge that he acquired under Ligeia's tutelage. In a rhetorical frenzy of self-justification, he acknowledges what he had begun to learn: "With how vast a triumph—with how vivid a delight—with how much of all that is ethereal in hope—did I *feel*, as she bent over me in studies but little sought—but less known—that delicious vista by slow degrees expanding before me, down whose long, gorgeous, and all untrodden path, I might at length pass onward to the goal of a wisdom *too divinely precious not to be forbidden!*" (*Tales*, 1:316; emphasis added). The narrator then recalls his feelings as Ligeia struggled with death while he was "entranced, to a melody more than mortal" (1:317). Yet he claims, in his narrative written years after her death, that he has "no power to portray" in words this intense yearning of hers to defer death (1:318).

Despite her incredible erudition, Ligeia fails to triumph over death, and the narrator's grief leads him not down the "long, gorgeous, and all untrodden path" to "forbidden" knowledge but to the panacea of skepticism and opium. He resigns himself to using other means to recover her, the most notable of which resemble the machinations described by Brewster. Brewster claims that the eye "may be considered as the sentinel which guards the pass between the worlds of matter and of spirit, and through which all their communications are interchanged."[38] This belief suggests a "scientific" path rather than a mystical one: "The optic nerve is the channel by which the mind peruses the handwriting of Nature on the retina, and through which it transfers to that material tablet its decisions and its creations. . . . Hence it is not only an amusing but an useful occupation to acquire a knowledge of those causes which are capable of producing so strange a belief, whether it arises from the delusions which the mind practises upon itself, or from the dexterity and science of others."[39] Having witnessed Ligeia's failure to achieve the "goal of a wisdom too divinely precious not to be forbidden," the narrator, unlike his mentor, turns to "such follies" or other means to conquer death and bring Ligeia back to "life."

The narrator ascribes Rowena's death to the mystical appearance of "ruby drops" that fall into her wine goblet. Describing his vigil beside her deathbed, he recalls the numerous "wild visions" that purportedly emerged from his opium-drenched mind (*Tales*, 1:326). Kennedy notes that "this scene has occasioned much debate about the narrator's reliability,"[40] and the narrator's depiction of his sudden horror at seeing the final transformation makes the means of Rowena's death and Ligeia's "ascension" appear fantastic. Yet this uncertainty is itself illusory, based on *our* forgetting (or not seeing) the narrator's role in producing "the phantasmagoric chamber" with its anamorphic potential.

All of this is no less true for the narrator himself. Close attention to the narrator's descriptions of both anamorphosis and the various phantasms that Rowena saw before her death suggest that the narrator's helplessness in the last scene, which he attributes to his opium-enhanced state, is illusory. Indeed, his subsequent retelling of the event can be read as a written confession of Rowena's murder. His horror uncloaks "the great invention—an invention proper": the purposeful use of the "marvellous expedients" of optics that shock in their virtual reality. The narrator's role as both agent and recipient of these delusional perceptions is revealed in a "circle of analogies" whose pivot is the anamorphic perspective point (*Tales*, 1:314). The story of Rowena's demise, then, becomes the confession of a murderer, albeit cloaked in the disguise of his "innocent" horror at the "supernatural" events that occur in the bridal chamber.

Poe relies on his audience's desire to be awed by the fantastic rather than acknowledge that "ordinary" means can produce such spectacles. He uses this tendency to produce the desired effect of fear and horror in the reader, which mirrors that of the narrator—a fear and horror that emerge from a sense of purported vulnerability and helplessness. The scene of mourning is especially conducive to this conjunction, since often, without conscious choice, a layering of one loved one's loss onto the death of another occurs, regardless of whether the mourner wishes this to happen. The universal appreciation of this unintentional emotional response reinforces the reader's willingness to grant credibility to the narrator's avowed passivity. All of this works to enhance the conditions under which appearance becomes more powerful than reality.

Curiously, both "Ligeia" and "A Descent into the Maelström" contain epigraphs attributed to Glanvill. And in both instances these epigraphs are used as foils. They suggest man's awe of God's unknowable ways and man's inability to build models that resemble God's design. Yet the ability to construct such a model saves the narrator of "Descent" from drowning, while the narrator of "Ligeia" indicts himself by revealing his fascination with mathematical models that can manipulate human perception, specifically anamorphosis and aerial optical illusions. The disjunction between the epigraph and the plot in "Descent" seems somewhat obvious. That is, the narrator's ability to tell his tale depends not on the grace of God but on his own ability to save himself from demise using induction and peripheral vision. However, the same disjunction is occluded in "Ligeia." As the plot unfolds, the narrator realizes, much to his despair, that even with her admirable store of esoteric knowledge, Ligeia cannot conjure the willful resistance to death promised by the story's epigraph. The epigraph clearly purports that through the power of his will, man might overcome the law of nature—that is, the finality of death. The narrator fails to believe the "truth" of this statement, even as both he and Ligeia reiterate it in the narrative. In the end, instead of joy, the narrator experiences horror at Ligeia's "reappearance," suggesting that he never fully believed such willfulness could prevail.

Poe's fascination with visual tricks and his reading of Brewster combine to help decipher an undercurrent of meaning in "Ligeia." In an overt display of the narrator's fascination with "supernatural" occurrences, the story's epigraph is reiterated by the characters in the tale proper. This reference to supernaturalism distracts the reader from the narrator's less obvious obsession—to outshine Ligeia, his mentor in the occult, by using "other means." She had failed to overcome death through her vast store of occult wisdom, so how could he accomplish more, being merely a student of her vastly superior knowledge? Her failure enhances his determination to satisfy his goal of outdoing her powers by bringing her back to "life," as if through occult means. By setting up an anamorphic apartment, marrying Rowena, and smoking opium, he successfully creates the final scene in the drama of his devised desire: he manipulates Ligeia's "spiritual revival," if only in the self-delusional "manufacture" of her image. As Roy Basler concluded in 1944—"In brief, it must be recognized that the hero has murdered Rowena"[41]—and as J. Gerald Kennedy concluded in 1993, the narrator's culpability is clearly drawn as he tells the tale of his "horror" at witnessing the "virtual reality" he has created—"ruby drops" and all. The story emerges, then, as a confession of the narrator's obsession with Ligeia's influence and its result: Rowena's murder, a murder obfuscated by the anamorphic manipulation that Poe hides in plain sight. Poe must have enjoyed introducing these visual tricks into his narratives, especially during a time when the populace was not only fascinated by these occurrences but also duped by them. Additionally, his use of these tricks ensures that the "graphicality" of his works remains central to their interpretation. Like the shrouded figure that appears at the end of *The Narrative of Arthur Gordon Pym* and in the anamorphic scene in "Ligeia," such visual puzzles continue to fascinate critics, readers, and visual artists alike, spawning unending literary and visual interpretations.

5

POE'S ART CRITICISM

Early in his career, Poe's art criticism was mainly found in his reviews of books and magazines. In his May 1836 review of Frances Trollope's *Paris and the Parisians in 1835*, for example, Poe takes time to describe each of its eleven engravings of drawings by Auguste Hervieu. Curiously, however, Poe's descriptions of these drawings veer away—sometimes dramatically—from the actual image on the page. Regarding the first plate, for example, he describes Hervieu's depiction of people at the Louvre, but it appears that this description is taken directly from Trollope's text and not from looking at the drawing. This is evident in a comparison of their strikingly similar wording:

Poe: Accordingly, the plate shows, among a variety of pretty *toques, cauchoises, chaussures*, and other more imperial equipments, a sprinkling of round-eared caps, awkward *casquettes*, filthy *blouses*, and dingy and ragged jackets (*Works*, 9:192).

Trollope: Dingy jackets, uncomely *casquettes*, ragged *blouses*, and ill-favoured round-eared caps, that look as if they did duty night and day, must all be tolerated; and in this toleration appears to consist, at present, the principal external proof of the increased liberty of the Parisian mob.[1]

The drawing itself (fig. 20) shows no "filthy blouses" or "ragged blouses" or "dingy and ragged jackets." True, we do see a woman in a "round-eared cap" next to a woman in a bonnet. In fact, the first row of people provides a sampling of

Fig. 20 Auguste Hervieu, *Louvre*, in *Paris and the Parisians in 1835*, by Frances Trollope (New York: Harper and Brothers, 1836).

the varied classes present: the military, the peasantry, and the well-to-do. However, neither filthiness nor raggedness can be seen.

To Poe's credit, he defers to Trollope's description of the second plate, *Morning at the Tuileries*, and simply gives a cursory overview of the composition. He does the same for the third plate and only ventures into interpretation when describing the fourth plate, "*Ce soir, à la Porte S^{t}. Martin!*" "*J'y serai*," by noting that it "is full of humor," even though the men pictured seem intent and serious. Most of Poe's other overviews do not go beyond objective description, until he gets to the last plate, "*V'la les restes de notre revolution de Jullet*": "Like all of the other engravings in the volume [this one] is admirable in its design, and especially in its expression. . . . [Hervieu's] theme is evidently the treatment of the prisoners at the Luxembourg. We cannot too highly praise the exquisite piquancy of the whole of these designs" (*Works*, 9:192–93).

Fig. 21 Auguste Hervieu, "*V'la les restes de notre Revolution de Juillet,*" in *Paris and the Parisians in 1835,* by Frances Trollope, vol. 2 (New York: Harper and Brothers, 1836).

In his February 1842 review of Charles Dickens's *Barnaby Rudge*, Poe bluntly criticizes the illustrations: "The wood-cut designs . . . are occasionally good. The copper engravings are pitiably ill-conceived and ill-drawn" (*Works*, 11:61). And in his January 1842 review of Oliver Goldsmith's *The Vicar of Wakefield*, Poe pays particular attention to the illustrated volumes. In short, Poe believed that illustrations enhance the pleasure derived from reading, even if the illustrations do not match the reader's interpretation of the text. If the artist's finesse is greater than the reader's, Poe argues, then "each picture will stimulate, support, and guide the fancy" (11:9); if the illustrations are weak, the astute reader will take pleasure in knowing that his interpretation is superior to the artist's conception.

To reinforce this perspective, Poe compares reading an illustrated book to viewing a painting and overhearing a bystander talk about that painting. The bystander's judgments, Poe asserts, are "easily and keenly appreciable, while these comments interfere, in no perceptible degree, with the force or the unity of our own comprehension." Following these overarching claims, Poe praises the overall quality of Francis W. Gimber's engravings of Hervieu's drawings in *Paris and the Parisians in 1835*: "They are sketchy, spirited cuts, depending for effect upon the higher merits rather than upon the minor morals of art—upon skillful grouping of figures, vivacity, *naiveté*, and originality of fancy, and good drawing in the mass—rather than upon finish in details, or too cautious adherence to the text. . . . A great number of them are of the nature to elicit enthusiastic praise from every true artist" (*Works*, 11:9). Poe must have abandoned this view of illustrations by 1845, since in his letter to James Russell Lowell of October 28, 1844, he rejects the use of illustrations in his prospective literary journal, the *Stylus*: "Plates, of course, would be disdained" (*Letters*, 2:265). Writing to Charles Anthon a month later, Poe reiterates this disdain by claiming that "absurd steel plates" are too costly (2:270). Notably, Poe's approach to reviewing magazines included critiquing their illustrations—often harshly. For example, he took the much-loved and highly respected painter Henry Inman to task in his 1844 review of John Inman's *Columbian Lady's and Gentleman's Magazine*, written for the *Columbia Spy*.

The editors of the *Columbia Spy*, a magazine published in the small town of Pottsville, Pennsylvania, approached Poe in the spring of 1844, just after he arrived in Manhattan, about contributing a weekly "letter" to the magazine to apprise their readers of the "doings of Gotham."[2] Poe contributed seven such letters between May 14, 1844, and June 25, 1844. He configured these contributions as "gossip" so that he could forgo the formal restrictions that apply to an essay. In his first letter, he explained, "As for law, he [the gossiper] is cognizant of but one, and that negative—the invariable absence of all. And, for his road . . . [he would] be malcontent without a frequent hop-skip-and-jump, over the hedges, into the tempting pastures of digression beyond."[3] In these columns, Poe did digress; he wrote about everything from road paving to the Croton Aqueduct, from Dickens's and Bulwer's visits to New York to the effects of the "water-cure." He also devoted part of his last letter to discussing art. This foray into art criticism gestures toward an interest that emerged with even more emphasis when Poe joined Charles Briggs on the staff of the *Broadway Journal* in the spring of 1845.

In his last contribution to the *Columbia Spy*, Poe reviewed the July 1844 issue of the *Columbian Lady's and Gentleman's Magazine*, which had begun publication six months earlier. This issue of the *Columbian*, he wrote, "in many respects, is peculiar," ostensibly because all of the articles were written by its editor, John Inman. A few sentences later, Poe describes Inman as "one of the most industrious men of the day" and his writing as "well done, and in good taste."[4] Printed in the issue was a long column on art-related topics, which includes a response to Hans Holbein's *The Dance of Death* and a dissertation on the neoclassical pastoral painting *View Near Cold-Spring*, commonly known by the title *Chapel of Our Lady of Coldspring*, by the English artist William Henry Bartlett (fig. 22). Pictures were a regular part of the *Columbian*, and the July issue was no exception, containing a portrait of John Inman by H. S. Sadd; a portrait of John Inman's daughter by Stephen Ormsby, from a painting by Henry Inman; and a reproduction of *View Near Cold-Spring* by Bartlett. In his letter for the *Columbia Spy*, Poe ignored John Inman's unabashed self-promotion by including both his own portrait and his daughter's in the same issue; normally such puffing would not have escaped Poe's tomahawk. We can deduce, then, that Poe chose not to be vitriolic because he was keenly aware of John Inman's influence in the magazine world. Poe had already mentioned Inman's *Columbian* in an earlier letter, noting its distinction from other journals and praising Inman as "a man of talent": "The Magazines, here, are 'dragging their slow lengths along.' Of the 'Knickerbocker' I hear little, and see less. The 'Columbian,' edited by Inman, crows most lustily; whether for good cause, or not, I really am not in condition to say. Mr. Inman, however, is undeniably a man of talent. You know he is, or was, the factotum of the Harpers—decided, generally, upon MSS offered for publication—read their proofs, now and then—wrote occasional puffs—and did other little '*chores*' of that nature."[5] That Poe was "not in condition to say" whether he thought that the *Columbian*'s "crowing most lustily" was justified is more than a subtle hint that he probably thought otherwise. But he was not wont to say so openly.

In his letter for the *Columbia Spy*, Poe made a point of noting the illustrations in the July issue of the *Columbian*, calling the painting of John Inman's daughter "an exquisite thing" and praising *View Near Cold-Spring* as "a very sweet landscape." This language hardly seems characteristic of Poe, and his praise of John Inman as an "industrious man," in light of his pious and didactic overview of *View Near Cold-Spring*—certainly not "well done, and in good taste," in Poe's terms—seems even queerer. Although Poe did not take exception to Inman's description of the painting in an overt way, he did so by innuendo, noting that both John Inman and his brother, the painter Henry Inman, were

Fig. 22   William Henry Bartlett, *Chapel of Our Lady of
Coldspring*, n.d. Hand-colored engraving by R. Brandard.
New York State Library, Manuscripts and Special
Collections. William H. Bartlett Prints, 1837–1842,
PRI5584, item 18.

"in England [where] they will meet with appreciation."[6] The undercurrent of
deprecation in this remark would have only been noticed by those acquainted
with Poe's negative attitude toward American writers and artists who sought
critical acclaim from the British. "There is not a more disgusting spectacle under
the sun than our subserviency to British criticism," Poe wrote in his marginalia.
"It is disgusting, first, because it is truckling, servile, pusillanimous—secondly,
because of its gross Irrationality. We *know* the British to bear us little but ill
will—we know that, in no case, do they utter unbiased opinions of American
books—we know that in the few instances in which our writers have been treated
with common decency in England, these writers have . . . openly paid homage to

English institutions" (*Works*, 2:509–10). This contradiction in Poe's seeming regard for John Inman despite his pious review of *View Near Cold-Spring* can only be understood as a way for Poe to gain Inman's good regard.

John Inman's response to *View Near Cold-Spring* is entirely unlike any of Poe's analyses of visual, musical, or literary art and lacks his requirements of formal precision, compositional order, and aesthetic effect. Instead, Inman simply appeals to the viewer's inclination to be "uplifted" in the same way he was when he looked at this painting:

> For my own part I can never stand on such an eminence as that, whence the eye commands an extensive view, without being filled with thoughts of Almighty power and of the consummate wisdom by which the plastic hand of that power was guided in the formation of hill, river, mountain, plain and valley—all designed by Almighty goodness also to delight the eye and subserve the varied interests of man. The majesty and beauty of the scene appeal to the mind as well as to the heart. . . . Far from the works of man, the greatest . . . are petty in comparison of those of Him who made man also. . . . In the scene before us, the mind should suffer no disturbance from the sights and sounds of worldly occupation; the eye should dwell only upon suggestive tokens of God's handiwork.[7]

Poe would have hardly agreed with the notion that an artist's role is to mimic nature or that nature provides the beauty that an artist can only hope to transcribe accurately. In fact, Poe believed the opposite, as seen in the aesthetic principles he outlined in numerous works, such as "The Landscape Garden." Yet Poe ostensibly chose to avoid openly criticizing Inman's moralistic critique of *View Near Cold-Spring* even though Inman's review would have been an easy target. This is most likely because Poe was looking to place one of his own stories in Inman's *Columbian*. The *Columbian* did indeed publish "The Angel of the Odd" in its October 1844 issue, so Poe's uncharacteristic critical restraint served him well in this instance. However, another reason that Poe chose not to disagree with the positive review of William Henry Bartlett's painting could have been Poe's relationship with N. P. Willis, who hired Poe on at the *New-York Evening Mirror* in October 1844. In 1839 London publisher George Virtue had sent Bartlett to the United States "to make wash drawings of cities and places of great natural beauty."[8] During that time, Bartlett became good friends with Willis, who was his traveling companion on trips to sites of natural beauty, such as Niagara Falls and the Hudson River Valley. Virtue also commissioned Willis "to write the letter press to accompany the steel engravings based on Bartlett's views,"[9] and the engravings and text were published as *American Scenery; or, Land, Lake, and River Illustrations of Transatlantic Nature* in 1840.

Although Poe avoids maligning John Inman, he does not hesitate to criticize Henry Inman in the same letter for the *Columbia Spy*. Aside from his cursory praise of Henry Inman's portrait of John Inman's daughter, Poe cannot control his need to disparage the painter's overall skill, and he takes two long paragraphs of his letter to do so. Poe must have realized that he would be free to express criticism of Inman's paintings, without repercussion, to the Pennsylvanians who read the *Columbia Spy*. However, these views would have been unpopular among New Yorkers, who greatly admired Inman for his portraiture. Indeed, at this time, Inman was "the painter of greatest repute and esteem in the city of New York."[10] He was also one of the founders of the National Academy of Design and served as its vice president from 1826 to 1831. Following his death in January 1846, the arts community in New York rallied in support of his widow by organizing a successful benefit exhibition of 126 paintings in the American Art-Union rooms, which yielded a profit of almost $2,000. Included in this exhibition were paintings by Inman that illustrated literary texts:

> The literary pictures, *Bimam Wood, Bride of Lammermoor, Lake of the Dismal Swamp* [sic],[11] *Rip Van Winkle Awaking from His Dream*, and *Maria* are accompanied by quotations from Shakespeare, Scott, Moore, Irving, and Stern[e], respectively, while *The Boyhood of Washington* is described by a passage from Jared Sparks' *Life of Washington*, and *Mumble-the-Peg*, from which an engraving had been made to illustrate Charles Fenno Hoffman's *Nick Ten-Vlyck*, published in *The Gift*, 1844, is accompanied by an excerpt from that story. Inman's *Trout Fishing in Sullivan County, New York* and *The Brothers* are annotated by extracts from contemporary poems, and three paintings done during his visit to Wordsworth at Rydal Mount in England—a portrait of the poet, *Rydal Water*, and *Rydal Falls*—are documented and accompanied by poems by Byron and Wordsworth.[12]

Whether Poe felt that his own work had been snubbed by this prominent New York painter cannot be known. Yet it seems likely that Poe, whose works often appeared in *The Gift*, would have seen these illustrations with their accompanying literary annotations and resented being overlooked. Either way, despite Inman's widespread respect among the New York arts community, Poe did not withhold his negative responses to Inman's paintings or to his technique. In this letter for the *Columbia Spy*, he takes exception to two of Inman's most popular paintings: *Fanny Elssler* and *Village School in an Uproar*. Poe faults both for their lack of accurate perspective: "The most striking defect [of *Fanny Elssler*] lies in the perspective (aerial and linear) of the floor, which seems to be inclined toward the spectator, so that the chair of the *danseuse* is in danger of sliding off. A similar error is very noticeable in the 'Village School in an Uproar.'"[13]

Poe had been aware of Henry Inman's work well before writing this response to his paintings. One of Inman's engravings, *The Newsboy*, appeared in *The Gift Book for 1843*, which also included Poe's "The Pit and the Pendulum." Poe also may have seen a review of Inman's paintings at the 1831 National Academy of Design in the May 7, 1831, edition of the *New-York Mirror*; a review of Poe's poem "A City in the Sea" by John P. Morris appears in the same issue. And, of course, it is simply improbable that Poe escaped hearing about an artist whose paintings, such as *Fanny Elssler*, were so immensely popular. As George Chaffee notes, Inman's portrait of Elssler, a famous ballerina, "was greatly admired and later it enjoyed the distinction of being the first—and [remained until 1947] perhaps the only—American dance subject of which an art-print was published in Europe."[14] In fact, Thomas Sully, a well-known and respected American painter, liked this painting so much that he made a copy of it in 1842. Poe was acquainted with Sully during this period—they were both living and working in Philadelphia—and therefore Poe could not have remained unaware of *Fanny Elssler*. Nonetheless, he seemed not to care about its popularity—nor about that of the beloved and admired dancer it depicted—when berating it as an example of Inman's inability to create accurate perspective. When referring to the painting in his letter, Poe acknowledges that "everyone" would have had the opportunity to see it: "Have you seen his 'Fanny Elssler'? It is a full exemplification of his principal merits and defects."[15]

In his critical overview of Henry Inman's work, Poe compares his painting style to that of Peter Frederick Rothermel, whose paintings Poe would have seen in the National Academy of Design's 1844 show and on exhibit at the

Fig. 23   Henry Inman, *Fanny Elssler*. Landesmuseum
Burgenland, Eisenstadt.

Pennsylvania Academy of the Fine Arts in Philadelphia. Rothermel's role in the
arts scene was similar to Inman's; both men were not only painters but also
museum administrators. Rothermel became the director of the Pennsylvania
Academy of the Fine Arts in 1847, just after the great fire that had destroyed
much of the museum's collection. As an artist, he was well known for his portraits and historical paintings. Poe describes Rothermel's painting technique as

"round or perfected," as compared to that of Inman, which is *massed* or suggestive." He follows this comparison with an even stronger criticism of Inman's style, implying that his paintings are so suggestive that they lose their effect. Poe further criticizes *Fanny Elssler* for a detail he finds especially problematic: "I cannot think . . . that the false *tournure* should have been introduced; more particularly as it disfigures, in this instance, rather than embellishes the person."[16] Evidence of the tournure (or bustle) in this painting is quite subtle, indicated only by the way Elssler sits on the chair. Sitting down while wearing a bustled dress was a difficult task, since the bustle got in the way of maintaining an upright posture, requiring the woman to sit in a tilted position, at best.

Poe had a strong dislike for the bustle, as evidenced in a tale he wrote and published eight months after this critique of Inman's painting. "The Thousand-and-Second Tale of Scheherazade," which appeared in *Godey's Lady's Book* in February 1845, is a rewriting of *The Arabian Nights* and transforms the ending dramatically. In Poe's story, instead of marrying the king and providing him with many progeny—as the tale originally unfolded—Scheherazade is strangled by a bowstring or garrote precisely because she describes a bustle as the means of assessing a woman's beauty in what will be the last tale she tells the king:

> [Scheherazade said,] "One of the evil genii, who are perpetually upon the watch to inflict ill, has put it into the heads of these accomplished ladies that the thing which we describe as personal beauty, consists altogether in the protuberance of the region which lies not very far below the small of the back. Perfection of loveliness, they say, is in the direct ratio of the extent of this hump. Having been long possessed of this idea, and bolsters being cheap in that country, the days have long gone by since it was possible to distinguish a woman from a dromedary—"
>
> "Stop!" said the king—"I can't stand that, and I won't. . . . Do you take me for a fool? Upon the whole, you might as well get up and be throttled."
>
> These words . . . both grieved and astonished Scheherazade; but, as she knew the king to be a man of scrupulous integrity, and quite unlikely to forfeit his word, she submitted to her fate with a good grace. (*Tales*, 2:1169–70)

Such is Scheherazade's demise in Poe's story. The king's continued impatience with the outrageousness of her tales finally culminates in his complete frustration with her assertion that a woman's beauty depended on the size of her "false *tournure*." The king orders Scheherazade's execution for her impertinence, and the story ends.

The story's denouement could have been triggered by Poe's memory of the painting by Henry Inman, since he had chosen this seemingly insignificant detail to criticize; the "false tournure" clearly made a strong negative impression on him. That Poe even noticed this minor detail is not uncharacteristic of his aesthetic sensibility, since he believed that every detail should contribute to an overall desired effect. Inman's choice to include a tournure in his portrait of Elssler must have triggered Poe's strong aversion to such "fashionable" absurdities, especially in the dress of a nimble ballerina. Indeed, Inman would have been at the forefront of Poe's consciousness while he was writing "The Thousand-and-Second Tale of Scheherazade," since the painter's death on January 17, 1846, prompted a public response that Poe could not have ignored, especially given that he was then living on Amity Street, the fashionable center of the arts community. Could the memory of Inman's "disfigurement" of Elssler have contributed to Poe's decision to make this detail the ultimate cause of Scheherazade's demise? It would seem likely.

This last letter for the *Columbia Spy* was only the beginning of Poe's writing about the visual art he saw while in New York. Poe's work on the *Broadway Journal* from January to May 1845 provided him with an opportunity to become thoroughly acquainted with the art on exhibit and with Charles Briggs's main contribution to the journal: art criticism. At its inception, most of the *Broadway Journal* was taken up with his reviews of the various exhibits at the National Academy of Design, the American Art-Union, and the New-York Gallery of the Fine Arts. Briggs's critical style was similar to Poe's in its unwillingness to bow to political exigencies. Although Briggs parted ways with Poe in less than a year's time, their months together at the *Broadway Journal* would have allowed for many discussions about art, and Poe would have benefited from Briggs's knowledge of the New York arts scene. The following background on their relationship and the analysis of Briggs's art criticism provide an overview of the kinds of paintings and sculptures Poe would have known intimately by seeing them, reading Briggs's reviews, and, we can surmise, discussing them with Briggs.

Poe and Briggs at the *Broadway Journal* (January–July 1845)

In December 1844, Charles Briggs, owner and editor of the soon-to-be published *Broadway Journal*, wrote to his friend James Russell Lowell asking if he knew "of any available talent, or genius rather"—someone who would be available to contribute to this new publication (*Poe Log*, 479). Prompted by Briggs's inquiry, Lowell shared with Briggs his biography of Poe. Lowell's short biographical sketch was published in the February 1845 issue of *Graham's Magazine*:

> Mr. Poe has that indescribable something which men have agreed to call *genius*. No man could ever tell us precisely what it is, and yet there is none who is not inevitably aware of its presence and its power. Let talent writhe and contort itself as it may, it has no such magnetism. . . . Genius claims kindred with the very workings of Nature herself. . . . Mr. Poe has two of the prime qualities of genius, a faculty of vigorous yet minute analysis, and a wonderful fecundity of imagination. The first of these faculties is as needful to the artist in words as a knowledge of anatomy is to the artist in colors or in stone. This enables him to conceive truly, to maintain a proper relation of parts, and to draw a correct outline, while the second groups, fills up, and colors.[17]

It is interesting to note that Lowell uses visual metaphors in describing Poe. In comparing his facility with words to an artist's method—that is, an artist's keen knowledge of anatomy and his ability to outline first before completing a painting with color—Lowell describes, if inadvertently, one of the outstanding qualities of Poe's work: its "graphicality."

Briggs was convinced by Lowell's estimation of Poe. On December 19, 1844, Briggs wrote to Lowell that he had met Poe; thereafter, he invited Poe to write a review of Elizabeth Barrett Barrett's new book of poems for the first two issues of the *Broadway Journal*.[18] Poe accepted the offer. Briggs was pleased with Poe's contributions and continued to regard him favorably. In fact, in the third number of the *Broadway Journal*, Briggs publicly announced his admiration for Poe in a review of the most recent issue of *Godey's Lady's Book*. He claimed that despite the numerous contributions by sixteen authors that filled forty-two pages of the issue, "the only article in the Magazine that will ever be read a second time" was Poe's "The Thousand-and-Second Tale of Scheherazade" (*BJ*, 1:60). Briggs praised Poe's "exact knowledge and lively imagination; two qualities that we rarely find united in the same person" (1:60–61). In the very next article in that same issue, Briggs again took Poe's side by criticizing the portrait of him that appeared in *Graham's Magazine*: "It is a gross wrong to Mr. Poe, and a fraud upon the purchasers of the Magazine. It bears no more resemblance to that gentleman than to any other of Mr. Graham's contributors. But if it were much worse that [sic] it is, which is hardly conceivable, it would be amply compensated by the fine sketch of Mr. Poe's genius, by Lowell, which accompanies it" (1:61). In the February 8, 1845, issue of the *Broadway Journal*, Briggs published "The Raven" "on account of its unusual beauty" (1:90). And by the end of the month, he had offered Poe "a work-and-share contract . . . [for] performing certain editorial duties each week . . . [for] one-third of the profits."[19]

By March 1845, Poe agreed to Briggs's terms and joined the *Broadway Journal* as associate editor. Readers had become accustomed to Briggs's pointed art criticism, and Poe's reputation as literary critic promised more of the same fare. Poe's new job took up most of his day, and, by inference, he must have had many opportunities to engage with Briggs and his associates. Not only was Briggs familiar with the New York arts scene as an art critic, but for three years, from 1842 to 1845, he served on the Committee of Management for the American Art-Union.[20] Through this association, Briggs came into personal contact with New York artists, had the opportunity to see paintings before public exhibitions, and was keenly aware of the politics of the New York arts community. Briggs was also a close friend of the painter William Page, a member of the National Academy of Design and author of "The Art of the Use of Color in Imitation in Painting," which Briggs published serially in the *Broadway Journal*. Certainly, Briggs and Poe would have discussed their opinions of these artists and their work, and there may have been opportunities for Poe to meet the artists Briggs knew as well.

Despite Briggs's high regard for Poe's genius upon their first meeting and while working with him closely, this opinion was short-lived, lasting a mere five months.[21] Although Poe worked exceedingly long hours on the *Broadway Journal* as associate editor, according to Lowell, he lapsed into drunkenness in May 1845. This alcoholic bout dramatically altered Briggs's relationship with Poe, and Briggs's initial enthusiasm turned into bitterness. Critics have used the correspondence between Lowell and Briggs as evidence of his disillusionment with

Poe; however, the following excerpt from Briggs's letter of June 4, 1846, to artist William Page also affirms these feelings:

> I am thankful for your generous offer to hammer Poe on my account. But I would hammer him myself if I cared anything about him. He is altogether the poorest devil (I beg the devil's pardon) I ever knew. I was indebted to James [Lowell] for an introduction to him and having his ideal in my mind all the while thought I had a great liking for him. But, as I gradually discovered his poltroonish character and at last saw what a humbug I had imposed upon myself my disgust was so strong that I could not tolerate him, and passed him without returning his how d'ye do when I saw him.[22]

In another letter to Page, Briggs continues his denigration of Poe: "When I first became intimate with him I liked him exceedingly well, but I soon discovered that he was the merest shell of a man, but I could not, then, easily get rid of him. In addition to his other unpleasant qualities he is a drunken sot, and the most purely selfish of human beings. He has a very little very showy talent but it is small in amount."[23] Briggs had to give up ownership of the *Broadway Journal* in July 1845 because he could not pay the publisher, John Brisco, the price he had set to purchase the journal. It was then that Poe took over the editorship on July 12, 1845, working with music critic Henry Cood Watson until October, when Poe became sole owner and editor of the *Broadway Journal*.

Because of Briggs's break with Poe, it is certain that Briggs did not write the art reviews published in the *Broadway Journal* after July 12, 1845. Although no definitive attribution of the art criticism printed after this time has been made (with the exception of the few reviews Poe marked with a "P" in the set of *Broadway Journal* issues he gave to Helen Whitman), the tone of the art reviews published immediately after the break with Briggs diverges greatly from the precedent set by his harsh critiques. The writing after July is tempered—almost conciliatory. This may suggest that Watson was the author of most of the art reviews at this time. The conciliatory tone is especially evident in a column about the opening of the New-York Gallery of the Fine Arts published in the August 1845 issue of the *Broadway Journal*. Reviews written months later, however, have the same biting tone as those written by Briggs during the journal's first seven months, suggesting that Poe may have assumed responsibility for writing about art even though he did not attribute these columns to himself.

The question of attribution, then, is open to speculation, but before attempting to identify the art critic or critics after July 1845, it will be useful to consider an overview of Briggs's criticism. This will help set the later art reviews apart from the approaches of Briggs or Watson. An analysis of Briggs's reviews not only reveals his theoretical approach to art criticism but also suggests that Poe's affinity to Briggs's approach afforded Poe a model of art criticism (one that differed from Henry Inman's moralistic evaluations of paintings and Watson's conciliatory reviews) that Poe could eventually apply to his own responses to visual art. Briggs was a sophisticated art critic whose reviews were far more detailed than any other American art reviews written during this period in newspapers or magazines. Not only did he evaluate various artists' skills, but he also considered the impact that the politics of the arts community had on the ways in which artists' works were exhibited and promoted. His reviews were pointed, particular, and often caustic.

Briggs's Art Criticism in the *Broadway Journal*

On the very first page of the inaugural issue of the *Broadway Journal*, Charles Briggs makes it clear that he will "devote a good part of our columns to the interests of American Art; especially to Painting and Architecture" (*BJ*, 1:1). He later reinforced this commitment in the January 18, 1845, issue by observing that "there is a growing interest for Art manifested among us, which, for the sake of both artists and public, should not be allowed to decrease; and the press being the only channel through which a knowledge of what is done in Art can be communicated to the public, we have determined to devote a portion of our Journal to that cause" (1:36). In the first issue, Briggs included a lengthy review of the American Art-Union exhibit in which he commented on the politics of the association. He praised the Art-Union's Committee of Management for its purchases that year, saying that the choices "evinced a discriminating taste" (1:12). This is no small compliment from Briggs, since just a month later, in the February 22, 1845, issue, he would ravage the collection at the Pennsylvania Academy of the Fine Arts:

Considering that this institution has only been in operation thirty-nine years, it has succeeded in accumulating an amount of bad pictures that would seen almost incredible, were it not that sincere conviction may be purchased for a quarter of a dollar. There seems to have existed a kind of chemical affinity, by which all the worst specimens of Art which came within the sphere of its attraction were drawn irresistibly toward it. . . . Institutions of this kind seem to be the threads around which all the bad taste hitherto held in solution in general society hastens to crystallize itself. They are the ravens sent by Providence to supply mediocrity with bread in the shape of patronage. . . . We have confined ourselves in this notice chiefly to the bad pictures in this exhibition, partly because they form by far the largest proportion, and partly because we think that most of them disgrace the walls where they hang. We are indignant that the public taste should continue any longer to be miseducated by such examples. (1:121)

This review of the management of the Pennsylvania Academy of the Fine Arts stands in distinct contrast to Briggs's earlier compliments of the choices made by the American Art-Union management. In his review of the artwork in the Art-Union exhibit, he critiques paintings by well-known and established artists such as Asher Durand, Thomas Cole, Peter Frederick Rothermel, Charles Weir, and Charles Deas. He follows these close analyses with praise for the paintings of Jasper Francis Cropsey, "a young artist of great promise," and he advises American artists to avoid looking for praise from "Englishmen [who] cannot appreciate the merits of a purely American landscape" (*BJ*, 1:13). This was Poe's sentiment exactly. In the process of critiquing these paintings, Briggs reveals a theoretical principle that informs his art criticism: a painter's overall sensibility should direct his choice of subject. As an example, Briggs distinguishes Thomas Cole from Asher Durand. He believes that, following this principle, Durand's paintings should reflect his peaceful, homely personality: "Mr. Durand is a gentle spirit; he loves quiet sunny places, rippling brooks, fleecy clouds, and willows that grow by water courses. The name of the street which he has chosen for his dwelling is an indication of his nature—Amity Street." (Interestingly enough, Poe would also end up living on Amity Street after he and Briggs parted ways on unfriendly terms.) Briggs then criticizes the paintings by

Durand that don't fit into this framework: "In the solemn solitudes, which Cole loves so well, [Durand] is out of his element, and only a man of fine talent" (1:12).

In direct parallel, Briggs goes on to characterize Thomas Cole's nature: "Cole loves the solemn stillness of our forests and prairies, and he has selected the foot of the Catskill mountains for his studio." Describing the only painting by Cole in the Art-Union exhibit, Briggs writes that it "possessed much of his character": "A still lake, a clear sky without a cloud, the ruins of a majestic tree stretching out its scathed but giant branches; and hoary old rocks; it is the very poetry of solitude." Briggs then provides an overall description of Cole's work: "He loves to represent Nature as she looked before living beings began to bustle about upon her surface. Before the serpent had begun to hiss, or the wolf to howl. . . . Nothing is easier with him than to produce an effect of grandeur and wildness; nothing harder than to be soft and fanciful" (*BJ*, 1:13).

In the next issue of the journal, Briggs continues his review of the Art-Union exhibit, this time emphasizing the paintings' size and tone rather than subject matter. He expresses decided opinions on these topics. "The finest landscapes that have ever been painted are small," he writes, concluding that "nearly all of Cole's paintings are too large." This opinion directly conflicts with Poe's belief that large paintings are the only ones worthy of being hung in a parlor, as he claims quite adamantly in "The Philosophy of Furniture." However, clearly Briggs does not agree. When paintings are too large, Briggs argues, the foreground is overemphasized if a viewer cannot stand far enough away, and when he can get enough distance, "the best part of [the painting] is lost entirely" (*BJ*, 1:21). This, of course, would have been the norm in most art shows of the time; the walls were crowded with paintings from ceiling to floor, and it would have been hard for a viewer to find space to step back from a large painting in order to see it in its full expanse. Briggs continues his argument by concluding that tone is also compromised in large paintings: "The tone of a small picture is not only more easily preserved than that of a large one, but much greater freedom of touch can be given" (1:22).

Apparently, these two reviews created an uproar in the arts community, because in the third issue of the *Broadway Journal* Briggs defended his views. Doing so gave him a platform to express his opinions on art criticism and arts administration—or, as Briggs calls it, "our position." He concluded that art criticism should not be written to please artists and, in fact, that indiscriminate, unmeaning praise hurts artists; most importantly, art critics should always be truthful. In his consideration of the administrative aspects of art organizations, Briggs faults Samuel Morse for continuing as president of the National Academy of Design, since he had turned from art to science: "We think that the artists in this city suffer much wrong from having a President of their Academy who has abandoned his profession." Briggs concludes quite boldly, "No true artist ever abandoned his profession." This comment, obviously, could easily be construed as an insult to Morse, but Briggs includes it nonetheless. His harsh criticism of some of the most influential artists of the time—Morse, Durand, Sully, Allston, and Cole—showed that Briggs either clearly practiced what he professed by being completely "truthful" or simply wanted to stir controversy and draw attention to his new journal. And he didn't stop with criticizing influential artists and arts administrators; he also issued a general warning that artists who do not show their best work do harm not only to themselves but to painting in general. "The public have a right to think, when they see a picture, that it is the best the painter can do," Briggs argues; if an artist does not heed this expectation, "he must be prepared for the consequences" (*BJ*, 1:37).

In a review of the recently published *Harper's Illuminated and New Pictorial Bible* in the February 8, 1845, issue of the *Broadway Journal*, Briggs makes a very clear aesthetic statement: "In all an artist attempts to do, he must seek to imitate nature. Nothing can be accomplished if this be forgotten" (*BJ*, 1:85). In the next issue, Briggs expands the parameters of his aesthetic theory by stating his views on beauty and its relation to morality in a review of the newly established New-York Gallery of the Fine Arts. But before he discusses the works on exhibit, he criticizes the gallery for charging too much for admission. Briggs believed that, the reason for "establishing a Gallery of Art being the good of the people, every inducement that can possibly be held out to them to make it a place of resort, should be adopted. The rich and well educated stand in little need of any such aids to refinement, but to the poor and ignorant, a public gallery of pictures is a real blessing, and it is for their aid that such places are, or should be established" (1:102). The tone of the article becomes acerbic as Briggs then launches into a lecture on the function of art and its relationship to morality. He harshly criticizes Thomas Cole's five-painting series *The Course of Empire* for being overtly moralistic. Here, Poe would agree completely with Briggs. Briggs strongly believed that such moralistic design in paintings was both unnecessary—since beauty refines the soul without the need for didactic moralizing—and offensive. "The pictures in themselves are truly beautiful, but the plan of them is against nature," Briggs objects. "Their beauty is marred by being seen together. We perceive directly that we are being imposed upon. Instead of looking upon beautiful landscapes, we discern that they are sermons in green paint; essays in gilt frames. The charm of nature is destroyed, the moment that the discovery is made; and we turn from them in disgust" (1:103). As Briggs continues his diatribe, his words begin to sound vaguely familiar; in fact, they are reminiscent of Poe's short story "The Imp of the Perverse," published months later in the June 1845 issue of *Graham's Magazine*. This is evident in a close comparison of the two works:

Briggs: There is nothing better than nature. Man cannot be wiser than God. It is idle, then, to think of improving on his manner of teaching. (*BJ*, 1:103)

Poe: If we cannot comprehend God in his visible works, how then in his inconceivable thoughts, that call the works into being? If we cannot understand him in his objective creatures, how then in his substantive moods and phases of creation? (*Tales*, 2:1220)

Despite this agreement that man cannot perceive God's thoughts or teachings, Poe did not agree with Briggs's assertion that "nothing is better than nature." Briggs and Poe would have parted ways completely on this issue, if the narrator's opinion in "The Landscape Garden"—"No such Paradises are to be found in reality as have glowed upon the canvass of Claude"—can be taken as a reflection of Poe's aesthetics (*Tales*, 1:707). Nonetheless, Poe clearly learned from Briggs's art criticism, both borrowing from his expertise and reacting to his philosophy of art. The similarity between Briggs's and Poe's ideas noted above is just one of many. Though they disagreed on how painters should depict nature, in general Poe's insistence on the importance of "effect" in writing and the plastic arts and his disdain for didactic art closely match Briggs's concerns.

Continuing his criticism of Thomas Cole, Briggs uses Cole's paintings to accuse him of avarice and insincerity, suggesting that his earlier work provoked a more pleasurable immediate response from its viewers. Briggs specifically points to Cole's *View on the Catskill* (number 65 in the National Academy of Design exhibit; fig. 24) as being more true to art than the paintings in the *Course of Empire* series:

Let any one test the truth of our principle by looking at this "savage state" painting, and then turning to the little piece by the same artist at the opposite end of the gallery, numbered 65, and *interpreting honestly the effect which each has upon his feelings.* This last picture is one of Mr. Cole's earlier works, painted when he seemed to love nature more than newspaper applause, or bank notes; it has more real merit than all of his allegorical pictures together; the pure morning sky, the still lake, the cool shadows of the dark woods, the feeling of nature over all, are unsurpassed by any landscape that has been painted in this country. (*BJ*, 1:103; emphasis mine)

Briggs's exceedingly scathing review of *The Course of Empire*—a series that, like Poe's "The Raven," had placed its creator in the limelight—is particularly bold and went against public opinion. Years earlier, for example, in the November 1836 issue of the *American Monthly Magazine*, the editor praised Cole's series, claiming that "these pictures . . . will hereafter mark a new era in the history of painting. They constitute a grand moral epic . . . the whole together comprising a system which, for completeness and grandeur of conception, may be classed with the noblest works of imagination."[24] *The Course of Empire* was largely responsible for Cole's preeminence in the arts community; thus, Briggs's criticism in 1845, almost ten years after the series was first exhibited, would have been quite shocking to his readers.

Even after Briggs praised the twentieth annual exhibition at the National Academy of Design in 1845 for showing "more good ones [paintings] than any exhibition has contained since the first opening of the Academy" (*BJ*, 1:254), he couldn't help but criticize the institution for hanging some "bad" pictures alongside them in a front-page review in the next issue of the *Broadway Journal*: "It is no disgrace to an artist to paint a poor picture, but it is a disgrace to an institution like the National Academy, which assumes the responsible duty of fostering and encouraging Art, to exhibit pictures to the public, which have no artistic merit of any kind" (1:257). Briggs also found fault with the selection committee for having included five "foreign" engravings, since he thought that the Academy should abide by its principle of showing only original work by American artists. In his most vicious criticism, Briggs berates the institution for hanging a specific painting that he judges to be "poor," and he calls the painter a "murderer" (presumably of beauty): "Every visitor to the exhibition will feel that the committee of arrangement have done themselves—the cause of Art, and one of their own

Fig. 24   Thomas Cole, *View on the Catskill*, 1836–37.
The Metropolitan Museum of Art, New York. Gift in
memory of Jonathan Sturges by his children, 1895,
95.13.3. Image copyright © The Metropolitan Museum
of Art. Photo: Art Resource, New York.

members, a grievous wrong, by the admission of the landscape numbered 28 on the catalogue. . . . The artist committed murder, and therefore was hung; to which we agree, but then he should have been hung out of sight: the law of the state says that no criminal shall be hung in public" (1:257). The painting in question, entitled *Evening, Landscape Composition*, was by James Hamilton Shegogue of 7 Amity Street. Shegogue was a member of the National Academy of Design's Committee of Arrangements that year and became the institution's corresponding secretary in 1849. Born in Charleston, he lived in New York City from 1833 to 1862 and showed work in nearly every annual show at the Academy from 1834 to 1858. Clearly, Briggs was again making himself vulnerable to backlash, since Shegogue was an insider at the National Academy of Design and the brutal denunciation of his painting would have angered many people.

But Briggs's most disturbing indictment appeared at the end of his serial reviews of the National Academy of Design show in the May 17, 1845, issue of the *Broadway Journal*. He broadly insults all of the "associates" of the National Academy of Design by stating that "everybody will acknowledge that the very worst performances in the exhibition are by academicians." Based on that judgment, he calls for the emergence of a rival institution, for "if the interests of art in the city are placed in the hands of such men, what can be hoped for Art? Nothing." He sums up the 1845 show—which he previously called the best show since the founding of the institution—as follows: "Taken altogether, the exhibition gives but little hope for the cause of Art in the United States. . . . There is an incubus weighing upon Art, which, if not removed, will destroy her altogether; and this incubus we believe in our heart is the Academy that was instituted for her nourishment" (*BJ*, 1:307).

No wonder Briggs was attracted to Poe and Poe to Briggs, even though the attraction was short-lived. Both were acerbic, bold, and sometimes even purposefully contentious in their criticism. Curiously, Poe's entry on Briggs in "The Literati of New York City," written for the May 1846 issue of *Godey's Lady's Book* after Poe and Briggs had parted ways, seems strongly (and suspiciously, I might add) to contradict their affinity for each other's critical style: "Among the principal papers contributed by Mr. B. [to the *Broadway Journal*] were those discussing the paintings at the last exhibition of the Academy of Fine Arts in New York. I may be permitted to say that there was scarcely a point in his whole series of criticisms on this subject at which I did not radically disagree with him."[25] Despite this overt rejection, Poe and Briggs shared a similar sensibility with regard to the value and purpose of art: neither appreciated allegory, both hated didactic art and New England "transcendentalism," and both saw beauty as the province of the soul.[26] Both wrote reviews that condemned pretense and posturing, and neither was afraid to condemn outright. For example, harshly criticizing a painting by W. Winner of Philadelphia based on the first chapter of the biblical book of First Kings, Briggs bluntly wrote, "The artist has allowed the whole beauty of the passage to escape him. He has placed David in his royal robes on the top of a high throne and the fair Shunamite at his feet too far removed to impart any heat to the old monarch though she were as hot as a furnace. There is hardly more nature in this picture than in the decorations of a China tea cup. It is idealized to the extremist point of inanity" (*BJ*, 1:305). This kind of condemnation could easily have come from Poe's pen. As Sidney Moss so succinctly states, "At a time when American critics, as well as American writers, confused a moralistic intent with literary value, Poe condemned didacticism both as a critical principle and as an aesthetic purpose, and insisted on Beauty."[27] So did Briggs.

One of the few differences between Briggs and Poe was Briggs's concern for the common man; again and again, he reminded his readers that arts institutions had a responsibility to set the standards for taste and to be places where the public could gain a greater appreciation of beauty. Briggs was highly critical of those who forgot this responsibility. He lambasted the Pennsylvania Academy of the Fine Arts for showing vastly inferior work that might leave viewers with a false sense of aesthetic standards. He also critiqued the founders of the New-York Gallery of the Fine Arts for having no guidelines in their constitution for future purchases: "It leaves a wide door open to admit anything and everything which the whims or incapacity of any future trustees may choose to purchase, or accept as a donation" (*BJ*, 1:134). Both institutions, Briggs believed, needed to be reminded that they should set standards for public taste: "Such institutions should lead the public taste in some measure, and the purchase of a picture by them should precede the verdict of popular taste, and not follow it" (1:122).

Overall, Briggs's style of criticism is quite similar to Poe's, and although they disagreed on particular aesthetic principles, Poe certainly gained valuable knowledge of the arts community while he was on good terms with Briggs. However, the *Broadway Journal*, because of its limited production life, did not review any other major New York exhibitions similar to those that Briggs had reviewed in such a comprehensive way. Briggs's art criticism was replete with specific critiques of artists' styles and paintings as well as the politics of arts institutions. He reinforced the prevailing notion that the arts community had a responsibility to set aesthetic standards and, in doing so, educate the public about the value and appreciation of great art.

Poe's Art Reviews in the *Broadway Journal*

According to Burton Pollin's research for his published collection of Poe's writings in the *Broadway Journal*, two reviews of sculptures exhibited in New York can be definitively attributed to Poe: one on the *Ivory Christ*, by an Italian monk, and the other on *La sortie du bain* (or *Nymph Entering the Bath*, as Thomas Cummings called it,[28] or *Coming from the Bath*, as Poe named it in his first notice on the sculpture), by a Belgian artist. Two articles that discuss Titian's painting *Venus of Urbino* (fig. 25), exhibited in "rooms at Broadway," are also attributed to Poe; he marked them with a "P" in the *Broadway Journal* issues he gave to Helen Whitman. However, as Pollin has indicated, these reviews may not constitute all of the art criticism that Poe wrote or directly supervised. Poe, of course, also reviewed books on art such as Charles Edwards Lester's *The Artist, the Merchant, and the Statesman, of the Age of the Medici, and of Our Own Times* and commented on the quality of plates in periodicals, gift books, and illustrated books (*Works*, 4:217).

In Poe's first article on the Titian painting, which appeared in the May 17, 1845, issue of the *Broadway Journal*, he addresses the difficulty of assessing whether the painting is an original or a copy. It was common practice for American artists—for example, John Vanderlyn—to make copies of important European paintings, and thus Poe questions why "no story is told of the manner in which so remarkable a work came to this country. All this looks very suspicious." (He specifically wonders how such a large painting by such a great "Old Master" could have been purchased by an individual, when "any European government would buy it at a price which few individuals could afford to pay.") Poe's attention in this column, at first, is drawn to the politics of authenticity, but he quickly turns to aesthetics and seems to suggest that the value of a work of art depends not on the name of the artist or the work's authenticity but on the amount of pleasure the viewer receives: "The only test . . . by which we should try a work of art is the delight it gives us; and we believe that there are very few persons who could honestly say that Titian's real paintings gave them more real pleasure than this of Venus" (*BJ*, 1:316).

Six months later, in the November 8, 1845, issue, Poe notes that this same painting was shown again in "rooms at Broadway." Poe begins the fine arts column almost peevishly by remarking, "Under this head we have very little to observe." Nonetheless, he gives strong praise to the painter and inventor Joshua Shaw.[29] Shaw's landscape paintings, as described by Milo Naeve, featured "a dark foreground, generalized trees or hills framing the composition in the foreground and middleground, a stream or lake and distant hills. All of these elements are a direct influence of Claude Lorraine's 17th-century idealized landscapes of the Roman countryside" (see fig. 26).[30] Poe does mention Claude in his tales, and his admiration for Shaw could have arisen from recognizing Claude's influence on Shaw's work. Poe may also have praised Shaw's paintings because the two met in Philadelphia,[31] and Poe knew the hardships that Shaw had faced in trying to make a living from his art. That Poe acknowledges the appeal of Shaw's paintings is another indication that Poe's visual aesthetics had turned toward an appreciation of the beautiful and a desire for repose, both characteristics of Shaw's work.

Poe saw Shaw's paintings on exhibit in the 1844 and 1845 National Academy of Design shows and at the American Art-Union in 1845: "At the rooms of the Art Union there are two very exquisite landscapes by Shaw—an artist whose merits (all of the loftiest order) will perhaps never be appreciated by his countrymen, until Death has mellowed down some of the personal ill-will with which his brother artists regard him" (*BJ*, 2:276). Shaw's work had also been shown at the Art-Union's predecessor, the Apollo Society. He exhibited a painting entitled *Shipwreck* in its 1839 show and the paintings *English Sea-Coast Scene*, *View on the Susquehanna*, and *View of the Falls on Reedy River* in the 1842 show. Poe specifically compliments one of Shaw's paintings in the 1845 Art-Union show, entitled *The Indian's First Sight of a Ship*, calling it one of his best works.

However, before this positive nod to Shaw, Poe makes disparaging remarks about Titian's *Venus of Urbino*. He notes that the painting's authenticity has been proven—a question he raised in his first review of the work—but in a curious turn, he then expresses a complete disinterest in the painting's beauty, a quality he clearly admired the first time he saw it in May: "We cannot force ourselves into any very enthusiastic admiration of the work. As a composition it is

Fig. 25   Titian (Tiziano Vecellio), *Venus of Urbino*, 1538.
Uffizi Gallery, Florence. Photo: Scala / Ministero per i
Beni e le Attività culturali / Art Resource, New York.

full of defects. Its color alone redeems it" (*BJ*, 2:276). Clearly, this contradiction
does not make sense; either Poe was seriously depressed when he forced himself
to write this column (by that time, he knew that the *Broadway Journal*'s viability
was waning) or he was overcome by the complications of his personal life.

Nonetheless, the comments in his first entry on the Titian painting regarding a viewer's responsiveness to a work of art are similar to those offered in his
October 11, 1845, review of the *Ivory Christ*, "brought from Italy by *C. Edwards
Lester*." Poe's positive appraisal of the *Ivory Christ* in this review may have been
based on his own aesthetic principles, but he also was aware that Lester, in
The Artist, the Merchant, and the Statesman—a book Poe reviewed—noted that
the sculpture was "esteemed by [Hiram] Powers to be the best representation of

Fig. 26 Joshua Shaw, *Landscape with Cattle*, 1818.
Collection of The Butler Institute of American Art,
Youngstown, Ohio, 961–0-117.

the Saviour he had ever seen."[32] In any case, in Poe's notice on the *Ivory Christ*, he encouraged "all lovers of the true and beautiful in art" to visit the sculpture, "now being exhibited in Broadway opposite the Park" (*BJ*, 2:214). One such "lover of the true and beautiful" was Anne Lynch, as evidenced by her poem "Sonnet—On Seeing the Ivory Statue of Christ," published in 1848:

> The enthusiast brooding in his cell apart
>   O'er the sad image of the Crucified,—
>   The drooping head, closed lips and pierced side,—
> A holy vision fills his raptured heart;
>   With heavenly power inspired, his unskilled arm
>   Shapes the rude block to this transcendent form.
> Oh Son of God! Thus, ever thus, would I
>   Dwell on the loveliness enshrined in Thee;
>   The lofty faith, the sweet humility;
> The boundless love, the love that could not die.
>   And as the sculptor, with thy glory warm,
>   Gave to this chiseled ivory thy fair form,
> So would my spirit, in thy thought divine,
> Grow to a semblance, fair as this, of Thine.[33]

The sentiment in Lynch's sonnet echoes Poe's contention in his *Broadway Journal* review of the *Ivory Christ* that the artist's enthusiasm for his subject gave him the power to create beauty out of "the tusk of an antique elephant." He observes, "A deep enthusiasm—an overwhelming passion to do justice to the intellectual and physical character of the God-man, seems to have been in this case at once the instigation and the instruction" (2:214). The artist was not schooled as a sculptor, according to Poe's knowledge, but this lack of training did not deter him from creating beauty, communicated to those who saw the figure.

Poe's review in the October 11, 1845, issue of the *Broadway Journal* sounds much like the following description of the *Ivory Christ* from the *American Review* for July 1845:

> There is now in this city, brought over from Italy by the American Consul at Genoa, Mr. C. Edwards Lester, a more exquisite and noble work of art than has probably ever been in this country. It is a Christ on the Cross,

wrought out of a single piece of ivory by a Genoese monk. . . . The first
great impression emanates to the beholder from the entire appearance of
the frame, as it hangs upon the cross, distended with the immortal pains
that have hardly departed. The exactness of detail, and the wonderful
effect of the whole combined, are truly astonishing. The anatomical structure, to the most experienced eyes that have scrutinized it, is found perfect. . . . The wonderful union, in the features, of manly massiveness and
exquisite womanish delicacy—the contrast, above all, of intellectual agony,
knit into the brows and frozen upon the lofty forehead, with the sublime
composure of sweet and calm resignation . . . we have never seen idealized
in any work of art.[34]

In his own review, Poe likewise praises the artist's ability to express Christ's
"intellectuality," an attribute that is very different, he concludes, from other representations of Christ that portray him as "merely benevolent, dignified, meek,
self-sustained and beautiful in feature." In this sculpture of Christ, Poe points
out, the artist recognizes that "intellectuality" is a necessary attribute of the
"God-man": "In this, mind—genius—predominates. The whole face is eminently intellectual." Poe also calls attention to the "absolute truth of the entire
design," which he finds in the "perfect" anatomy of the figure and in the way that
Christ "depends" on the cross: "The figure depends from the cross *precisely* as
the human form would depend under the circumstances" (*BJ*, 2:228, 214).

Poe's method of evaluating works of visual art, as revealed in this review, is
similar to how he assessed poetry. He emphasizes the value of accurate craftsmanship, since form is the vehicle for artistic expression in the visual arts as
much as it is in writing. And his admiration for the "absolute truth of the entire
design" in sculpture is much like his requirement that poetry display a keen
sense of meter or that the details in a fictional work contribute to its denouement. Most important, the writer of both fiction and poetry, first and foremost,
must be concerned with how to produce a desired effect. In a review of Elizabeth Oakes Smith's poetry, for example, Poe makes it clear that meter is of the
utmost importance to effective poetry and that the beginning of a poem should
demonstrate the poet's grasp of prosody:

A rhythm should always be distinctly marked by its first foot—that is to
say, if the design is iambic, we should commence with an unmistakeable

iambus, and proceed with this foot until the ear gets fairly accustomed to it before we attempt variation; for which, indeed, there is no *necessity* unless for the relief of monotone. When the rhythm is in this manner thoroughly recognised, we may sparingly vary with anapæsts (or if the rhythm be trochaic, with dactyls). Spondees, still more sparingly, as absolute discords, may be also introduced either in an iambic or trochaic rhythm. In common with a very large majority of American, and, indeed, of European poets, Mrs. Smith seems to be totally unacquainted with the principles of versification—by which, of course, we mean its *rationale*. (*Works*, 13:91)

The familiar beginning of "The Philosophy of Composition" asserts a similar concern for craftsmanship. Poe uses the example of Edward Bulwer-Lytton's fiction to suggest that an admirable story must reveal, like a poem marked by its "first foot," a fiction writer's rationale. By this, Poe means that the writer must have the ability to conceive the end of his story before he begins to write; he must employ the tools of composition to accomplish this end, but only after he has the denouement in sight. "Nothing is more clear than that every plot, worth the name, must be elaborated to its *dénouement* before anything be attempted with the pen," Poe explains. "It is only with the *dénouement* constantly in view that we can give a plot its indispensable air of consequence, or causation, by making the incidents, and especially the tone at all points, tend to the development of the intention" (*Works*, 14:193). Artistic method (that is, the path of prosody or plot) is crucial to Poe's aesthetic, but as always he acknowledges over and over that art must offer something more than accurate form. As the anonymous letter writer in Poe's *Eureka* concludes, truth and beauty come from "the Soul which loves nothing so well as to soar in those regions of illimitable intuition which are utterly incognizant of 'path'" (16:195).

Poe finds such beauty in *La sortie du bain*, a sculpture by "De Kuyper." In the first of his three entries on this sculpture in the *Broadway Journal*, Poe informs his readers that it was brought by "an American gentleman, who saw it in Belgium, and being struck by its extraordinary merit, purchased it at a great price." The gentleman granted Poe a private viewing of the sculpture in a "room at Broadway," and although Poe writes that he intends to "defer his critical accounting of it" until the exhibit is opened to the public, he could not refrain from extolling its merits: "In all attributes of female loveliness, delicacy and roundness of form, perfection of proportion, intellectuality, gentleness, and modesty, it could hardly be excelled" (*BJ*, 2:155). The sculpture was also highly praised by Thomas Cummings, then treasurer of the National Academy of Design, as "one of the most exquisitely beautiful creations of the chisel that ever appeared in the city."[35]

Poe's "De Kuyper" (and Cummings's "De Keypers") is actually Jean-Baptiste De Cuyper of Antwerp, Belgium, according to Burton Pollin, who uncovered an article in Antwerp's *Bijdragen tot de Geschiedenis* claiming that "he showed in New York 'a Venus at the water's edge.'"[36] De Cuyper was part of the new arts movement that emerged after Belgium gained independence from the northern Netherlands in 1830, and his sculptures of angels can be seen in "Sint-Paulus" Cathedral in Antwerp, where three paintings by Peter Paul Rubens also hang. De Cuyper also specialized in sculptures for graveyard monuments, a detail Poe would have certainly appreciated. Today the Royal Museum of Fine Arts Antwerp holds a De Cuyper sculpture of a *cupido* (fig. 26), the overall design of which would have pleased Poe, had he had the opportunity to see it. The gentleness of the cupid's hands, mirrored by the position of the legs and toes, catches the eye. The figure's beauty emanates from these features and from its yearning repose. Poe described the female figure of *La sortie du bain* with these words: "The attitude is easy, and full of truth" (*BJ*, 2:260). The same is true of this *cupido*.

Despite the mixed reviews *La sortie du bain* received, Poe's careful description of the sculpture reveals the pleasure he found in it, even though the anatomical flaws he observed should have detracted from a positive evaluation:

> The figure—of white marble, slightly impaired by blue veins—is the size of life, and represents a young and exquisitely beautiful woman, reclining on the sea-shore. . . . The name given the sculpture—*La Sortie du Bain*—and the shell-strown shore on which we see the girl—denotes that she has lately emerged from the sea, in which she has been bathing. She has thrown herself listlessly on the sand. . . . The face is of surpassing loveliness—its expression that of girlish innocence, and the languor consequent from bathing. The attitude is easy, and full of truth. The toes, in especial, convey the idea of one luxuriating in the sense of comfort—of refreshment—of animal life and health. . . . *La Sortie du Bain* is undoubtedly the work of genius; and should be visited by all who have a regard for the pure and truthful in Art. (*BJ*, 2:260)

Fig. 27   Jean-Baptiste De Cuyper, *Cupido*, n.d.
Koninklijk Museum voor Schone Kunsten Antwerpen.
From *Beeldhouwwerken en assemblages 19de en 20ste*
eeuw, edited by Dorine Cardyn-Oomen et al. (Antwerp:
Koninklijk Museum, 1986).

This attitude of ease and innocence is also seen in De Cuyper's sculpture *Madonna and Child*, located in the church of Saint Barbara College, a Jesuit school in Ghent, Belgium.

Poe's Visual Aesthetics

Like Briggs, Poe knew that the public was vulnerable to fashion's whims and lacked an appreciation for aesthetic principles, but unlike Briggs, Poe simply disdained that tendency and was not concerned with educating the public. His disdain is evident in "The Philosophy of Furniture," first published as "House Furniture" in the May 1840 issue of *Burton's Gentleman's Magazine*. The revised version appeared as the first article in the May 3, 1845, issue of the *Broadway Journal*, when Poe was still working with Charles Briggs and Henry Cood Watson. Two weeks later, George Pope Morris reprinted it in the May 17, 1845, issue of the *New-York Mirror*. The sketch, ostensibly about home decoration, incorporates a set of aesthetic principles that apply equally to art criticism. Poe argues that those aspects of home decoration that are "offensive to the eye" are also found in inferior paintings.

Poe explicitly states that the critical principles he uses to judge the layout and "keeping" of a room are also used when analyzing paintings: "We speak of the keeping of the room as we would of the keeping of a picture—for both the picture and the room are amenable to those undeviating principles which regulate all varieties of art; and very nearly the same laws by which we decide on the higher merits of a painting, suffice for decision on the adjustment of a chamber." He follows this assertion with a complaint about the composition of a poorly arranged room: "A want of keeping is observable sometimes in the character of the several pieces of furniture, but generally in their colors or modes of adaptation to use. *Very* often the eye is offended by their inartistical arrangement. Straight lines are too prevalent—too uninterruptedly continued—or clumsily interrupted at right angles. If curved lines occur, they are repeated into unpleasant uniformity. By undue precision, the appearance of many a fine apartment is utterly spoiled" (*Tales*, 1:497). By inference, Poe would have the arrangement of a room follow the rules of pictorial composition; rather than being aligned linearly, furniture should radiate from a focal point, in a way similar to the composition of a painting.

When Poe discusses the "keeping" of a room, his foremost consideration—like that of Briggs for painting—is overall "effect." The carpet, Poe asserts, is "the soul of the apartment" and, like the background of a painting, must be chosen in relation to all aspects of the composition (*Tales*, 1:497). Yet it is most often offensive because of an excessive mixture of color, pattern, and texture: "A carpet should *not* be bedizzened out like a Riccaree Indian—all red chalk, yellow ochre, and cock's feathers. In brief—distinct grounds, and vivid circular or cycloid figures, *of no meaning*, are here Median laws." Poe's prose in this section of the essay displays a frenetic quality, culminating in an angry rant against capitalism and its disastrous influences: "Cloths of huge, sprawling, and radiating devices, stripe-interspersed, and glorious with all hues, among which no ground is intelligible—these are but the wicked invention of a race of time-servers and money-lovers—children of Baal and worshippers of Mammon—Benthams, who, to spare thought and economize fancy, first cruelly invented the Kaleidoscope, and then established joint-stock companies to twirl it by steam" (1:498).

Clearly, Poe finds rooms filled with dizzying colors and shapes to be offensive and blames those who have the power to promote such bad taste. Here he implies that the popular fascination with the kaleidoscope has had disastrous effects on choices made in home decoration. In this respect, Poe is similar to Briggs; both men admonished those with the power to set trends. The only difference between the two, of course, is that Briggs believed that those with influence should be responsible for establishing standards of good taste, while Poe blasted those whose influence overrode what he considered to be good taste and derided those who were vulnerable to such influences. "It is an evil growing out of our republican institutions, that here a man of large purse has usually a very little soul which he keeps in it," Poe contends. "The corruption of taste is a portion or a pendant of the dollar-manufacture" (*Tales*, 1:500).

Poe continues his rant against popular taste while discussing the importance of light in room decoration. He believes that the pervasive attraction to glare, cut glass, and glitter reflects a public that blindly follows fashion. The focus on light and its effects applies as much to painting as it does to home decoration, of course. Just as the play of light in a painting can distract or enhance the subject matter, so too does bad lighting destroy the overall effect of a room's "keeping." Good composition and engaging content are nullified by ineffectual lighting, especially the "unquiet light" produced by cut glass. "The cut-glass shade is a weak invention of the enemy," Poe declares. "The eagerness with which we have adopted it, partly on account of its *flashiness*, but principally on account of its *greater cost*, is a good commentary on the proposition with which we began. It is not too much to say, that the deliberate employer of a cut-glass shade, is either radically deficient in taste, or blindly subservient to the caprices of fashion." He goes on to assert that not only is furniture negatively affected by flashy lighting, but "female loveliness, in especial, is more than one-half disenchanted beneath its evil eye" (*Tales*, 1:499).

Overall, the overt purpose of "House Furniture" is to admonish Americans for their willingness to decorate their homes based merely on what's fashionable, to value costliness over aesthetics, and to choose glitter and glare over repose. The aesthetic principles Poe applies to home decoration easily translate into the principles that underlie Poe's responses to the visual arts: composition that revolves around a focal point, lighting that reflects mood, color and texture that combine in harmonious ways, and an overall sense of spirituality enhanced by quietude. All that notwithstanding, the final aesthetic measure, Poe seems to say, depends on the viewer's pleasurable response to a painting or home decor. Although he acknowledges that most people would not be able to articulate why a good painting or a tastefully decorated room provokes a sense of pleasure, he believes that the viewer can feel the difference: "The veriest bumpkin, on entering an apartment so bedizened, would be instantly aware of something wrong, although he might be altogether unable to assign a cause for his dissatisfaction. But let the same person be led into a room tastefully furnished, and he would be startled into an exclamation of pleasure and surprise" (*Tales*, 1:500).

Poe was keenly aware that the reception of art is key, that the viewer's perspective—not just his aesthetic sensibility but quite literally his physical vantage point—makes all the difference in how something is seen and whether the intended effect can be achieved. His awareness of point of view is not only demonstrated in his descriptions in "Landor's Cottage" but also plays a pivotal role in "Ligeia," "The Sphinx," and "The Spectacles." The narrator in "Landor's Cottage," for example, in concluding that he did "no more than give, in detail, a picture of Mr. Landor's residence—*as I found it*," nonetheless did so from a "point of view [that] . . . was not *altogether*, although it was nearly, the best point from which to survey the house" (*Tales*, 2:1340, 1335). The narrator is constantly coming to spots where he becomes transfixed and stationary, knowing full well that any deviation from that point of view might alter the perception of the beauty before him.

When he first sees Landor's cottage, he remarks, quite revealingly, "Its marvellous *effect* lay altogether in its artistic arrangement *as a picture*. I could have fancied, while I looked at it, that some eminent landscape-painter had built it with his brush" (*Tales*, 2:1335). Later, the narrator compares what he sees with what could easily be a painting: "The shingles were painted a dull gray; and the happiness with which this neutral tint melted into the vivid green of the tulip-tree leaves that partially overshadowed the cottage, can readily be conceived by an artist" (2:1337). The description of a parlor table near the end of the story reveals a still-life painting: "On the table were a few books; a large, square, crystal bottle of some novel perfume; a plain, ground-glass *astral* (not solar) lamp, with an Italian shade; and a large vase of resplendently-blooming flowers" (2:1340). This evocation of a still life signals Poe's embrace of the beauty of homeliness and may reflect a desire to recover the idealized sense of his cottage in Fordham when his wife, Virginia, was alive—his own Landor's cottage and a place of repose.

Coda

This book pictures Poe as many may not have known him before. As the evidence presented here reveals, Poe's youthful dedication to beauty did not fade; in fact, his mature work shows a move away from the grotesque and the sublime and toward an appreciation of homeliness and beauty, most clearly seen in his last published work, "Landor's Cottage." Had Poe lived longer, this story would have been the second in a trilogy of domestic landscapes. The first of these pieces, "The Domain of Arnheim," features his ideal artist: the landscape gardener Ellison. In his grace, poetic sentiments, and great love of beauty, Ellison is a far cry from the frenetic, murderous narrators of "The Tell-Tale Heart," "The Black Cat," "The Imp of the Perverse," and "William Wilson," and from disturbed, obsessive characters such as Montresor, Usher, and Legrand.

Thus, despite his popular image as a writer of stories that invoke fear and horror, Poe had a high regard for beauty and its expressions. Unfortunately, unlike the character of Ellison, Poe was not independently wealthy and, as a result, needed to cater to the public's desire for sensationalist tales in order to make money. Indeed, he had an astute ability to pen stories expressing the depths of human depravity and to critique the cultural concerns of his time through satire and humor. Yet he also knew and valued pastoral scenes like those depicted by Asher Durand, Frederic Church, and Claude Lorrain, among others. Such artists' works influenced his visual sensibilities, and their expressions of domestic paradise call to mind the first stanza of his 1834 poem "To One in Paradise," "always considered one of Poe's most important poems" (*Poems*, 211), which he gave to the protagonist in "The Assignation":

> Thou wast that all to me, love,
>   For which my soul did pine—
> A green isle in the sea, love,
>   A fountain and a shrine,
> All wreathed with fairy fruits and flowers,
>   And all the flowers were mine.
>
> (Poems, 214)

Such visions of paradise never reappear in his poetry, but they do find a place in stories such as "Landor's Cottage," albeit in a homely way. Poe wrote about ideals of beauty at both the beginning and the end of his career. And throughout his life—despite his often caustic literary criticism and his sensationalist tales—he alluded to the beautiful in his references to landscape painters and in his creation of "word paintings." It is this Poe, with his painterly sensibilities, who appears in the written recollections of Elma Mary Letchworth. As a child growing up in Fordham, her encounters with Poe were deeply impressed upon her memory:

> It was my privilege, when quite young, to be taken often to see Edgar Allan Poe, and to listen to many discussions between him and literary people as well as to the monologues in which he indulged when with sympathetic listeners. . . . Long and interesting was the talk in the sitting-room after luncheon. . . . I remember the . . . little grove by the house seemed a wood of romance to me. I dare say it was only a group of trees, and I sat in their shade with Poe, who interested himself in my education and called my attention to beauties of nature. "Look up over your head into the trees," he said, as he sat beside me, "and see how beautiful is the play of sunlight among the leaves—how the shadow of one leaf falls on another." I had never noticed these things, being a city child, but I have often thought of that afternoon since when sitting under sunlit trees. . . . At that time Fordham was an insignificant village set in a very pretty country. There flowed the beautiful Bronx river, made famous by contemporary poets. It ran through forest and dale. On its banks, high above the stream, was a lovely wood with great trees—a charming place for a picnic: and the group of friends already mentioned often came out for an afternoon, bringing their baskets full of good things. It became their custom to call at Poe's cottage and invite him to join the party. He entered pleasantly into their companionship, and it was a memorable occasion when he sat beneath the biggest oak in the wood. It was a balmy summer's day, birdsong mingled with the murmur of the Bronx below. Sunshine flecked the brown earth and shimmered in the leaves above our heads. The party grouped themselves about the poet, and he recited in his melodious voice "The Bells." And when
>
> "Bells, bells, bells"
>
> were uttered, it was like the sound of ringing and resounding bells. I hear it in my memory.[37]

Such bucolic peace and resounding bells are a part—if not the most valued part—of Poe's poetic and artistic sensibility. This Poe is a far cry from the popular twenty-first-century perception of his work as coming from the tortured soul of a demented madman. "The Island of the Fay," a plate piece published first in *Graham's Magazine* in June 1841 with an engraving by Sartain and then republished by Poe in the October 4, 1845, issue of the *Broadway Journal*, stands as a strong counter to this benighted image, mirroring the picture of Poe that I have presented in this book. In "The Island of the Fay," the narrator admits that a devotion to music—found in Poe's poetry and praised in his reviews—takes second place to "the happiness experienced in the contemplation of natural scenery. . . . I love, indeed, to regard the dark valleys, and the grey rocks, and the waters that silently smile, and the forests that sigh in uneasy slumbers, and the proud watchful mountains that look down upon all—I love to regard these as themselves but the colossal members of one vast animate and sentient whole" (*BJ*, 2:188). This sentiment of nature being "one vast animate and sentient whole" anticipates Poe's most powerful spiritual conclusion, voiced at the end of *Eureka*. The wholeness of landscape beauty, as expressed in "The Island of the Fay," emerges in *Eureka* in this cosmological conclusion: "The long succession of ages . . . must elapse before these myriads of individual Intelligences become blended—when the bright stars become blended—into One. Think that the sense of individual identity will be gradually merged in the general consciousness—that Man, for example, ceasing imperceptibly to feel himself Man, will at length attain that awfully triumphant epoch when he shall recognize his existence as that of Jehovah."[38] Poe's high regard for natural beauty, seen as a "sentient whole," serves as a prelude to this spiritual vision of everlasting life, reinforcing the importance of landscape art in Poe's artistic vision.

Appendix

POE'S REFERENCES TO ARTISTS, PAINTINGS, DRAWINGS, AND SCULPTURES

Artist	Cited in	Title of artwork
William Henry Bartlett (1809–1854)	Review of the *Columbian Lady's and Gentleman's Magazine*	*View Near Cold-Spring*
Edmé Bouchardon (1698–1762)	Pinakidia 79	Statue of Louis XV
Antonio Canova (1757–1822)	"The Assignation"	*Venus*
John Gadsby Chapman (1808–1889)	"The Philosophy of Furniture"	*The Lake of the Dismal Swamp*
Cimabue (1240–1302)	"The Assignation"	
Claude Lorrain (1600–1682)	"The Domain of Arnheim" "The Landscape Garden"	
George Cruikshank (1792–1878)	Review of Henry Cockton's *Stanley Thorn*	
Jean-Baptiste De Cuyper (aka De Kuyper and De Keypers) (1807–1852)	Review in the *Broadway Journal*	*La sortie du bain*
Balthasar Denner (1685–1749)	Marginalia 243 Review of Henry F. Chorley's *Memorials of Mrs. Hemans*	
John Flaxman (1755–1826)	Review of Henry Wadsworth Longfellow's *Ballads and Other Poems*	
Henry Fuseli (1741–1825)	"The Fall of the House of Usher"	*The Nightmare*
Auguste Hervieu (1794–1858)	Review of Frances Trollope's *Paris and the Parisians in 1835*	

Artist	Cited in	Title of artwork
Henry Inman (1801–1846)	Review of the *Columbian Lady's and Gentleman's Magazine*	*Fanny Elssler* *Village School in an Uproar*
Bernard-Romain Julien (1802–1871)	"Landor's Cottage"	
Leonardo da Vinci (1452–1519)	"The Oblong Box"	*The Last Supper*
Michelangelo (1475–1564)	"The Assignation" Review of Henry Wadsworth Longfellow's *Ballads and Other Poems* "Al Aaraaf"	
Parrhasius (5th century B.C.)	Review of Henry Wadsworth Longfellow's *Ballads and Other Poems*	
Jean-Baptiste Pigalle (1714–1785)	Pinakidia 79	Statue of Louis XV
Nicolas Poussin (1594–1665)	"The Landscape Garden"	
Guido Reni (1575–1642)	"The Assignation"	*Madonna della Pieta*
Moritz Retzsch (1779–1857)	"The Man of the Crowd" Review of Henry F. Chorley's *Memorials of Mrs. Hemans* Review of Henry Wadsworth Longfellow's *Ballads and Other Poems*	
Salvator Rosa (1615–1673)	"Morning on the Wissahiccon" "Landor's Cottage"	
Peter Frederick Rothermel (1817–1895)	Review of the *Columbian Lady's and Gentleman's Magazine*	
Joshua Shaw (1776–1860)	Review in the *Broadway Journal*	*The Indian's First Sight of a Ship*
Clarkson Stanfield (1793–1867)	"The Philosophy of Furniture" "The Landscape Garden"	

Artist	Cited in	Title of artwork
Jan Steen (1626–1679)	Review of Henry Wadsworth Longfellow's *Ballads and Other Poems* Review of Charles James Lever's *Charles O'Malley* "Lionizing"	
Thomas Sully (1783–1872)	"The Philosophy of Furniture"	
John Frederick Tennant (1796–1872)	Review of *The Gift for 1836*	*Smuggler's Repose*
Titian (1485–1576)	Review in the *Broadway Journal*	*Venus*
Zeuxis (464–323 B.C.)	Marginalia 243 Review of Henry Wadsworth Longfellow's *Ballads and Other Poems*	

Notes

————————————

Introduction

1. Poe, *Complete Poems*, 146. Further references to Poe's poems will be noted parenthetically in the text as *Poems*.

2. Poe, *Collected Letters*, 1:47. Further references to Poe's letters will be noted parenthetically in the text as *Letters*.

3. Poe, *Tales and Sketches*, 1:707 and 2:1272. Further references to Poe's short stories and sketches will be noted parenthetically in the text as *Tales*.

4. This story originally appeared in Snowden's *Ladies' Companion* for October 1842, and the end of the quoted sentence read "of Claude, or Poussin or Stanfield." When Poe revised this tale for publication in the *Broadway Journal*, he removed the references to Poussin and Stanfield.

5. Poe, *Writings in the "Southern Literary Messenger,"* 117.

6. Poe, "Letter to B———," 7.

7. Poe, *Writings in the "Southern Literary Messenger,"* 117.

8. Poe, *Complete Works*, 10:152–53. Further references to Poe's reviews will be from this edition and noted parenthetically in the text as *Works*.

9. Poe, *Brevities*, 385.

10. Ljungquist, *The Grand and the Fair*, 92, 82.

11. See, for example, Osipova, "Aesthetic Effects," and Hayes, "One-Man Modernist."

12. Hayes, "One-Man Modernist," 237.

13. Pollin, *Images of Poe's Works*, 1.

14. Cantalupo, "Interview with Burton Pollin," 109. Pollin notes in *Images of Poe's Works*, "Such passages [Poe] said, 'are unrivalled for *graphicality* (why is there not such a word?)'" (2).

15. Quoted in Thomas, "Poe in Philadelphia," 70.

16. About two years before his death on June 30, 2009, Burton Pollin sent me all of his handwritten notes regarding Poe and the visual arts, with this note: "As for Poe and art—please forgive the dreadful condition of these very old and nasty notes. May they be of use, in strange ways!" (February 18, 2007). I am indebted to Dr. Pollin for this and for the valuable advice he gave me over the years, and I am especially thankful that he shared his detailed research on this topic with me.

17. Thomas and Jackson, *Poe Log*, xliv. Further references to this book will be noted parenthetically in the text as *Poe Log*.

18. Thomas, "Poe in Philadelphia," 741.

19. Lewis, "Felix O. C. Darley," 1.

20. Keyes, "Daguerreotype's Popularity," 118.

21. My appreciation goes to Mary DeJong for referring me to Samuel Stillman Osgood in an email on August 3, 2005.

22. Here I would have to disagree with Silverman's assessment that "except the triumph of 'The Raven,' [Poe] spent most of 1845 in an uproar. . . . His writing and editorial labor for the

Broadway Journal were both ground and outlet for many of his woes." Silverman, *Mournful and Never-Ending Remembrance*, 293.

23. According to an 1840 map of Philadelphia, Sixteenth Street was then named North Eighth Street. See Martinez and Talbott, *Philadelphia's Cultural Landscape*.

24. Thomas, "Poe in Philadelphia," 25.

25. Martinez and Talbott, *Philadelphia's Cultural Landscape*, 4.

26. Quinn, *Edgar Allan Poe*, 274.

27. Lewis, "Felix O. C. Darley," 1.

28. Webb, *History of Pennsylvania Hall*, 6. See also Caust-Ellenbogen, "Pennsylvania Hall Association."

29. Wilson and Coval, "City of Unbrotherly Love."

30. "History and Timeline."

31. See Cantalupo, "Interview with Jefferson Moak."

32. Homberger, *Scenes from the Life of a City*, 218.

33. Spannuth, *Poe's Contributions*, 25.

34. Stokes, *Iconography of Manhattan*.

35. For a concise narrative overview of the history of art galleries in New York from 1800 to 1850, see Bender, *New York Intellect*.

36. *Transactions of the American Art Union*.

37. Spannuth, *Poe's Contributions*, 33.

38. Strong, *Diary*, 264–65.

39. *New-York Mirror*, 1.

40. Myers, "Public Display of Art," 37.

41. Important paintings that influenced Poe's work will be described in a later chapter.

42. Dearinger and Barry, "Annual Exhibitions," 57. See Dearinger, *Paintings and Sculpture*, xi, n. 2, for discussion of the actual date that the Academy was established.

43. Stone, *History of New York City*, 64 (appendix X).

44. Dearinger and Barry, "Annual Exhibitions," 57.

45. Myers, "Public Display of Art," 37.

46. For a detailed overview of Luman Reed's collection, see Foshay, *Mr. Luman Reed's Picture Gallery*.

47. Gerdts, "Newly Discovered Records," 3.

48. Stokes, *Iconography of Manhattan*, 5:1783.

49. Gerdts, "Newly Discovered," 9.

50. Pollin, *Writings in the "Broadway Journal*," 177.

51. *Broadway Journal*, 2:154. Further references to the periodical will be noted parenthetically in the text as *BJ*.

52. Sperling, "'Art, Cheap and Good.'"

53. Mann, *American Art-Union*, 90.

Chapter 1

1. For an account of Sartain and Poe's friendship, see Tuerk, "John Sartain and E. A. Poe"; see also Silverman, *Mournful and Never-Ending Remembrance*, 416–18.

2. Deas, *Portraits and Daguerreotypes*, 66.

3. F. D. Miller, "Basis for Poe's 'The Island of the Fay,'" 138.

4. For an account of Poe and Robert Sully's friendship, see Deas, *Portraits and Daguerreo-types*, 143–45.

5. "Philadelphia Academy."

6. Piggush, "Visualizing Early American Art Audiences," 722–23.

7. In this and subsequent lists compiled from exhibition records, I have retained the original spelling of artwork titles.

8. Trollope, *Paris and the Parisians*, 35.

9. Verdi, "Poussin's 'Deluge,'" 388.

10. Ibid., 390.

11. Poe, *Imaginary Voyages*, 514–15.

12. Ljungquist, *The Grand and the Fair*, 92.

13. Poe, *Imaginary Voyages*, 543.

14. Ibid., 575.

15. Pickering, *Painting*, 133.

16. *Burton's Gentleman's Magazine*, 185.

17. Quoted in Manwaring, *Italian Landscape*, 49–50.

18. Quoted in ibid., 153.

19. Cummings, *Historic Annals*, 179.

20. Mann, *Francis William Edmonds*, 7.

21. Ibid.

22. See Clark, *Francis W. Edmonds*, 27.

23. Adams, "A Study of Art Unions," 8.

24. Clark, *Francis W. Edmonds*, 23.

25. Ibid., 21.

26. Matheson, "Poe's 'The Black Cat,'" 4–5.

27. Mann, *Francis William Edmonds*, 24.

28. Avery, *American Drawings*, 174.

29. Johnson, "William Sidney Mount," 27.

30. Ibid., 12.

31. Ibid.

32. *National Academy of Design Exhibition Record*.

33. Durand, *Life and Times*, 141.

34. Ibid., 173.

35. Burns, *Painting the Dark Side*, 21.

36. Ibid., 3, 7.

37. See Jacobs, "Poe's Earthly Paradise," 406. See also Sanford, "Edgar Allan Poe," 55.

38. Downing, *Treatise on the Theory*, 49.

39. Poe, "Literati of New York City," 200.

Chapter 2

1. Poe's comic tale "The Oblong Box" includes references to both Leonardo da Vinci and a follower of Rubens. However, their relevance to the overall story is superficial at best. The narrator simply comes to a conclusion about the oblong box that satisfies his inquisitiveness: "Now here was a box which, from its shape, *could* possibly contain nothing in the world but a copy of Leonardo's 'Last Supper'; and a copy of this very 'Last Supper,' done by Rubini the younger, at Florence, I had known, for some time, to be in the possession of Nicolino" (*Tales*, 2:925).

2. A complete list of these references can be found in the appendix.

3. Gallanti, "Mapping a National Identity," 23.

4. Benjamin, *Art in America*, 58.

5. Hirshler, "'Claiming Our Property,'" 70.

6. Manwaring, *Italian Landscape*, 54.

7. Quoted in N. Powell, *Fuseli*, 87.

8. I am grateful to Burton Pollin's notes in his edition of Mabbott's *Collected Works* for this connection.

9. N. Powell, *Fuseli*, 77.

10. Ibid., 34, 49.

11. Jowett, "Editing Shakespeare's Plays," 131.

12. See Pollin, "Edgar Allan Poe and John G. Chapman."

13. Ramsey, "Poe and Modern Art," 212.

14. See Brennan, "Turnerian Topography."

15. Wilbur, "House of Poe," 265–66.

16. Ibid., 267.

17. Renza, *Edgar Allan Poe*. See Hayes, "Retzsch's *Outlines*," for a contextual overview of Retzsch's impact on nineteenth-century readers and writers, from Shelley to Hawthorne.

18. Ibid., 32, 34.

19. Vaughan, *German Romanticism*, 128, 132.

20. Renza, *Edgar Allan Poe*, 63.

21. Reinis, *Reforming the Art of Dying*, 40.

22. D'Israeli, *Curiosities of Literature*, 96.

23. See Cantalupo, "The Lynx in Poe's 'Silence.'"

24. Sutton and Butler, "Life and Art of Jan Steen," 3.

25. Poe, *Brevities*, 385.

26. Cikovsky, "Democratic Illusionism," 39.

27. Pelizzari, "Thomas Sully," 269–70.

28. Fabian, *Mr. Sully, Portrait Painter*, 14.

29. For more information on Sully's role in the Philadelphia art scene, see ibid., 20–22.

30. Thomas, "Poe in Philadelphia," 806.

31. See Deas, *Portraits and Daguerreotypes*, esp. 120–23.

32. Ibid., 143.

33. Poe, *Writings in the "Southern Literary Messenger,"* 41.

34. *European Magazine*, 357.

35. Pollin, "Edgar Allan Poe and John G. Chapman," 246.

36. Campbell, *John Gadsby Chapman*, 13–14.

37. Chapman's aunt sold the fire screen to Bill Lewis of Little Washington, Virginia. This provenance is courtesy of Katherine Wilkins, assistant librarian at the Virginia Historical Society, where the fire screen is currently held. Email communication, June 17, 2011.

38. According to John McGuigan, the sale is entry 221 in Chapman's revised memoranda book. My thanks to Bob Mayo, whose gallery held the fire screen before it was sold to the Virginia Historical Society; he introduced me to John McGuigan, who is working on a book about Chapman. In a phone conversation in June 2011, McGuigan provided me with the details related to George Bancroft's purchase of the oil painting from Chapman.

39. Pollin, "Edgar Allan Poe and John G. Chapman," 253.

40. Ibid., 255–56.

41. Ibid., 246.

42. D. C. Miller, *Dark Eden*, 30–31.

43. Langdon, *Claude Lorrain*, 9.

44. Taylor, *America as Art*, 98.

45. Lagerlöf, *Ideal Landscape*, 17–18.

46. For a thorough overview of Cole's reputation, see Parry, *Art of Thomas Cole*.

47. Gallanti, "Mapping a National Identity," 25.

48. Renza, "'Ut Pictura Poe,'" 320.

49. Wallach, "Thomas Cole," 67.

50. See Fisher, "More Pieces in the Puzzle," for possible sources that Poe used in writing "The Assignation."

51. Quoted in Honour, "Canova's Work in Clay," 67.

52. See Poe, *Brevities*, 183, for further explication of this idea.

53. Russell, *Claude Lorrain*, 160.

54. *Academy*, 7.

55. Wallace, *Salvator Rosa*, 6.

56. Ibid., 35.

57. Ibid., 106.

Chapter 3

1. Lee, "Introduction," 11.

2. The ad is pictured in ibid.

3. Quoted in ibid., 16.

4. Ibid.

5. Ohl and Arrington, "John Maelzel." This claim is also noted in Thomas, "Poe in Philadelphia."

6. Goldstein, *Philadelphia and the China Trade*, 2.

7. Rees, *Rees's Manufacturing Industry*.

8. Wolfe, *Brandy, Balloons, and Lamps*, xiii.

9. Quoted in ibid., 7.

10. Ibid., 19.

11. Sherman, "Central Draft Burner."

12. Munger, "Sèvres Porcelain."

13. Kurland, "Aesthetic Quest," 169–70.

14. Mabbott's *Tales and Sketches* omits the latter sentence, following the version of "Landor's Cottage" that appeared in Rufus Griswold's *Works of the Late Edgar Allan Poe*. I have restored it to reflect the story's first printing in the June 9, 1849, issue of the *Flag of Our Union*.

Chapter 4

1. Saltz, "'Eyes Which Behold,'" 26n22. For other scholarship on Poe's use of Brewster's *Letters on Natural Magic*, see Scheick, "An Intrinsic Luminosity"; Pollin, "'MS. Found in a Bottle'"; and Wimsatt, "Poe and the Chess Automaton."

2. Saltz, "'Eyes Which Behold,'" 11.

3. Poe, *Brevities*, 165.

4. Crary, *Techniques of the Observer*, 2–3. See his chapter 4 for a discussion of the inventions noted above and their impact on theories of perception in the early nineteenth century.

5. Poe, *Imaginary Voyages*, 203–5.

6. Ibid., 206.

7. See Farrell, "Dream Texts"; Peirce and Rose, "Poe's Reading of Myth"; and Kopley, *Poe's "Pym."*

8. Brewster, *Letters on Natural Magic*, 50–51.

9. Thanks to Louis Renza, who made this observation in the margins of my original manuscript.

10. Cicovacki, *Anamorphosis*, 8.

11. Brewster, *Letters on Natural Magic*, 2.

12. Ibid., 5, 10–11.

13. See Castle, "Phantasmagoria," for a description of the ways in which phantasmagoria fascinated the public.

14. Quoted in Wade, *Brewster and Wheatstone*, 99.

15. Brewster, *Letters on Natural Magic*, 28.

16. Pérez-Gómez and Pelletier, *Anamorphosis*, xi–xiv.

17. Baltrušaitis, *Anamorphic Art*, 47.

18. Brewster, *Letters on Natural Magic*, 92–93.

19. Ibid., 90, 92.

20. Della Porta, *Natural Magick*, 355.

21. Moxon, *Practical Perspective*, 63.

22. Ibid., 64.

23. Hayter, *Introduction to Perspective*, 41. The full title of the manual is *An Introduction to Perspective, Drawing, and Painting in a Series of Pleasing and Familiar Dialogues Between the Author's Children; Illustrated by Appropriate Plates and Diagrams, and a Sufficiency of Practical Geometry, and A Compendium of Genuine Instruction, Comprising a Progressive and Complete Body of Information, Carefully Adapted for the Instruction of Females, and Suited Equally to the Simplicity of Youth and to Mental Maturity.*

24. See Foister, *Holbein's Ambassadors*, for a description of Holbein's painting.

25. Dupin's respect for Minister D——'s peculiar acumen "as poet *and* mathematician" reflects Poe's facility in mathematics and his chosen profession as a poet. Dupin, in describing Minister D——, says, "As poet *and* mathematician, he would reason well; as mere mathematician, he could not have reasoned at all. . . . Mathematical reasoning is merely logic applied to observation upon form and quantity. . . . Mathematical axioms are *not* axioms of general truth" (*Tales*, 2:986–87).

26. Baltrušaitis, *Anamorphic Art*, 114. See his chapter "The First Anamorphoses and Their Dissemination: Sixteenth and Seventeenth Centuries," especially for descriptions of Erhard Schön's engravings (11–36).

27. Ketterer, *Rationale of Deception*, 192.

28. Dayan, *Fables of Mind*, 181.

29. Ibid., 182, 184.

30. Baltrušaitis, *Anamorphic Art*, 121. Plottel, in "Anamorphosis in Painting and Literature," identifies anamorphosis in both "Ligeia" and "The Gold Bug" but does not interpret its implications in "Ligeia."

31. Baltrušaitis, *Anamorphic Art*, 2.

32. Poe, *Thirty-Two Stories*, 55n2.

33. Baudelaire, "Edgar Poe," 86.

34. Plottel, "Anamorphosis in Painting and Literature," 15, 16.

35. Baltrušaitis, *Anamorphic Art*, 2.

36. Dayan, *Fables of Mind*, 182.

37. Kennedy, "'Ligeia' and the Problem," 123–24.

38. Brewster, *Letters on Natural Magic*, 10.

39. Ibid., 10–11.

40. Kennedy, "'Ligeia' and the Problem," 125.

41. Basler, "Interpretation of 'Ligeia,'" 368. For an overview of other interpretations of "Ligeia," see Carlson, "Tales of Psychal Conflict," 109–12.

Chapter 5

1. Trollope, *Paris and the Parisians*, 39.

2. Spannuth, *Poe's Contributions*, 23.

3. Ibid., 23–24.

4. Ibid., 74.

5. Ibid., 41.

6. Ibid., 73.

7. Inman, "View Near Cold-Spring."

8. Ibid.

9. Cowdrey, "William Henry Bartlett," 90.

10. Gerdts, "Henry Inman Memorial Exhibition," 2.

11. *The Lake of the Dismal Swamp* was not by Henry Inman, as this quote states, but rather by John Gadsby Chapman.

12. Gerdts, "Henry Inman Memorial Exhibition," 4.

13. Spannuth, *Poe's Contributions*, 74.

14. Chaffee, "Lost and Found American Ballet Masterpieces," 18.

15. Spannuth, *Poe's Contributions*, 73.

16. Ibid., 74.

17. Lowell, "Edgar Allan Poe."

18. Pollin, "Introduction," in *Writings in the "Broadway Journal,"* x. Also see P. Miller, *The Raven and the Whale*, 126.

19. Ehrlich, *"Broadway Journal,"* xviii.

20. Cowdrey, *American Academy of Fine Arts*, 106. See also McCoy, "'I Am Right.'"

21. See Ehrlich, *"Broadway Journal,"* xii–xxxi. (Note Pollin's reservations on xxxii.)

22. McCoy, "'I Am Right,'" 19.

23. McCoy, "Mr. Poe Called upon Me," 12.

24. "Cole's Pictures of the Course of the Empire."

25. Poe, "Literati of New York City."

26. See Moss, *Poe's Literary Battles*: "Through all of Briggs's early writing, including his magazine skits, runs a hostility to New England transcendentalism more than in keeping with the New York attitude" (53).

27. Ibid., ix.

28. Cummings, *Historic Annals*, 189.

29. Joshua Shaw invented the copper percussion cap used in firearms, which was patented in the United States in 1828. See Kinard, *Pistols*: "The invention of the percussion cap was arguably the greatest single development in nineteenth-century firearms history" (53). Poe's mention of Shaw is particularly interesting because of Poe's military experience, as Hecker explains in *Private Perry and Mister Poe*. While serving at West Point, Poe was promoted to the role of artificer, readying bombs for use: "The artificer calculated the projectile's ballistic time of flight to the target to ascertain the correct fusing and charging of the round. . . . Miscalculation in any aspect of the bomb's construction potentially had catastrophic consequences for either the artificer himself or the crew firing the round" (xxxv).

30. Naeve, *150 Years of Philadelphia Painters*, 26.

31. Shaw immigrated to the United States from England when he was forty-one and lived in Philadelphia from 1819 to 1843.

32. Lester, *The Artist, the Merchant*, 2:155.

33. Lynch, *Poems*, 24.

34. "A True Work of Art."

35. Cummings, *Historic Annals*, 189.

36. Poe, *Writings in the "Broadway Journal,"* 2:226.

37. My thanks to Chris Sempter of the Poe Museum in Richmond for sharing the manuscript "A Young Girl's Recollection of Edgar Allan Poe," by Elma Mary Letchworth (née Gove), with me by email (July 1, 2013). I heard his talk "A Young Girl's Recollections of Edgar Allan Poe" at the Positively Poe Conference on June 24, 2013.

38. Poe, *Eureka*, 106.

Bibliography

Academy: A Record of Literature, Learning, Science, and Art 3, no. 39 (1872).

Achilles, Jochen. "Edgar Allan Poe's Dreamscapes and the Transcendentalist View of Nature." *Amerikastudien / American Studies* 40, no. 4 (1995): 553–73.

Adams, Jane. "A Study of Art Unions in the United States of America in the Nineteenth Century." Master's thesis, Virginia Commonwealth University, 1990.

Avery, Kevin. *American Drawings and Watercolors in The Metropolitan Museum of Art*. New Haven: Yale University Press, 2002.

Bachinger, Katrina. "The Aesthetics of (Not) Keeping in Step: Reading the Consumer Mobocracy of Poe's 'The Devil in the Belfry' Against Peacock." *Modern Language Quarterly* 51, no. 4 (1990): 513–33.

Baigell, Matthew. *Thomas Cole*. New York: Watson-Guptill, 1981.

Baltrušaitis, Jurgis. *Anamorphic Art*. Translated by W. J. Strachan. New York: Harry N. Abrams, 1976.

Basler, Roy. "The Interpretation of 'Ligeia.'" *College English* 5, no. 7 (1944): 363–72.

Baudelaire, Charles. "Edgar Poe: His Life and Works." In *The Unknown Poe*, edited and translated by Raymond Foye, 79–91. San Francisco: City Lights, 1980.

Baym, Nina. "The Function of Poe's Pictorialism." *South Atlantic Quarterly* 65 (1966): 46–54.

Bender, Thomas. *New York Intellect: A History of Intellectual Life in New York City, from 1750 to the Beginnings of Our Own Time*. New York: Alfred A. Knopf, 1987.

Benjamin, S. G. W. *Art in America: A Critical and Historical Sketch*. New York: Harper and Brothers, 1880.

Benton, Richard P. "Poe's Acquaintance with Chinese Literature." *Poe Newsletter* 2, no. 2 (1969): 34.

Berman, Jacob. "Domestic Terror and Poe's Arabesque Interior." *English Studies in Canada* 31, no. 1 (2005): 128–50.

Biddle, Edward, and Mantle Fielding. *The Life and Works of Thomas Sully (1783–1872)*. Philadelphia: Kessinger, 1921.

Boucher, Bruce, ed. *Earth and Fire: Italian Terracotta Sculpture from Donatello to Canova*. New Haven: Yale University Press, 2001.

Brennan, Matthew. "Turnerian Topography: The Paintings of Roderick Usher." *Studies in Short Fiction* 27, no. 4 (1990): 605–8.

Brewster, David. *Letters on Natural Magic*. London: J. Murray, 1832.

Broadway Journal. 2 vols. 1845. New York: AMS Press, 1965.

Brooks, Cleanth. "Edgar Allan Poe as Interior Decorator." *Ventures* 8, no. 2 (1968): 41–46.

Budd, Henry. "Thomas Sully." *Pennsylvania Magazine of History and Biography* 42, no. 2 (1918): 97–126.

Burns, Sarah. *Painting the Dark Side: Art and the Gothic Imagination in Nineteenth-Century America*. Berkeley: University of California Press, 2004.

Burton's Gentleman's Magazine and American Monthly Review. Vol. 6. Philadelphia: William E. Burton, 1840.

Burwick, Frederick. "Edgar Allan Poe: The Sublime, the Picturesque, the Grotesque, and the Arabesque." *Amerikastudien / American Studies* 43, no. 3 (1998): 423–36.

Campbell, William. *John Gadsby Chapman.* Washington, D.C.: Smithsonian Institution Press, 1962.

Cantalupo, Barbara. "Interview with Burton Pollin." *Edgar Allan Poe Review* 2, no. 2 (2001): 98–120.

———. "Interview with Jefferson Moak." *Edgar Allan Poe Review* 8, no. 2 (2007): 92–98.

———. "The Lynx in Poe's 'Silence.'" *Poe Studies / Dark Romanticism* 28, nos. 1–2 (2009): 1–4.

Carlson, Eric. "Tales of Psychal Conflict: 'Berenice,' 'Morella,' 'Ligeia.'" In *A Companion to Poe Studies*, edited by Eric Carlson, 168–87. Westport, Conn.: Greenwood Press, 1996.

Castle, Terry. "Phantasmagoria: Spectral Technology and the Metaphorics of Modern Reverie." *Critical Inquiry* 15, no. 1 (1988): 26–61.

Caust-Ellenbogen, Celia. "Pennsylvania Hall Association." Quakers and Slavery Project, Haverford and Swarthmore Colleges. http://trilogy.brynmawr.edu/speccoll/quakersandslavery/commentary/organizations/pennsylvania_hall.php.

Chaffee, George. "Lost and Found American Ballet Masterpieces: The Inman-Sully Fanny Elssler." The Ballettophile. *Dance Magazine*, December 1947, 16–19.

Chamberlain, Georgia Stamm. *Studies on John Gadsby Chapman.* Alexandria, Va.: Robert S. Chamberlain, 1963.

Cicovacki, Predrag. *Anamorphosis: Kant on Knowledge and Ignorance.* New York: University Press of America, 1997.

Cikovsky, Nicolai. "Democratic Illusionism." In *America: The New World in Nineteenth-Century Painting*, edited by Stephan Koja, 33–41. Munich: Prestel Verlag, 1999.

Clark, H. Nichols. *Francis W. Edmonds: American Master in the Dutch Tradition.* Washington, D.C.: Smithsonian Institution Press, 1988.

Cole, Thomas. "Proceedings of the American Lyceum: Essay on American Scenery." *American Monthly Magazine* 7 (January 1836): 1–12.

"Cole's Pictures of the Course of the Empire." *American Monthly Magazine* 8 (November 1836): 513–15.

Cowdrey, Mary Bartlett. *American Academy of Fine Arts and American Art-Union: Introduction, 1816–1852.* New York: New-York Historical Society, 1953.

———. "William Henry Bartlett and the American Scene." *New York History* 2, no. 4 (1941): 380–400.

Crary, Jonathan. *Techniques of the Observer: On Vision and Modernity in the Nineteenth Century.* Boston: MIT Press, 1992.

Craven, Wayne. "Luman Reed, Patron: His Collection and Gallery." *American Art Journal* 12, no. 2 (1980): 40–59.

Cross, Joseph. "To the Editor." *Northern Christian Advocate*, 1845, 150.

Cummings, Thomas S. *Historic Annals of the National Academy of Design.* 1865. New York: Da Capo Press, 1969.

Dameron, Lasley. "Poe, 'Simplicity,' and *Blackwood's Magazine*." *Mississippi Quarterly* 51, no. 2 (1998): 233–42.

Danly, Susan. *Telling Tales: Nineteenth-Century Narrative Painting from the Collection of the Pennsylvania Academy of the Fine Arts.* Philadelphia: American Federation of Arts, 1991.

Dayan, Joan. *Fables of Mind: An Inquiry into Poe's Fiction*. New York: Oxford University Press, 1987.

Dearinger, David. "Asher B. Durand and Henry Kirke Brown: An Artistic Friendship." *American Art Journal* 20, no. 3 (1988): 74–88.

———. "An Introduction to the History of American Art Criticism to 1925." In *Rave Reviews: American Art and Its Critics, 1826–1925*, edited by David Dearinger, 17–29. New York: National Academy of Design, 2000.

———. "Nineteenth-Century Sculpture from the National Academy of Design." *Resource Library*, August 2004. http://www.tfaoi.com/aa/4aa/4aa554.htm.

———. *Paintings and Sculpture in the Collection of the National Academy of Design*. Vol. 1. New York: Hudson Mills Press, 2004.

———, ed. *Rave Reviews: American Art and Its Critics, 1826–1925*. New York: National Academy of Design, 2000.

Dearinger, David, and Elizabeth Barry. "Reviews of the Annual Exhibitions of the National Academy of Design, 1826–1925." In *Rave Reviews: American Art and Its Critics, 1826–1925*, edited by David Dearinger, 277–99. New York: National Academy of Design, 2000.

Deas, Michael J. *The Portraits and Daguerreotypes of Edgar Allan Poe*. Charlottesville: University of Virginia Press, 1988.

della Porta, John Baptista. *Natural Magick*. Edited by Derek J. Price. Facsimile edition of the 1658 English translation. New York: Basic Books, 1957.

Dictionary of National Biography. Vol. 53. Edited by Sidney Lee. New York: Macmillan, 1898.

D'Israeli, Israel. *Curiosities of Literature, First Series*. New York: William Pearson, 1835.

Downing, A. Jackson. *A Treatise on the Theory and Practice of Landscape Gardening, Adapted to North America*. New York: A. O. Moore, 1859.

Durand, John. *The Life and Times of A. B. Durand*. New York: Da Capo Press, 1970.

Ehrlich, Heyward. "*The Broadway Journal* (1): Briggs's Dilemma and Poe's Strategy." In *Writings in the "Broadway Journal": Nonfictional Prose*. Pt. 2, *The Annotations*. Volume 4 of *Collected Writings of Edgar Allan Poe*, edited by Burton Pollin, xii–xxxi. New York: Gordian Press, 1986.

———. "Charles Frederick Briggs and Lowell's *Fable for Critics*." *Modern Language Quarterly* 28, no. 3 (1967): 329–41.

European Magazine and London Review: Literature, History, Biography, Politics, Arts, Manners, and Amusements of the Age. Vol. 83. London: Lupton Relfe, 1823.

Fabian, Monroe H. *Mr. Sully, Portrait Painter*. Washington, D.C.: Smithsonian Institution Press, 1983.

Falk, Peter Hastings, ed. *The Annual Exhibition Record of the Pennsylvania Academy of the Fine Arts*. 3 vols. Madison, Conn.: Sound View Press, 1989.

Farrell, Grace. "Dream Texts: *The Narrative of Arthur Gordon Pym* and *The Journal of Julius Rodman*." In *A Companion to Poe Studies*, edited by Eric W. Carlson, 209–35. Westport, Conn.: Greenwood Press, 1996.

Fisher, Benjamin Franklin, IV. "More Pieces in the Puzzle of Poe's 'The Assignation.'" In *Myths and Reality: The Mysterious Mr. Poe*, edited by Benjamin Franklin Fisher IV, 59–88. Baltimore: Edgar Allan Poe Society, 1987.

Foister, Susan, Ashok Roy, and Martin Wyld. *Holbein's Ambassadors: Making and Meaning*. New Haven: Yale University Press, 1997.

Forshay, Ella. *Mr. Luman Reed's Picture Gallery: A Pioneer Collection of American Art*. New York: Harry N. Abrams, 1990.

Furrow, Sharon. "Psyche and Setting: Poe's Picturesque Landscapes." *Criticism* 15, no. 1 (1973): 16–27.

Gallanti, Barbara. "Mapping a National Identity: American Painting Before the Civil War." In *America: The New World in Nineteenth-Century Painting*, edited by Stephan Koja, 23–31. Munich: Prestel Verlag, 1999.

Gerdts, Abigail Booth. "Newly Discovered Records of the New-York Gallery of the Fine Arts." *Archives of American Art Journal* 21, no. 4 (1981): 2–9.

Gerdts, William H. *The Art of Henry Inman*. Washington, D.C.: National Portrait Gallery, Smithsonian Institution, 1987.

———. *The Great American Nude: A History in Art*. New York: Praeger, 1974.

———. "Henry Inman: Genre Painter." *American Art Journal* 9, no. 1 (1977): 26–48.

———. "The Henry Inman Memorial Exhibition of 1846." *Archives of American Art Journal* 14, no. 2 (1974): 2.

Glanvill, Joseph. *Saducismus Triumphatus*. Gainesville: Scholars Facsimiles, 1966.

Goldbaek, Henning. "Poe and Cooper: A Comparison, Between an American Democrat and a Southern Gentleman." Paper presented at the 11th Cooper Seminar, "James Fenimore Cooper: His Country and His Art," State University of New York College at Oneonta, July 1997.

Goldstein, Jonathan. *Philadelphia and the China Trade, 1682–1846: Commercial, Cultural, and Attitudinal Effects*. University Park: Pennsylvania State University Press, 1978.

Gordon, Margaret. *The Home Life of Sir David Brewster*. Edinburgh: Edmonston and Douglas, 1870.

Hayes, Kevin. *Edgar Allan Poe in Context*. Cambridge: Cambridge University Press, 2012.

———. "One-Man Modernist." In *The Cambridge Companion to Edgar Allan Poe*, edited by Kevin Hayes, 225–40. Cambridge: Cambridge University Press, 2002.

———. "Retzsch's *Outlines* and Poe's 'The Man of the Crowd.'" *Gothic Studies* 12, no. 2 (2010): 29–41.

———. "Visual Culture and the Word in Edgar Allan Poe's 'The Man of the Crowd.'" *Nineteenth-Century Literature* 56, no. 4 (2002): 445–65.

Hayter, Charles. *An Introduction to Perspective, Drawing, and Painting*. London: Black, Kingsbury, Parbury, and Allen, 1820.

Heath, Charles. *Heath's Picturesque Annual for 1832: Travelling Sketches in the North of Italy, the Tyrol, and on the Rhine. With Twenty Six Beautifully Finished Engravings from Drawings by Clarkson Stanfield*. London: Longman, Rees, Orme, Brown, and Green, 1832.

Hecker, William. *Private Perry and Mister Poe: The West Point Poems, 1831*. Baton Rouge: Louisiana State University Press, 2005.

Hess, Jeffrey A. "Sources and Aesthetics of Poe's Landscape Fiction." *American Quarterly* 22, no. 2 (1970): 177–89.

Hirshler, Erica E. "'Claiming Our Property Wherever We Find It': American Art After 1865." In *America: The New World in Nineteenth-Century Painting*, edited by Stephan Koja, 43–51. Munich: Prestel Verlag, 1999.

"History and Timeline." Pennsylvania Academy of the Fine Arts. http://www.pafa.org/museum/Research-Archives/History-and-Timeline/59/.

"History of the Museum and School." National Academy Museum. http://www.nationalacademy.org/about-us/history/.

Hoffman, Daniel. *Poe Poe Poe Poe Poe Poe Poe.* 1972. Baton Rouge: Louisiana State University Press, 1998.

Homberger, Eric. *Scenes from the Life of a City: Corruption and Conscience in Old New York.* New Haven: Yale University Press, 1994.

Hone, Philip. *Diary, 1828–1851.* Edited by Allen Nevans. Vol. 2. New York: Dodd, Mead, 1927.

Honour, Hugh. "Canova's Work in Clay." In *Earth and Fire: Italian Terracotta Sculpture from Donatello or Canova*, edited by Bruce Boucher, 69–81. New Haven: Yale University Press, 2001.

Howat, John K. *Frederic Church.* New Haven: Yale University Press, 2005.

Inman, John. "View Near Cold-Spring." *Columbian Lady's and Gentleman's Magazine*, July 1844, 43.

"Ivory Crucifix." *Catholic Telegraph* 14, no. 42 (1845): 335.

Jacobs, Robert D. *The Courage of a Critic: Edgar Poe as Editor.* Baltimore: Edgar Allan Poe Society of Baltimore, 1971.

———. *Poe: Journalist and Critic.* Baton Rouge: Louisiana State University Press, 1969.

———. "Poe's Earthly Paradise." *American Quarterly* 12, no. 3 (1960): 404–13.

Johnson, Deborah J. "William Sidney Mount: Painter of American Life." In *William Sidney Mount: Painter of American Life*, edited by Deborah J. Johnson, 17–108. New York: American Federation of Arts, 1998.

Jowett, John. "Editing Shakespeare's Plays in the Twentieth Century." In *Editing Shakespeare*, edited by Peter Holland, 1–19. Shakespeare Survey 59. Cambridge: Cambridge University Press, 2006.

Kasson, Joy S. "The Voyage of Life: Thomas Cole and Romantic Disillusionment." *American Quarterly* 27, no. 1 (1975): 42–56.

Kehler, Joel R. "New Light on the Genesis and Progress of Poe's Landscape Fiction." *American Literature* 47 (1975): 173–83.

Kelly, Franklin. "Nineteenth-Century Collections of American Paintings." In *America: The New World in Nineteenth-Century Painting*, edited by Stephan Koja, 194–99. Munich: Prestel Verlag, 1999.

Kelly, George. "Poe's Theory of Beauty." *American Literature* 27, no. 4 (1956): 521–36.

Kennedy, J. Gerald. "'Ligeia' and the Problem of Dying Women." In *New Essays on Poe's Major Tales*, edited by Kenneth Silverman, 113–29. Cambridge: Cambridge University Press, 1993.

Ketterer, David. *The Rationale of Deception in Poe.* Baton Rouge: Louisiana State University Press, 1979.

Keyes, Donald. "The Daguerreotype's Popularity in America." *Art Journal* 36, no. 2 (1976–77): 116–22.

Kinard, Jeff. *Pistols: An Illustrated History of Their Impact.* Santa Barbara: ABC-CLIO, 2003.

Klein, Rachel. "Art and Authority in Antebellum New York City: The Rise and Fall of the American Art-Union." *Journal of American History* 81, no. 4 (1995): 1534–61.

Kopley, Richard. *Poe's "Pym": Critical Explorations.* Durham: Duke University Press, 1992.

Kurland, Sydney. "The Aesthetic Quest of Thomas Cole and Edgar Allan Poe: Correspondences in Their Thought and Practice in Relation to Their Time." Ph.D. diss., Ohio University, 1976.

Lagerlöf, Margaretha Rossholm. *Ideal Landscape: Annibale Carracci, Nicolas Poussin, and Claude Lorrain.* New Haven: Yale University Press, 1990.

Langdon, Helen. *Claude Lorrain.* Oxford: Phaidon, 1989.

———. "Salvator Rosa and Claude." *Burlington Magazine* 115, no. 849 (1973): 778–85.

Lee, Jean Gordon. "Introduction: Philadelphians and the China Trade." In *Philadelphians and the China Trade, 1784–1844*, edited by Jean Gordon Lee, 11–19. Philadelphia: University of Pennsylvania Press, 1984.

Lester, C. Edwards. *The Artist, the Merchant, and the Statesman, of the Age of Medici, and of Our Times*. 2 vols. New York: Paine and Burgess, 1845.

———. "Henry Inman." In *The Artists of America: A Series of Biographical Sketches of American Artists; with Portraits and Designs on Steel*, 34–64. New York: Baker and Scribner, 1846.

Lewis, E. Anna. "Felix O. C. Darley." *Home Journal*, August 5, 1854, 37.

Ljungquist, Kent. *The Grand and the Fair: Poe's Landscape Aesthetics and Pictorial Techniques*. Potomac, Md.: Scripta Humanistica, 1984.

Lowell, James Russell. "Edgar Allan Poe." *Graham's Magazine* 27 (February 1845): 49–53.

"The Lower Part of the City in Ruins—Millions of Property Destroyed." *New-York Mirror: A Reflex of the News, Literature, Arts, and Elegancies of Our Time*, July 26, 1845, 1.

Luhrs, Kathleen. "Museum Accessions." *The Magazine Antiques*, November 2008, 36–38.

Lynch, Anne C. *Poems*. New York: George P. Putnam, 1848.

Lynes, Russell. *The Tastemakers: The Shaping of American Popular Taste*. New York: Dover, 1949.

Mackay, Mary Alice. "Sketch Club Drawings for Byron's 'Darkness' and Scott's 'Lay of the Last Minstrel.'" *Master Drawings* 35, no. 2 (1997): 142–54.

Mann, Maybelle. *The American Art-Union*. Otisville, N.Y.: ALM Associates, 1977.

———. *Francis William Edmonds*. Washington, D.C.: International Exhibitions Foundation, 1975.

Manwaring, Elizabeth. *Italian Landscape in Eighteenth-Century England: A Study Chiefly of the Influence of Claude Lorrain and Salvator Rosa on English Taste, 1700–1800*. New York: Oxford University Press, 1925.

Marryat, Captain R. N. *The Naval Annual, or Stories of the Sea for M.DCCC.XXXVI*. Philadelphia: DeSilver, Thomas, 1836.

Martinez, Katharine, and Page Talbott, eds. *Philadelphia's Cultural Landscape: The Sartain Family Legacy*. Philadelphia: Temple University Press, 2000.

Matheson, T. J. "Poe's 'The Black Cat' as a Critique of Temperance Literature." *Mosaic: A Journal for the Interdisciplinary Study of Literature* 19, no. 3 (1986): 69–81.

McCoy, Garnett. "'I Am Right and You Are Wrong': Letters of Advice to an Artist of the 1840s." *Archives of American Art Journal* 28, no. 4 (1988): 15–21.

———. "'Mr. Poe Called upon Me . . .'" *Archives of American Art Journal* 4, no. 4 (1964): 10–12.

Miller, Angela. *The Empire of the Eye: Landscape Representation and American Cultural Politics, 1825–1875*. Ithaca: Cornell University Press, 1993.

Miller, David C. *Dark Eden: The Swamp in Nineteenth-Century American Culture*. Cambridge: Cambridge University Press, 1989.

Miller, F. DeWolfe. "The Basis for Poe's 'The Island of the Fay.'" *American Literature* 14, no. 2 (1942): 135–40.

Miller, Linda. "Poe on the Beat: 'Doings of Gotham' as Urban, Penny Press Journalism." *Journal of the Early Republic* 7, no. 2 (1987): 147–65.

Miller, Perry. *The Raven and the Whale: Poe, Melville, and the New York Literary Scene*. Baltimore: Johns Hopkins University Press, 1956.

Moldenhauer, Joseph J. "Beyond the Tamarind Tree: A New Poe Letter." *American Literature* 42, no. 4 (1971): 468–77.

Moore, Lillian. "Found! A Lost Masterpiece—the Inman Elssler." *Dance Magazine*, December 1949, 14.

Moss, Sidney. *Poe's Literary Battles: The Critic in the Context of His Literary Milieu*. Carbondale: Southern Illinois University Press, 1963.

Moxon, Joseph. *Practical Perspective or Perspective Made Easy, Teaching By the Opticks, How to Delineate all Bodies, Buildings, or Landskips, &c, By Catoptricks, How to Delineate confused Appearances, so as when seen in a Mirror of Pollisht Body of any intended shape, the reflection shall shew a Designe, By the Dioptircks, How to draw parts of many Figures into one, when seen through a Glass or Christal cut into many Faces, Useful for all Painters, Engravers, Architects, &c. and all others that are any waies inclined to Speculatory Ingenuity*. London: Joseph Moxon, 1670.

Munger, Jeffrey. "Sèvres Porcelain in the Nineteenth Century." In *Heilbrunn Timeline of Art History*. New York: Metropolitan Museum of Art, 2000–. http://www.metmuseum.org/toah/hd/sevr/hd_sevr.htm.

Myers, Kenneth John. "The Public Display of Art in New York City, 1664–1914." In *Rave Reviews: American Art and Its Critics, 1826–1925*, edited by David Dearinger, 31–51. New York: National Academy of Design, 2000.

Myrone, Martin. *Gothic Nightmares: Fuseli, Blake, and the Romantic Imagination*. New York: Tate, 2006.

Naeve, Milo. *150 Years of Philadelphia Painters and Paintings: Selections for the Sewell C. Biggs Museum of American Art*. Philadelphia: Library Company of Philadelphia, 1999.

National Academy Museum and School. http://www.nationalacademy.org/museum/.

National Academy of Design Exhibition Record, 1826–1860. 2 vols. New York: New-York Historical Society, 1943.

Novak, Barbara. *American Painting of the Nineteenth Century: Realism, Idealism, and the American Experience*. 3rd ed. Oxford: Oxford University Press, 2007.

———. *Nature and Culture: American Landscape and Painting, 1825–1875*. New York: Oxford University Press, 1980.

Ohl, John F., and Joseph Earl Arrington. "John Maelzel, Master Showman of Automata and Panoramas." *Pennsylvania Magazine of History and Biography* 84, no. 1 (1960): 56–92.

Olson, Amanda. "Facing Celebrity in America: Thomas Sully's Theatrical Portraits of Fanny Kemble." Master's thesis, Southern Methodist University, 2008.

Osipova, Elvira. "Aesthetic Effects of 'King Pest' and 'The Masque of the Red Death.'" *Edgar Allan Poe Review* 8, no. 2 (2007): 25–33.

O'Toole, Judith Hansen. *Different Views in Hudson River School Painting*. New York: Columbia University Press, 2005.

Parry, Ellwood C. *The Art of Thomas Cole: Ambition and Imagination*. Newark: University of Delaware Press, 1988.

Parshall, Linda. "Hirschfeld, Pückler, Poe: The Literary Modeling of Nature." *German Historical Institute Bulletin Supplement* 4 (2007): 149–69.

Parsons, Coleman O. Introduction to *Saducismus Triumphatus*, by Joseph Glanvill, i–xxiv. Gainesville: Scholars Facsimiles, 1966.

Peeples, Scott. *The Afterlife of Edgar Allan Poe*. Rochester: Camden House, 2004.

Peirce, Carol, and Alexander G. Rose. "Poe's Reading of Myth: The White Vision of *Arthur Gordon Pym*." In *Poe's "Pym": Critical Explorations*, edited by Richard Kopley, 57–74. Durham: Duke University Press, 1992.

Pelizzari, Maria Antonella. "Thomas Sully." In *America: The New World in Nineteenth-Century Painting*, edited by Stephan Koja, 269–70. Munich: Prestel Verlag, 1999.

Pérez-Gómez, Alberto, and Louise Pelletier. *Anamorphosis: An Annotated Bibliography*. Montreal: McGill University Press, 1995.

"Philadelphia Academy." *New-York Mirror*, June 21, 1845, 120.

Phillips, H. Wells. "Poe's Usher: Precursor of Abstract Art." *Poe Studies* 5, no. 1 (1972): 14–16.

Pickering, T. C. *Painting: Its Rise and Progress from the Earliest Ages to the Present Time*. Boston: John P. Jewett, 1846.

Piggush, Yvette. "Visualizing Early American Art Audiences: The Pennsylvania Academy of Fine Arts and Allston's *Dead Man Restored*." *Early American Studies: An Interdisciplinary Journal* 9, no. 3 (2011): 716–47.

Plottel, Jeanine. "Anamorphosis in Painting and Literature." *Yearbook of Comparative and General Literature* 28 (1979): 10–19.

Poe, Edgar Allan. *The Brevities: Pinakidia, Marginalia, and Other Works*. Volume 2 of *Collected Writings of Edgar Allan Poe*. Edited by Burton Pollin. New York: Gordian Press, 1985.

———. *The Collected Letters of Edgar Allan Poe*. Edited by John Ward Ostrom, Burton R. Pollin, and Jeffrey Savoye. 2 vols. 1948. New York: Gordian Press, 2008.

———. *Complete Poems*. Edited by Thomas Ollive Mabbott. 1969. Urbana: University of Illinois Press, 2000.

———. *Complete Works of Edgar Allan Poe*. Edited by James A. Harrison. 18 vols. New York: AMS Press, 1965.

———. *Eureka*. Edited by Stuart Levine and Susan Levine. Urbana: University of Illinois Press, 2004.

———. *The Imaginary Voyages: "The Narrative of Arthur Gordon Pym," "The Unparalleled Adventure of One Hans Pfaall," "The Journal of Julius Rodman."* Volume 1 of *Collected Writings of Edgar Allan Poe*. Edited by Burton Pollin. New York: Gordian Press, 1981.

———. "Letter to B———." In *Critical Theory: The Major Documents*, edited by Stuart Levine and Susan F. Levine, 1–19. Urbana: University of Illinois Press, 2009.

———. "The Literati of New York City: Some Honest Opinions at Random Respecting Their Autorial Merits, with Occasional Works of Personality." *Godey's Lady's Book*, May 1846, 194–201.

———. "The Philosophy of Composition." In *Critical Theory: The Major Documents*, edited by Stuart Levine and Susan F. Levine, 55–76. Urbana: University of Illinois Press, 2009.

———. *Tales and Sketches*. 2 vols. Edited by Thomas Ollive Mabbott. 1978. Urbana: University of Illinois Press, 2000.

———. *Thirty-Two Stories*. Edited by Stuart Levine and Susan F. Levine. Cambridge, Mass.: Hackett, 2000.

———. *Writings in the "Broadway Journal": Nonfictional Prose*. Pt. 1, *The Text*. Volume 3 of *Collected Writings of Edgar Allan Poe*. Edited by Burton Pollin. New York: Gordian Press, 1986.

———. *Writings in the "Southern Literary Messenger": Nonfictional Prose*. Volume 5 of *Collected Writings of Edgar Allan Poe*. Edited by Burton Pollin. New York: Gordian Press, 1997.

Pollin, Burton. "Edgar Allan Poe and John G. Chapman: Their Treatment of the Dismal Swamp and the Wissahickon." *Studies in the American Renaissance*, 1983, 245–74.

———. *Images of Poe's Works: A Comprehensive Descriptive Catalogue of Illustrations*. New York: Greenwood Press, 1989.

———. "'MS. Found in a Bottle' and Sir David Brewster's *Letters*: A Source." *Poe Studies* 15, no. 2 (1982): 40–41.

———. "New York City in the Tales of Poe." *Bronx County Historical Society Journal* 2, no. 1 (1965): 16–22.

———. "Poe in Art, Music, and Dance." In *A Companion to Poe Studies*, edited by Eric W. Carlson, 494–517. Westport, Conn.: Greenwood Press, 1996.

———. "*Undine* in the Works of Poe." *Studies in Romanticism* 14, no. 1 (1975): 59–74.

———. "When Is a Church Not a Church?" *Edgar Allan Poe Review* 5, no. 1 (2004): 47–56.

———. *Writings in the "Broadway Journal": Nonfictional Prose.* Pt. 2, *The Annotations.* Volume 4 of *Collected Writings of Edgar Allan Poe.* New York: Gordian Press, 1986.

Powell, Earl A. *Thomas Cole.* New York: Harry N. Abrams, 1990.

Powell, Nicolas. *Fuseli: "The Nightmare."* Art in Context. New York: Viking Press, 1972.

Quinn, Patrick. *Edgar Allan Poe: A Critical Biography.* New York: Appleton-Century-Crofts, 1941.

Rainwater, Catherine. "Poe's Landscape Tales and the 'Picturesque' Tradition." *Southern Literary Journal* 16, no. 2 (1984): 30–41.

Ramsey, Paul. "Poe and Modern Art: An Essay on Correspondences." *College Art Journal* 18, no. 3 (1959): 210–15.

Rees, Abraham. *Rees's Manufacturing Industry (1819–20).* Vol. 3, *A Selection from "The Cyclopaedia, or Universal Dictionary of Arts, Sciences, and Literature."* Edited by Neil Cossons. Trowbridge, Wiltshire: David and Charles Reprints, 1972.

Reinis, Austra. *Reforming the Art of Dying: The "Ars Moriendi" in the German Reformation (1519–1528).* Aldershot, Hampshire: Ashgate, 2007.

Renza, Louis. *Edgar Allan Poe, Wallace Stevens, and the Poetics of American Privacy.* Baton Rouge: Louisiana State University Press, 2002.

———. "'Ut Pictura Poe': Poetic Politics in 'The Island of the Fay' and 'Morning on the Wissahiccon.'" In *The American Face of Edgar Allan Poe*, edited by Shawn Rosenheim and Stephen Rachman, 305–29. Baltimore: Johns Hopkins University Press, 1995.

Rosand, David. *The Invention of Painting in America.* New York: Columbia University Press, 2004.

Russell, H. Diane. *Claude Lorrain, 1600–1682.* New York: George Braziller, 1982.

Rutledge, Anna Wells. *Cumulative Record of Exhibition Catalogues: The Pennsylvania Academy of the Fine Arts, 1807–1870; the Society of Artists, 1800–1814; the Artists' Fund Society, 1835–1845.* Philadelphia: American Philosophical Society, 1955.

Saltz, Laura. "'Eyes Which Behold': Poe's 'Domain of Arnheim' and the Science of Vision." *Edgar Allan Poe Review* 7, no. 1 (2006): 4–30.

Sanford, Charles L. "Edgar Allan Poe: A Blight upon the Landscape." *American Quarterly* 20, no. 1 (1968): 54–66.

Scheick, William J. "An Intrinsic Luminosity: Poe's Use of Platonic and Newtonian Optics." In *American Literature and Science*, edited by Robert J. Scholnick, 77–93. Lexington: University Press of Kentucky, 1992.

Schuyler, David. *Apostle of Taste: Andrew Jackson Downing, 1815–1852.* Baltimore: Johns Hopkins University Press, 1996.

Sempter, Chris. "A Young Girl's Recollections of Edgar Allan Poe." Paper presented at the Positively Poe Conference, University of Virginia, June 24, 2013.

Sharp, Roberta. "Poe's Chapters on 'Natural Magic.'" In *Poe and His Times: The Artist and His Milieu*, edited by Benjamin Franklin Fisher, 154–66. Baltimore: Edgar Allan Poe Society, 1990.

Sherman, Mimi. "The Central Draft Burner: Ami Argand's Contribution to the American Home." *Encyclopedia of Earth.* http://www.eoearth.org/view/article/158703.

Silverman, Kenneth. *Edgar A. Poe: Mournful and Never-Ending Remembrance*. New York: HarperCollins, 1991.

Simpson, Marc. *The Rockefeller Collection of American Art at the Fine Arts Museums of San Francisco*. New York: Harry N. Abrams, 1994.

Soria, Regina. "Washington Allston's Lectures on Art: The First American Art Treatise." *Journal of Aesthetics and Art Criticism* 18, no. 3 (March 1960): 329–44.

Spannuth, Jacob. *Poe's Contributions to "The Columbia Spy": Doings of Gotham by Edgar Allan Poe*. Pottsville, Pa.: Jacob Spannuth, 1929.

Sperling, Joy. "'Art, Cheap and Good': The Art Union in England and the United States, 1840–60." *Nineteenth-Century Art Worldwide* 1, no. 1 (2002).

Stern, Madeleine. "The House of Expanding Doors: Anne Lynch's Soireés, 1846." *New York History* 23 (January 1942): 42–51.

Stokes, I. N. Phelps. *The Iconography of Manhattan Island, 1498–1909*. 6 vols. 1915–28. New York: Arno Press, 1967.

Stone, William. *History of New York City*. New York: Virtue and Yarston, 1872.

Strong, George Templeton. *Diary*. New York: Macmillan, 1952.

Sutton, Peter C., and Marigene H. Butler. "The Life and Art of Jan Steen." *Philadelphia Art Bulletin* 78, nos. 337/338 (1982–83): 3–63.

Sweeney, J. Gray. "'Endued with Rare Genius': Frederic Edwin Church's *To the Memory of Cole*." *Smithsonian Studies in American Art* 2, no. 1 (1988): 45–71.

Taylor, Joshua C. *America as Art*. Washington, D.C.: Smithsonian Institution Press, 1976.

Thomas, Dwight. "Poe in Philadelphia, 1838–1844." Ph.D. diss., University of Pennsylvania, 1978.

Thomas, Dwight, and David K. Jackson. *The Poe Log: A Documentary Life of Edgar Allan Poe, 1809–1849*. Boston: G. K. Hall, 1987.

Thompson, G. R. "The Face in the Pool: Reflections on the Doppelgänger Motif in 'The Fall of the House of Usher.'" *Poe Studies* 5, no. 1 (1972): 16–21.

Thornbury, Walter. *The Life of J. M. W. Turner, R. A., with Illustrations, Facsimiled in Colours, from Turner's Original Drawings*. New York: Holt, 1877.

Transactions of the American Art Union, for the Year 1845. New York: Office of the *Evening Post*, 1845.

Trollope, Frances. *Paris and the Parisians in 1835*. New York: Harper and Brothers, 1836.

"A True Work of Art." *American Review: A Whig Journal of Politics, Literature, Art, and Science* 2, no. 1 (1845): 12.

Tuerk, Richard. "John Sartain and E. A. Poe." *Poe Studies* 4, no. 2 (1971): 21–23.

Vaughan, William. *German Romanticism and English Art*. New Haven: Yale University Press, 1979.

Verdi, Richard. "Poussin's 'Deluge': The Aftermath." *Burlington Magazine* 123, no. 940 (1981): 388–401.

Wade, Nicholas, ed. *Brewster and Wheatstone on Vision*. London: Academic Press, 1983.

Wallace, Richard W. *Salvator Rosa in America*. Wellesley: Wellesley College Museum, 1979.

Wallach, Alan. "'This Is the Reward of Patronising the Arts': A Letter from Robert Gilmor, Jr., to Jonathan Meredith, April 2, 1844." *American Art Journal* 21, no. 4 (1989): 76–77.

———. "Thomas Cole: Landscape and the Course of American Empire." In *Thomas Cole: Landscape into History*, edited by William H. Truettner and Alan Wallach, 23–111. New Haven: Yale University Press, 1994.

Walters, C. T. "'The Philosophy of Furniture' and Poe's Aesthetics of Fictional Design." *Edgar Allan Poe Review* 5, no. 1 (2004): 57–79.

Warner, Marina. "Spirit Visions." Lecture delivered at the Tanner Lectures on Human Values, Yale University, October 20 and 21, 1999. Available at http://tannerlectures.utah.edu/_documents/a-to-z/w/Warner_01.pdf.

Webb, Samuel. *History of Pennsylvania Hall Which Was Destroyed by a Mob, on the 17th of May, 1838.* Philadelphia: Merrihew and Gunn, 1838.

Weidman, Bette. "Charles Frederick Briggs: A Critical Biography." Ph.D. diss., Columbia University, 1968.

Weigley, Russell Frank, ed. *Philadelphia: A 300-Year History.* New York: W. W. Norton, 1982.

Weisman, Morris. "Story and Webster—And the Bankruptcy Act of 1841." *Commercial Law Journal* 4 (January 1941).

Wilbur, Richard. "The House of Poe." In *The Recognition of Edgar Allan Poe,* edited by Eric W. Carlson, 255–77. Ann Arbor: University of Michigan Press, 1966.

Wilson, Kathryn, and Jennifer Coval. "City of Unbrotherly Love: Violence in Nineteenth-Century Philadelphia." Historical Society of Pennsylvania. http://hsp.org/sites/default/files/legacy_files/migrated/thephiladelphiariotsof1844.pdf.

Wimsatt, W. K. "Poe and the Chess Automaton." *American Literature* 11, no. 2 (1939): 138–51.

Wolfe, John J. *Brandy, Balloons, and Lamps: Ami Argand, 1750–1803.* Carbondale: Southern Illinois University Press, 1999.

Index

Page numbers in *italics* indicate illustrations.